The Story of

Pop Art

An Hachette UK Company
www.hachette.co.uk

First published in the United Kingdom in 2020 by Ilex, an imprint of
Octopus Publishing Group Ltd
Carmelite House
50 Victoria Embankment
London EC4Y 0DZ
www.octopusbooks.co.uk
www.octopusbooksusa.com

Distributed in the US by
Hachette Book Group
1290 Avenue of the Americas
4th and 5th Floors
New York, NY 10104

Distributed in Canada by
Canadian Manda Group
664 Annette St.
Toronto, Ontario, Canada M6S 2C8

Publisher: Alison Starling
Editorial Director: Zena Alkayat
Commissioning Editors: Zara Anvari and Ellie Corbett
Managing Editor: Rachel Silverlight
Editor: Jenny Dye
Art Director: Ben Gardiner
Designer: Evelin Kasikov
Picture Research Manager: Giulia Hetherington
Production Manager: Lisa Pinnell

ISBN 978-1-78157-611-3

A CIP catalogue record for this book is available from the British Library.

Printed and bound in China

10 9 8 7 6 5 4 3 2 1

The Story of Pop Art

Culture, Celebrity & Controversy in 100 Creative Milestones

Andy Stewart MacKay

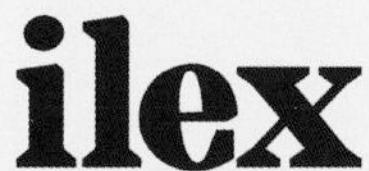

The Story of
Pop Art

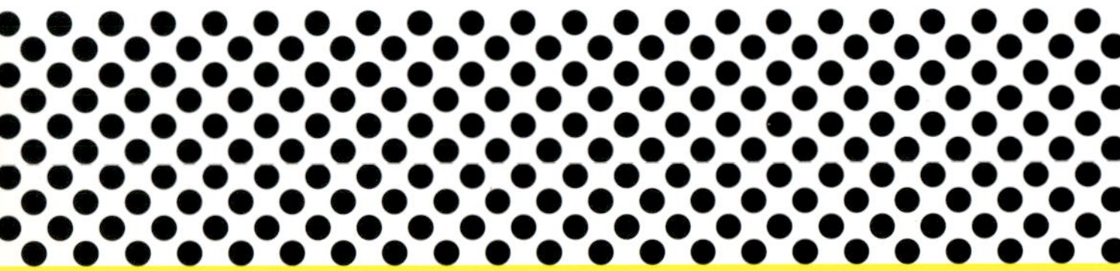

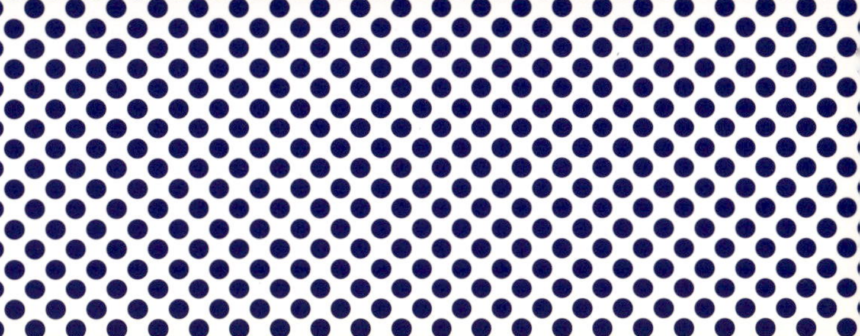

Introduction

Pop Art shocked the world with its irreverent, ironic attitude and its bold, diverse aesthetic. Since it emerged in London in the 1950s, through its heyday in the 1960s on both sides of the Atlantic and continuing into the present, it has influenced spheres of visual culture from street art to high fashion, and from publishing to film-making. Today it stands as perhaps the most arresting and recognizable 20th-century art movement.

Pop Art was the first vernacular Realist movement in avant-garde art in a century. Enlivened by the influence of modern mass media and the techniques of mass production, Pop Art's radical rejection of abstraction in favour of figurative motifs that engaged and held the viewer's attention made it direct and accessible. Pop artists were the first to fully immerse themselves in the language of advertising, and because, as consumers, we all understand that language we can all appreciate and admire Pop Art.

In the 1950s, with rising affluence and affordably priced goods, services and branded products, aspirational consumption became the new post-war Western ideal. This was a period when industry, technology, advertising and art coalesced in mainstream public life. In response, Pop artists appropriated the idioms of the advertising industry to embody, reflect and, in some cases, drive popular culture and its consumerist flavour. In doing so, they invented a new definition of art and made icons out of everything they touched, from **soup cans** 38 to comic books. They proclaimed that anyone could be an artist and that anything could be art. Critics found, often somewhat to their frustration, that to interpret Pop Art was simply to interpret modern life itself.

Because Pop was never just one thing, *The Story of Pop Art* uses 100 entries to delve into the patchwork of personalities, ideas and artworks that shaped its existence and continue to influence its afterlife. The book celebrates the creativity and variety of Pop – from London to **Los Angeles** 50, Blake to **Basquiat** 96, fetishism to the **Factory** 71.

Pop Pioneers, 1915–58

Although it took on different forms wherever it emerged, Pop Art epitomizes the convergence of art and advertising. After the Second World War, with American advances in printing and the advent of four-colour reproduction, the print media and the commercial advertising industry created an iconography of modernity that everyone wanted to be in on. Young Americans embraced this vision of a new consumerism and, rather than training as traditional fine artists, many young creatives – Roy Lichtenstein, Andy Warhol and James Rosenquist among them – worked as commercial illustrators, becoming **'Mad men'** 9 who sold the **American Dream** 4 .

In post-war Europe it was impossible to ignore the avalanche of gorgeous colour magazines coming from across the Atlantic. For young British artists such as Eduardo Paolozzi and Richard Hamilton, contending with food rationing and surrounded by the ruined cityscapes of war, the promise of affordable housing, modern **cars** 7 , **television sets** 25 and convenience foods could only be glimpsed in print. The aspirant vision of American advertising induced, for many ordinary people in Europe, a kind of reverence. The promise of a new life of affluence can be glimpsed in pioneering Pop works such as Paolozzi's *Real Gold* (1949), a giddying collage of cut-out colour magazine advertisements from what Paolozzi called the new 'exotic society' – its title lifted from the 'Real Gold' orange juice ad featured prominently on the right-hand side of the work. During the 1950s, new critiques of advertising by philosophers Marshall McLuhan and Roland Barthes began to gain influence. And soon, Hamilton for one took a step back, famously defining Pop Art as the 'sieved reflection of the ad man's paraphrase of the consumer's dream'. A more ironic take on Pop also emerged back in America, where, in a developing culture of material excess, artists began to recognize that as much was being discarded as was manufactured. Developing the principles and aesthetics of early 20th-century Dada – an art movement epitomized by the subversive collages of John Heartfield, the found-object sculptures of **Kurt Schwitters** 3 and the 'readymades' of **Marcel Duchamp** 1 – artists such as Robert Rauschenberg began to incorporate, or **'combine'** 11 , rubbish into their work.

During the late 1950s, something changed in the way Pop artists across the Western world thought about themselves and their work. They began to recognize in radical and individual ways how their direct style, seductive motifs and descriptive techniques reflected contemporary life more accurately and inclusively than any current – or indeed former – art movement. Rejecting the traditional convention that art should have an intellectual and metaphysical focus, avoiding contact with popular culture, Pop artists instead revelled in it and sought to understand how it shaped and informed modern life.

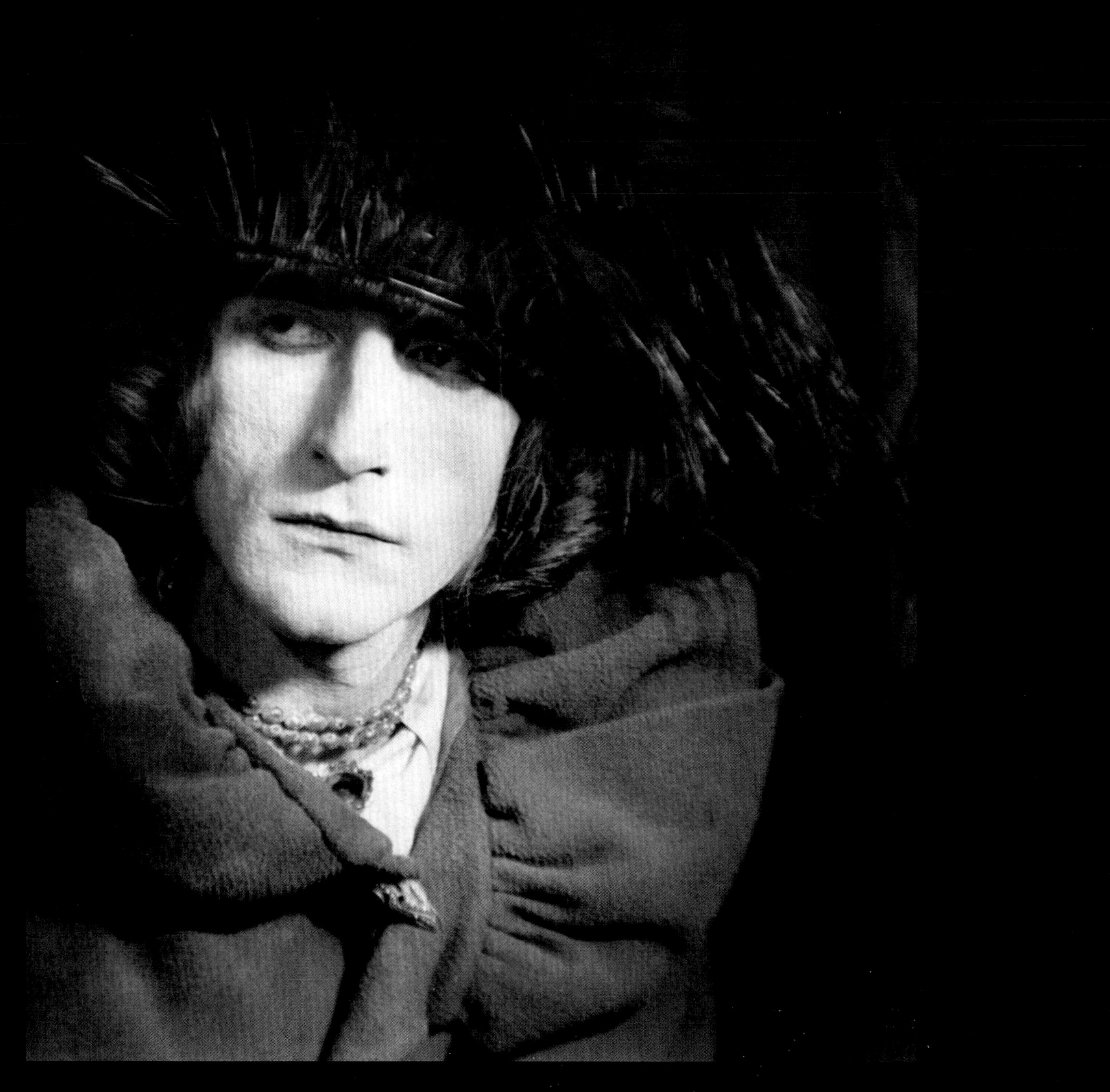

1

Marcel Duchamp

Associated with the Dada movement, French avant-gardist Marcel Duchamp was one of the 20th century's most influential artists. His 'anti-art' legacy – the idea that art need not be a manual activity but can be an intellectual one instead – had a huge influence on the development of Pop Art. Andy Warhol proclaimed that 'everything seen... is a Duchamp' and insisted that 'Dada must have something to do with Pop... the names are really synonyms'.

Duchamp emigrated to the United States in 1915, settling in New York. There he bought a snow shovel, inscribed it with the title *Prelude to a Broken Arm* and hung it from the ceiling of his studio. This was the first of his American 'readymade' sculptures. The most famous of them was the porcelain urinal *Fountain* (1917) – although recent evidence suggests it may, in fact, be the work of radical Dadaist Baroness Elsa von Freytag-Loringhoven. Signed (as if by the manufacturer) 'R. Mutt 1917', *Fountain* scandalized even the avant-garde Society of Independent Artists and, despite the 'No juries, no prizes' ethos of its annual exhibition, the work was never shown and somehow lost.

Forty years later, however, just as Duchamp became an American citizen, Warhol bought himself a reproduction *Fountain*. In innumerable ways, Duchamp laid the foundations for Pop Art's irreverent attitude to both art and convention. His use of everyday 'vulgar' objects was a direct influence on Robert Rauschenberg's **'combine'** sculptures from the 11 1950s; his readymades were a direct influence on the French **New Realists**. 24 Warhol's repetition of the *Mona Lisa* in the 1963 **silkscreen** 36 *Thirty Are Better Than One* displays the same disregard for tradition as Duchamp's graffitied 1919 postcard of the same artwork, *L.H.O.O.Q.*

Duchamp's 1920s **drag** performances as Russian émigré Rrose Sélavy anticipated Warhol's playful approach to gender in his drag **Polaroids** from the 1970s. Duchamp's last major work, *Étant donnés* (1946–66), even anticipates the voyeurism of 1960s Pop **pornography**. As Californian Pop artist **Ed Ruscha** put it, Duchamp was the undeniable 'real guiding light' of Pop Art.

OPPOSITE
Man Ray
Portrait of Rrose Sélavy, 1921
GELATIN SILVER PRINT

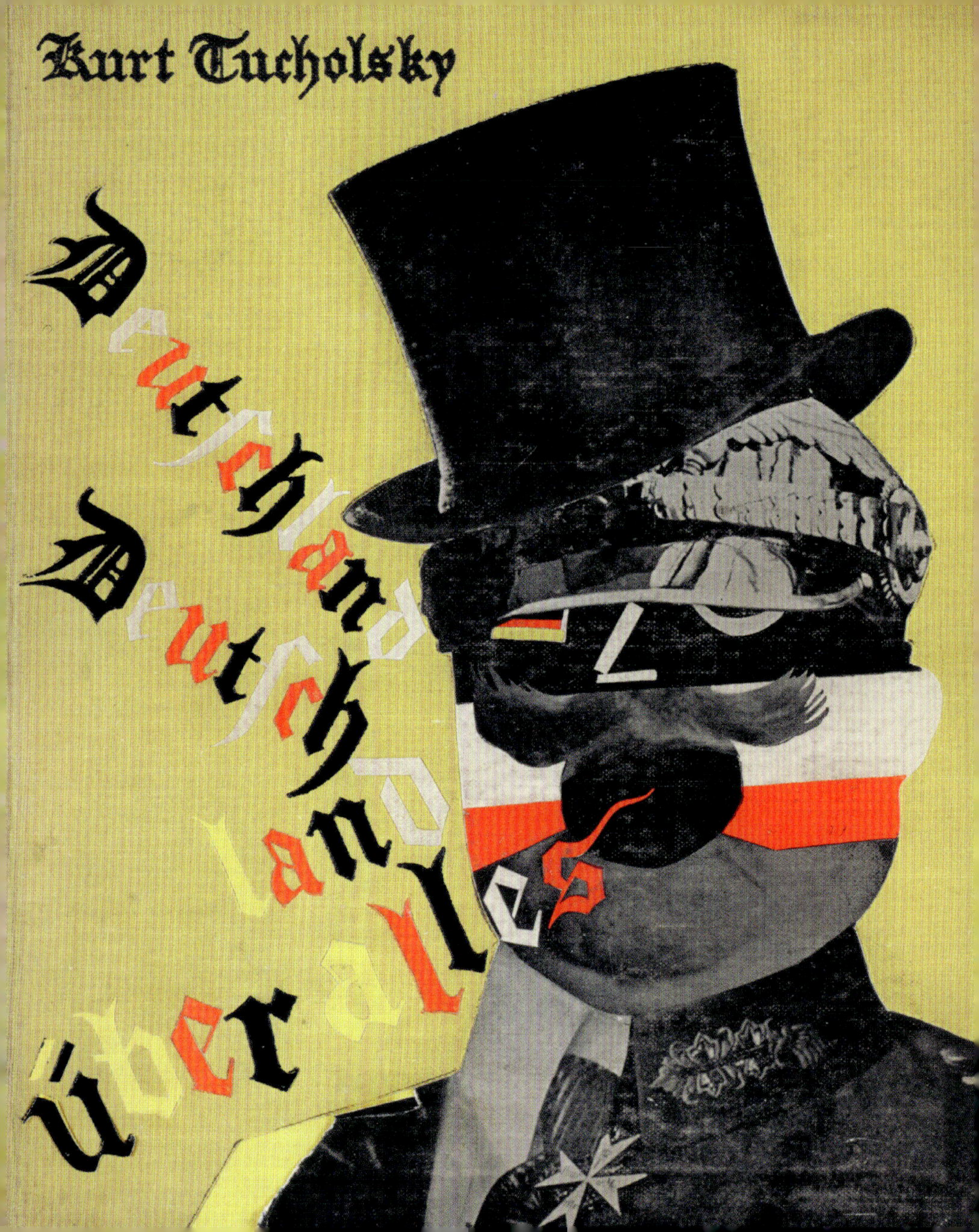
Kurt Tucholsky
Deutschland Deutschland
über alles

2

Photomontage

Pop Art was an explicit challenge to the traditions of fine art but also, perhaps inevitably, drew upon them. Subjects, methods, techniques and philosophies were both recycled and developed, with Pop artists seeking to blur the lines between high-art techniques such as painting and industrial methods including photographic reproduction.

While the collage technique was being developed in Paris by Cubist artists Pablo Picasso and Georges Braque around 1910, its variant, photomontage, emerged in Germany a few years later, during the First World War. Late one night in a Berlin studio in May 1916, Dada artists John Heartfield and George Grosz began playing with images from propagandist local newspapers including the *Berliner Lokal-Anzeiger*. Short on cash to buy traditional art materials, they were forced to appropriate the images and materials that surrounded them to create new work. Heartfield in particular became known for his anti-Nazi photomontages from the 1930s: 'I saw both what was being said and not being said with photos in the newspapers…how you can fool people with photos, really fool them.' These artworks created a new visual 'logic' that would be developed by Pop artists including Eduardo Paolozzi and Richard Hamilton.

The roots of photomontage, a form of collaging photographs, lie in the provocative Victorian technique of 'combination printing', which was advanced by Swedish photographer Oscar Rejlander. In 1857, over a six-week period, Rejlander developed 32 negatives to create one new composite image, the tableau *Two Ways of Life*. Rejlander's image, featuring female nudes, was ordered by Queen Victoria as a present for her husband, Prince Albert. When it was exhibited in Manchester and Edinburgh, it caused, perhaps predictable, outrage. A hundred years later, responding to technological innovations in colour printing and reproduction, Pop artists made photomontage their own, cutting, pasting, photographing, retouching and manipulating images from newspapers and magazines. The provocations of this kind of 'mash up' would be developed by, for example, Pop artist Richard Hamilton in his collage ***Just what is it that makes today's homes so different, so appealing?***. Separated by a century, Rejlander and Hamilton both reflect a voyeuristic desire to live – and consume – vicariously.

OPPOSITE
John Heartfield
Book cover from *Deutschland, Deutschland über alles* by Kurt Tucholsky, 1929

PHOTOMONTAGE

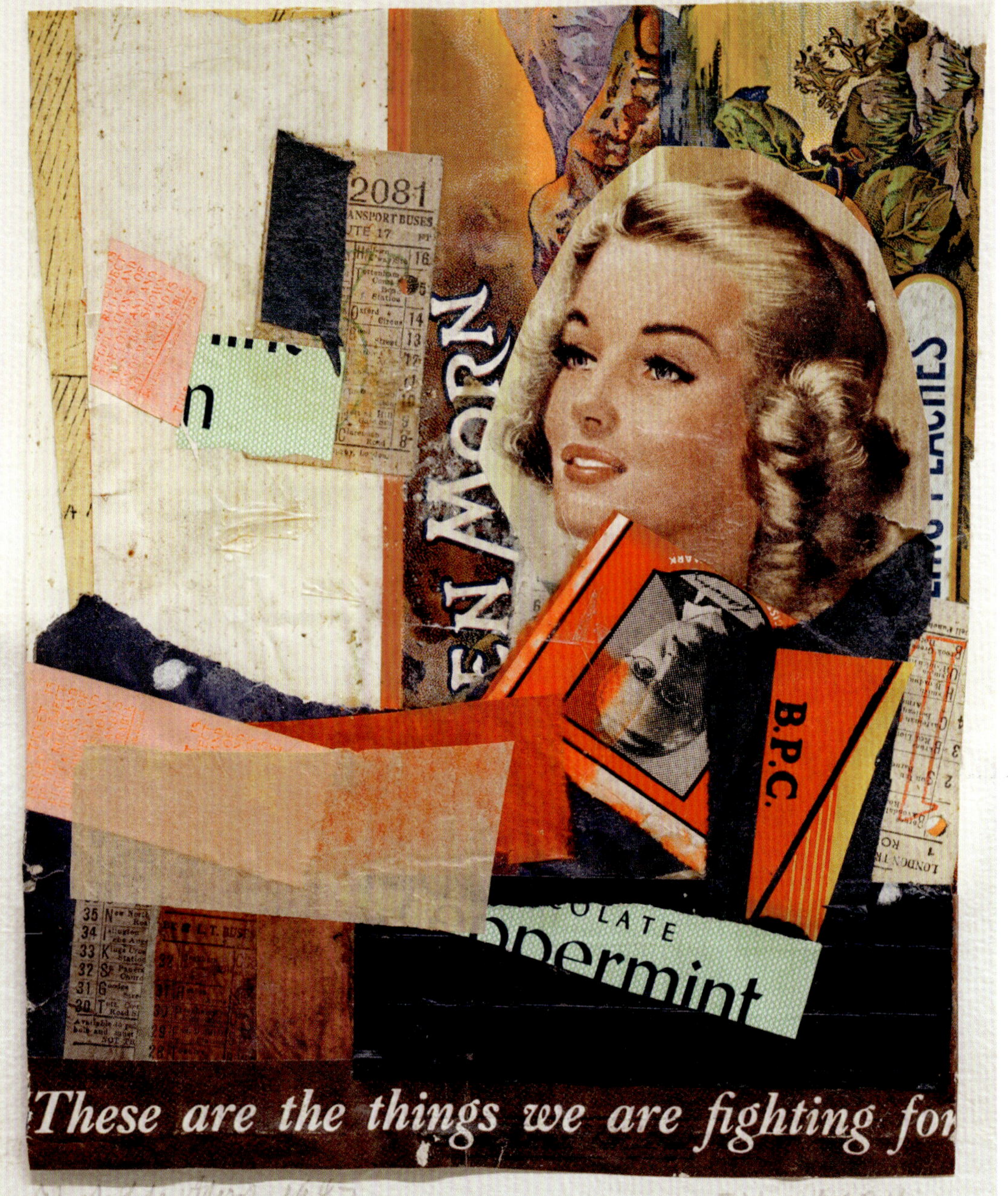
2081
EN MORN
B.P.C.
These are the things we are fighting for
EN MORN

3

Kurt Schwitters

Sometimes referred to as 'the grandfather of Pop Art', German-born Kurt Schwitters was one of the most inventive artists of the 20th century 1 and, like **Marcel Duchamp**, was associated with the Dada movement. Until his death in 1948, he produced newspaper collages, sculptures using 'bits of old rubbish', strange *Ursonate* sound performances and *Merzbau* installations that would prove powerfully influential on the development of Pop Art.

Schwitters famously said that he could 'see no reason why used tram tickets, bits of driftwood, buttons and old junk from attics and rubbish heaps should not serve well as materials for paintings'. He even invented the nonsense word *Merz* to describe his collages and sculptures incorporating these 'found objects'. Developing the German concept of *Gesamtkunstwerk* ('total work of art'), Schwitters arranged his pieces into fantastical interior installations he called *Merzbau* (*bau* means 'building' in German).

A social and artistic radical who fled Nazi Germany, Schwitters eventually found refuge in Britain, though initially as an 'enemy alien'. After the war, and with a grant from the Metropolitan Museum of Art in New York, he created his final *Merzbau* in an old barn near the village of Elterwater in the Lake District. Named the Merz Barn, it lay unfinished at the time of his death but was rescued in 1965 by Pop artist Richard Hamilton, who at the time was teaching just over the Pennines at Newcastle University. Schwitters's work was 'rediscovered' thanks in part to 1958 exhibitions at Lord's Gallery in London and Hatton Gallery in Newcastle, but it had already attracted the attention of the **Independent Group** of young British 6 Pop artists, which included Hamilton, Eduardo Paolozzi and John McHale. His last collages – such as *En Morn* (1947), with its blonde women, Golden Morn peaches label, London bus ticket, chocolate peppermint wrapper and propagandist slogan 'These are the things we are fighting for' – clearly anticipate, and went on to influence, the new iconography of Pop Art.

OPPOSITE
Kurt Schwitters
En Morn, 1947
COLLAGE

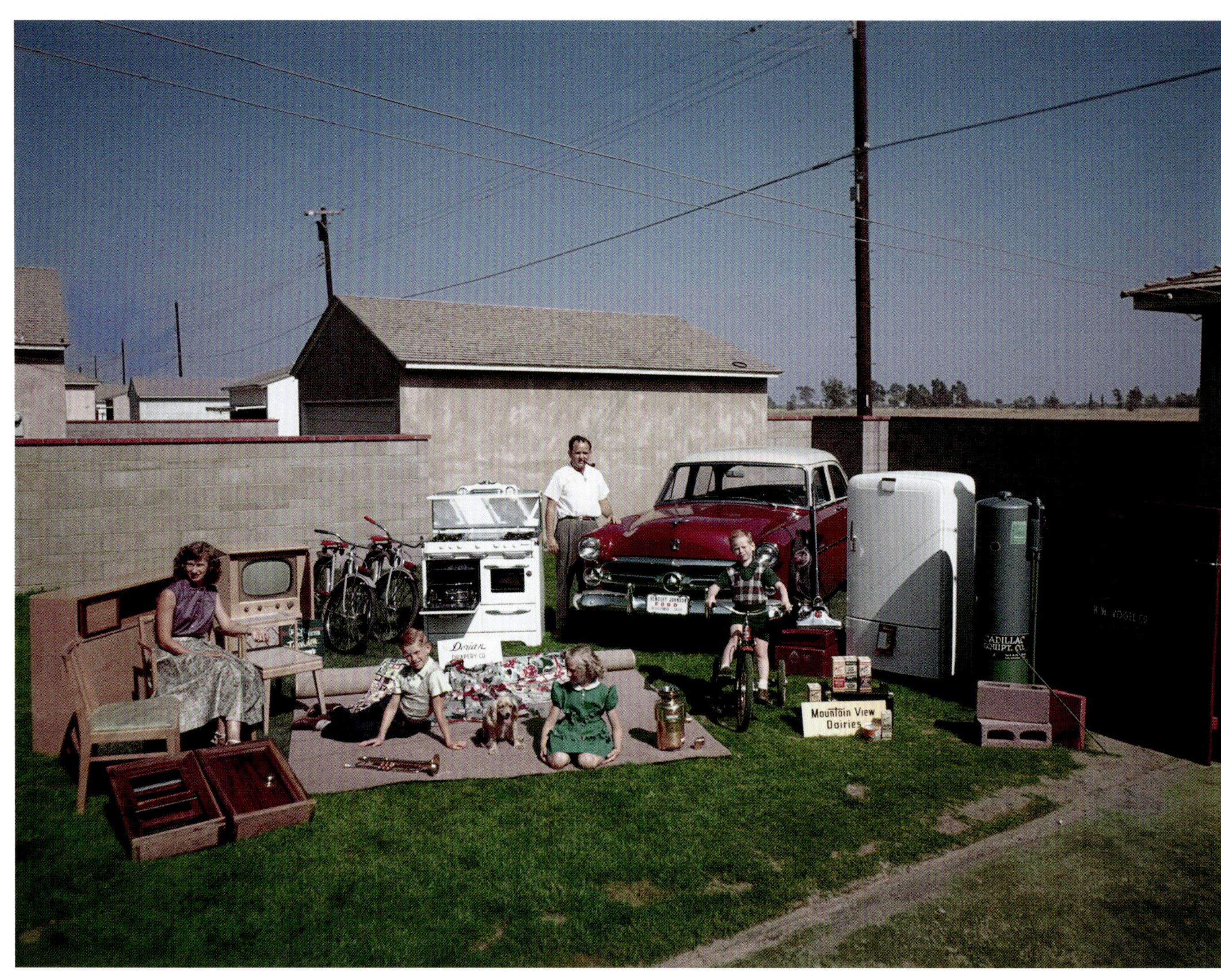
Dorian
DRAPERY CO
HENSLEY JOHNSON
FORD
Mountain View
Dairies
CADILLAC
EQUIPT. CO.
R.W. VOGEL CO

4

The American Dream

As a national myth, the American Dream has its origins in the 19th century, when new frontiers and gold rushes fuelled migrant aspirations for a bright new future. As a term, however, the 'American Dream' was coined during the Great Depression by the historian James Truslow Adams to convey the visionary ideal that 'life should be better and richer and fuller for everyone'. In the 1960s, it was civil rights leader Martin Luther King Jr who developed this national vision, encouraging his fellow citizens to stand up 'for the best in the American dream'.

As far back as 1893, the historian Frederick Jackson Turner had spoken of American democracy, and by extension the American Dream, as being characterized by a national resistance to elitist high culture. Pop Art, then, is an accessible and mass-market expression of this idea. And the recurring consumerist motifs of the 1940s and 1950s – the tract housing, billboards, processed food, 'white
7 goods' and **cars** of the new American Dream – are the central motifs of Pop Art. Artists such as Andy Warhol saw such manufactured standardization as a positive development. For him, even the drinking of **Coca-Cola** – enjoyed 34
by Hollywood stars and factory workers alike – was a ritualized national 'right', an equality of daily experience that was historically unique. 'Once you thought Pop, you could never see America the same way again,' he declared.

Pop Art came to embody the iconography of affluence on both sides of the Atlantic. After the Second World War, at the height of its global influence, the American Dream was everyone's dream. Eduardo Paolozzi, 'the father of **British Pop Art**', immediately 6
realized that American 'food and automobile ads spoke more eloquently and economically of dreams than any conventional art was able to do'. With this in mind, in 1947 he created his magazine collage *I Was a Rich Man's Plaything* (see pages 20–1, the first to feature the word 'POP'). Heavily suggestive of sensationalized sexual violence, it evokes **popular fantasies** 56
of pulp fiction and Hollywood movies.

OPPOSITE
Example of suburban growth in Los Angeles County, *c.*1952

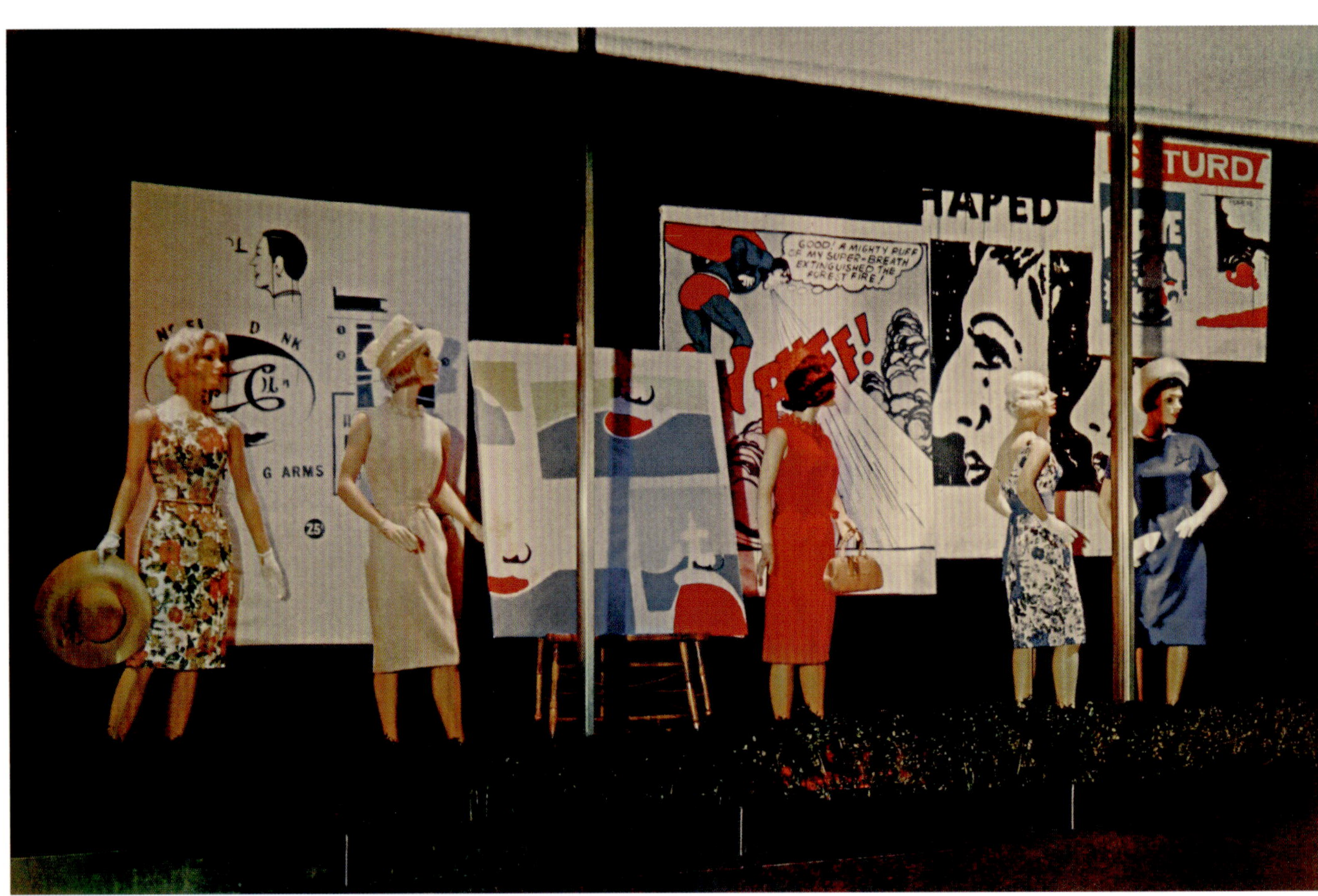
GOOD! A MIGHTY PUFF OF MY SUPER-BREATH EXTINGUISHED THE FOREST FIRE!
HAPED
TURD
G ARMS

5

The 'staple-gun queens'

In 1951, Gene Moore, displays director at the famed New York department store Bonwit Teller – a 'sparkling jewel' whose window displays of the 1930s featured works by artists such as René Magritte and Salvador Dalí – hired two new display designers and window dressers: 23-year-old commercial illustrator Andy Warhol and 26-year-old art student Robert Rauschenberg. Three years later they were joined on the display team by Korean War veteran Jasper Johns, who would soon become Rauschenberg's romantic partner. Warhol – who had himself been dismissed by the writer Truman Capote as a 'window-dresser type' – later liked to disparage Rauschenberg and Johns as the 'staple-gun queens'.

Rauschenberg and Johns became successful business partners, producing innovative and widely acclaimed window designs for companies such as Tiffany & Co. They worked as Matson Jones Custom Display (Matson being Rauschenberg's mother's maiden name and Jones a stand-in for Johns), but, at a time when their sexuality could have landed them – and Warhol too – in jail, Rauschenberg and Johns kept their six-year relationship hidden. Unlike his conventionally handsome colleagues, Warhol found the anxieties brought about by this hidden lifestyle were compounded by a painful self-consciousness about his body, and snide comments were his defence. Warhol clearly respected Rauschenberg, though, creating in 1962 a series of
biographical **silkscreen** portraits 36
of him called *Now Let Us Praise Famous Men*. Within a decade of their working together, all three men would gain extraordinary success as some of the most significant artists of the 20th century.

With its vast window spaces, Bonwit Teller was the ideal place for emergent Pop artists to cut their teeth. The store showcased some of the earliest examples of Pop Art, which were produced initially as displays: Rauschenberg's *Untitled (Red Painting)* (c.1953), Johns's first
flag painting, *Flag on Orange Field* 10
(1957), and Warhol's ***Superman*** 
(1961) and *Before and After* (1961, see pages 36–7). Unknowingly, and for almost a decade, Fifth Avenue shoppers were passing the very first exhibitions of American Pop Art.

OPPOSITE
Andy Warhol's window display at the Bonwit Teller department store, 1961

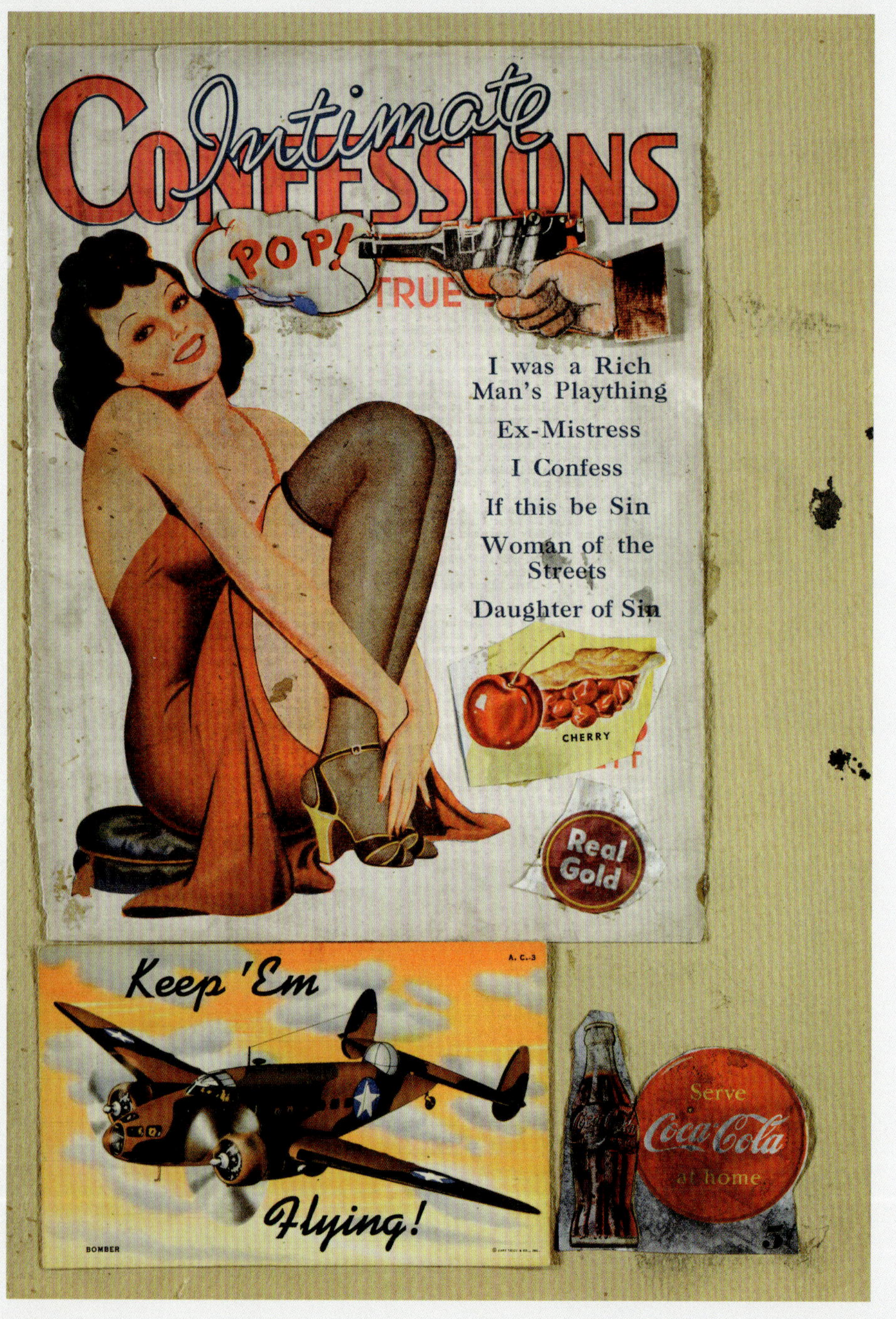

Intimate Confessions
POP!
TRUE
I was a Rich Man's Plaything
Ex-Mistress
I Confess
If this be Sin
Woman of the Streets
Daughter of Sin
CHERRY
Real Gold
A. C.-3
Keep 'Em Flying!
BOMBER
Serve Coca-Cola at home

6

The Independent Group

1952–5

In the lecture theatre of London's Institute of Contemporary Arts in 1952, Scottish-born artist Eduardo Paolozzi presented his collage series *Bunk!* (1947–52) to the first session of the newly founded Independent Group. Chaired by the design critic Reyner Banham, this group was a diverse artistic think-tank made up of artists including Richard Hamilton, John McHale and Magda Cordell, art critic Lawrence Alloway, and a number of sculptors, photographers, composers and architects. Progressive and anti-establishment, they were united in their dislike of high-minded elitist culture and their chosen aesthetic was accessible, popular, 'vulgar', voyeuristic and everyday. In other words, pure Pop Art.

Considered the standard-bearer of British Pop Art, Paolozzi created his images while he was living in Paris. *Bunk!* makes inventive use of mass-media motifs and the clichés of American culture. While artists such as Francis Bacon were using film stills and photographs as source material for their work at this time, Paolozzi was directly cutting and pasting his sources into collage.

His references took in Hollywood celebrities, **Disney** characters,  **Californian** beach culture, canned  fruit and manufactured sweets, tinned fish and processed sausages, cocktails and **Coca-Cola**, pulp  novels and comic books, as well as ancient sculpture. Paolozzi wove these seductive images – about as far from post-war European austerity as could be – into a continuous dream-like narrative.

Short-lived and only ever loosely affiliated, the Independent Group disbanded in 1955. Nevertheless, in the three years of their existence, the Independents held a series of controversial and important exhibitions. Their first, and perhaps most radical, was the 1953 *Parallel of Life and Art* at the ICA. It featured crudely enlarged magazine photographs, children's drawings, and graffiti, not framed and hung neatly on the walls, but cut out and crudely stuck to both walls and ceilings. The effect was reminiscent of the *Merzbau* of **Kurt Schwitters**,  whose work was explored by the young Independents the following year at their next ICA exhibition, *Collages and Objects*.

OPPOSITE
Eduardo Paolozzi
I Was a Rich Man's Plaything, from the *Bunk!* series, 1947
PRINTED PAPERS ON CARD

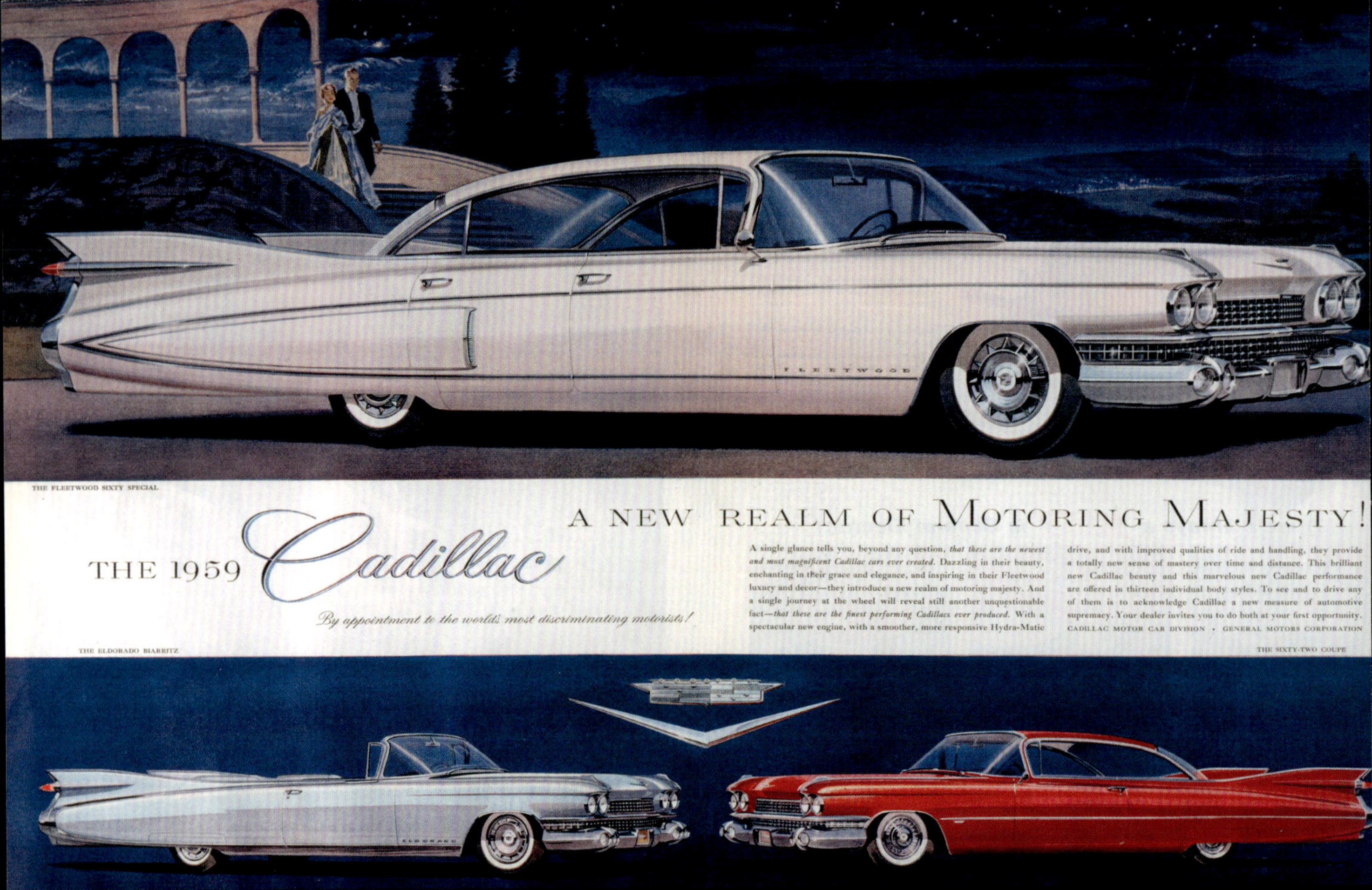

THE FLEETWOOD SIXTY SPECIAL

THE 1959 *Cadillac*

A NEW REALM OF MOTORING MAJESTY!

By appointment to the world's most discriminating motorists!

A single glance tells you, beyond any question, *that these are the newest and most magnificent Cadillac cars ever created.* Dazzling in their beauty, enchanting in their grace and elegance, and inspiring in their Fleetwood luxury and decor—they introduce a new realm of motoring majesty. And a single journey at the wheel will reveal still another unquestionable fact—*that these are the finest performing Cadillacs ever produced.* With a spectacular new engine, with a smoother, more responsive Hydra-Matic drive, and with improved qualities of ride and handling, they provide a totally new sense of mastery over time and distance. This brilliant new Cadillac beauty and this marvelous new Cadillac performance are offered in thirteen individual body styles. To see and to drive any of them is to acknowledge Cadillac a new measure of automotive supremacy. Your dealer invites you to do both at your first opportunity.

CADILLAC MOTOR CAR DIVISION • GENERAL MOTORS CORPORATION

THE ELDORADO BIARRITZ

THE SIXTY-TWO COUPE

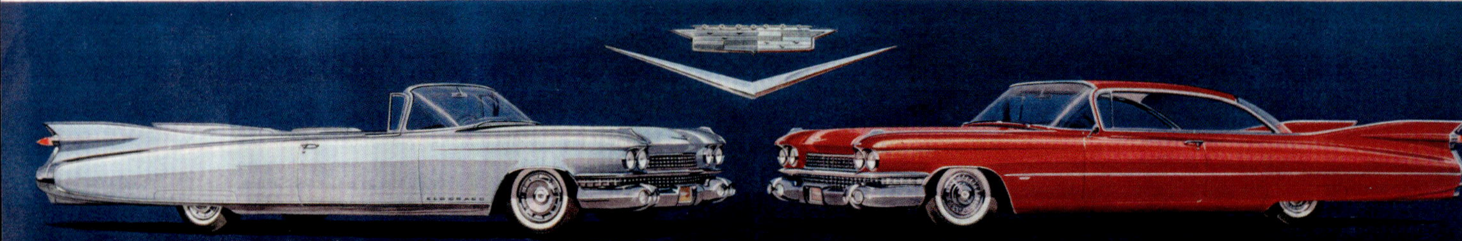

7

Cars

During the 1950s, American disposable income increased significantly. With the expansion of automobile manufacturing and the construction of new roads, cars became more practical and affordable than ever before. In 1953, the American car manufacturer Cadillac launched their now-iconic Eldorado. With its slick, finned exterior and luxurious interior trimmings, the Eldorado became an aspirational status symbol and it soon began to feature prominently – alongside American highways and freeways – as a powerful Pop Art motif.

Cars fascinated Pop artists on both sides of the Atlantic. In 1955, Reyner Banham gave a lecture
6 to the **Independent Group** on
the subject of modern car design (he would go on to publish a book about Los Angeles, the ultimate car city, 16 years later). Also in 1955, the group held an exhibition entitled *Man, Machine and Motion* at London's Institute of Contemporary Arts. In the late 1950s, group member Richard Hamilton produced several paintings that incorporated motifs from American car adverts and the glamorous young women often draped across them.

The American neo-Dada sculptor John Chamberlain, acting with consummate reverent irreverence, smashed up cars and put the pieces back together again as assemblage sculptures, many of which were exhibited at *The Art of Assemblage* in 1961 at the Museum of Modern Art in New York. Pop artist Andy Warhol created endless stand-alone, and often repeated, images of cars – suburban Cadillacs, folksy Volkswagens, police cars and speeding trucks – even exploring,
like **J. G. Ballard**, the fascination 89
prompted by car crashes.

Several Pop artists became bespoke BMW designers for the German car manufacturer's exclusive Art Car series. Roy Lichtenstein was the first to be commissioned in 1977 and, using
his trademark **Ben-Day dots**, painted 53
what he imagined passengers might see from the windows of the car. David Hockney's 1995 design looked like a cross between an abstract painting by idiosyncratic Cubist Fernand Léger and his own figurative, and more familiar, Yorkshire landscapes.

OPPOSITE
Cadillac advertisement, 1958

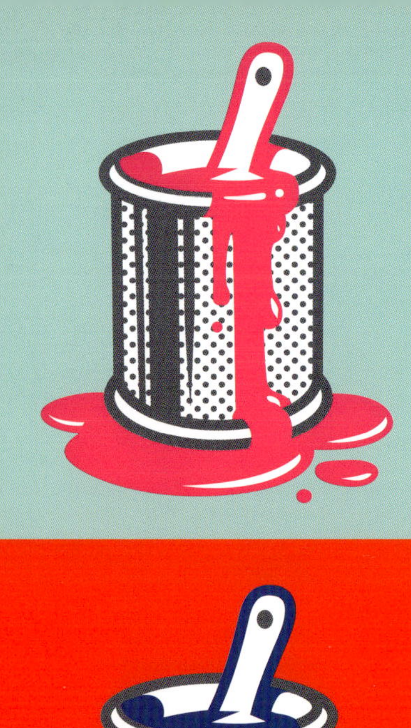
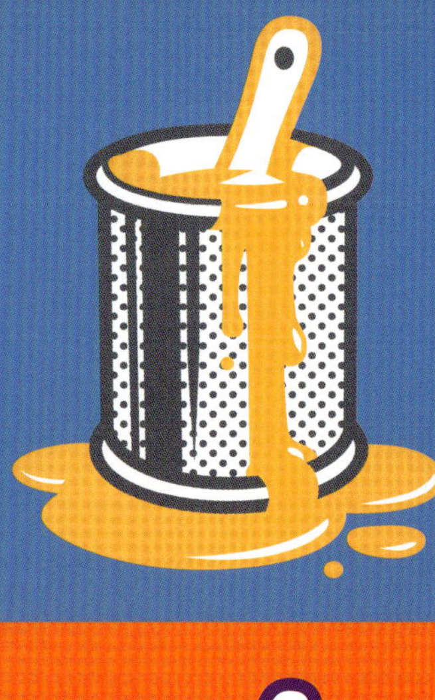
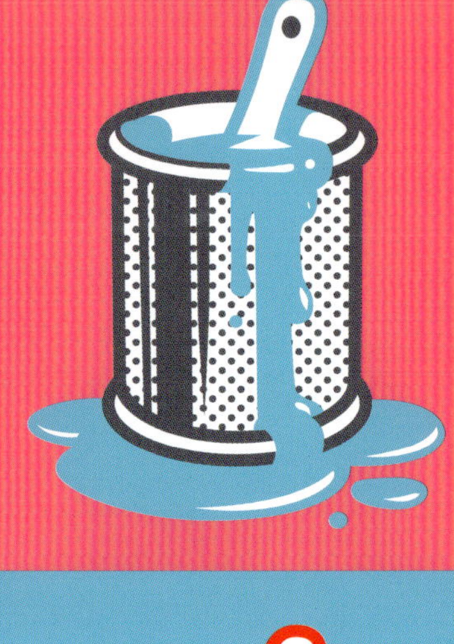
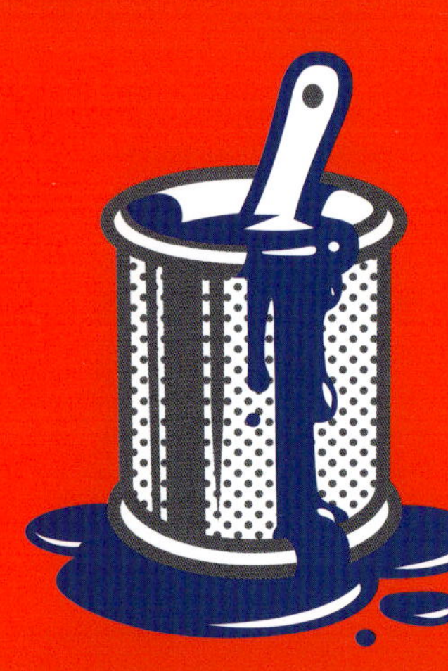
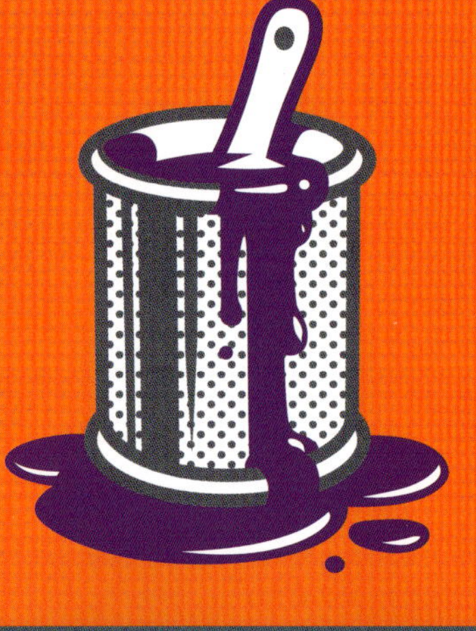

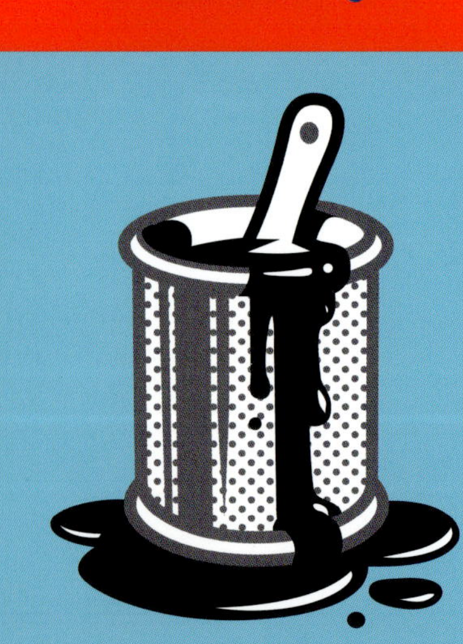
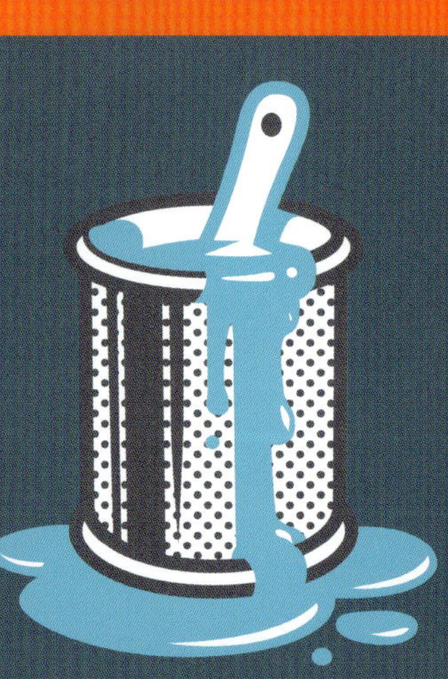
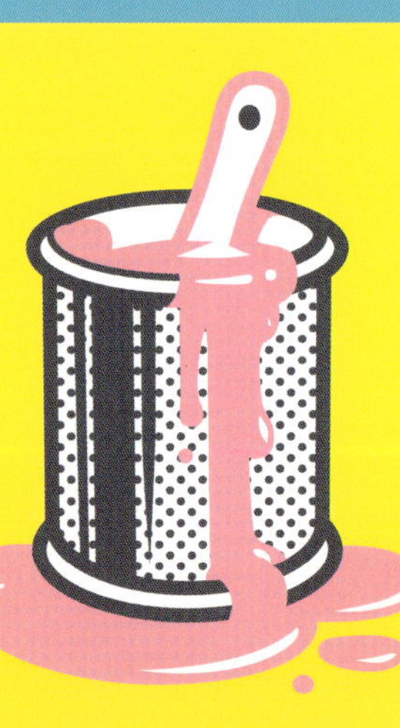

8

Magna

Perfect for Pop Art because it was cheaper than oil paint, fast-drying and sold in any number of brilliant synthetic colours, Magna acrylic resin paint was first produced in 1947 after experiments by American manufacturers Leonard Bocour and his nephew Sam Golden. Industrial developments such as these meant that American artists of the 1950s and 1960s often favoured new products such as Magna over traditional oils.

When he founded Bocour Artist Colors Inc. in New York in 1932, Bocour was already famous for grinding mineral pigments by hand in the studio at the back of his shop. As a former art student and apprentice to the German-American painter Emil Ganso, he understood what artists wanted and needed from the paint they used and was admired for his high-quality products. He gave the painter Morris Louis the first batch of Magna paints to try out in exchange for product feedback. Bocour's shop became something of a hang-out for artists during the 1950s and he got to know Abstract Expressionists including Mark Rothko and Willem de Kooning. In response to their huge canvases, Bocour's fashionable tubes of acrylic paint went king-size. Sometimes impoverished artists would even give Bocour their work in exchange for a clutch of hallowed tubes. By the end of the 1950s, Pop artists such as Roy Lichtenstein had become Magna customers.

When he eventually retired in 1986, Bocour owned a large collection of paintings, which he donated to St Mary's, a liberal arts college in Maryland. His departure from the company that bore his name meant the discontinuation of Magna, but Lichtenstein favoured the brand so much he famously bought as much of the last stock as he could get his hands on. Over four decades, Bocour's volcanic eruption of electric colours defined an era. Without Magna, Pop Art wouldn't exist.

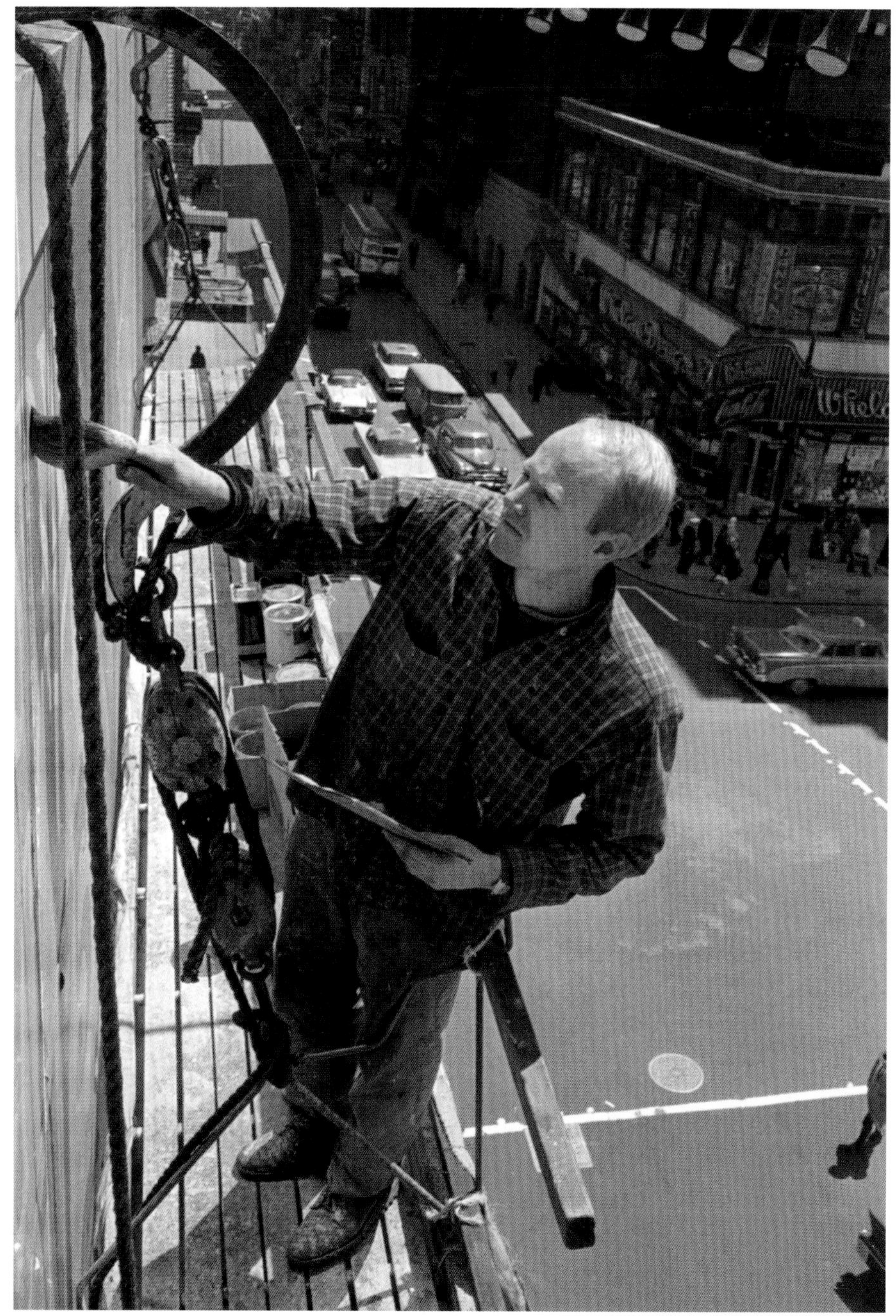

9

'Mad men'

It's no coincidence that some of the best-known Pop artists started out as 'Mad men' in the advertising industry of 1950s America. Young artists needed to earn a living, but the early training they received in the commercial field also contributed significantly to the fine art they produced out of hours and defined their later success. Pop Art was, then, a powerful – and often ironic – response to not only the visual imagery of mass markets but also the seductive techniques of advertising.

Roy Lichtenstein began his career as a commercial draughtsman and designer for electrical and steel firms, a catering company and a department store, while Claes Oldenburg started out drawing insects for insecticide
33 advertisements. **Ed Ruscha** worked as a commercial artist in California, while Andy Warhol – who drew advertisements for a women's shoe manufacturer – was known as the most successful illustrator in New York. James Rosenquist worked as a Times Square billboard painter for the Strauss Sign Corporation and was hailed by an industry magazine in 1958 as 'Broadway's Biggest Painter'.
18 Pop sculptor **Chryssa** was so taken by Times Square that she too tried – unsuccessfully – to get a job there as a sign painter. Meanwhile, in London, Pop artist Peter Blake worked as a graphic designer. Characteristically, however, the artists of the period were keen to mock the industry that paid their wages. As early as April 1956, the satirical American magazine *MAD* ran a spoof of the phenomenally successful 1954 Marlboro cigarette rebrand featuring rugged cowboy-style models. Marlboros were smoked by millions, including several emerging Pop artists, and soon, in a neat loop, cigarettes – and their distinctive branding – became part of the iconography of Pop Art.
Pop artist **Tom Wesselmann**, for 30
example, produced a series of *Mouth* paintings in the late 1960s that developed into the *Smoker* series. Here, the smoking cigarette – between parted, red-lipsticked lips – is directly suggestive of sex. And as ad men well know, sex sells.

Before Pop Art was officially defined by critics, it already existed as commercial art. Pop Art is commercial art and Mad men were, more often than not, Pop artists. Even in the 1980s, Warhol could assert, 'I'm still a commercial artist. I was always a commercial artist.'

OPPOSITE
James Rosenquist painting a billboard in New York City, 1960

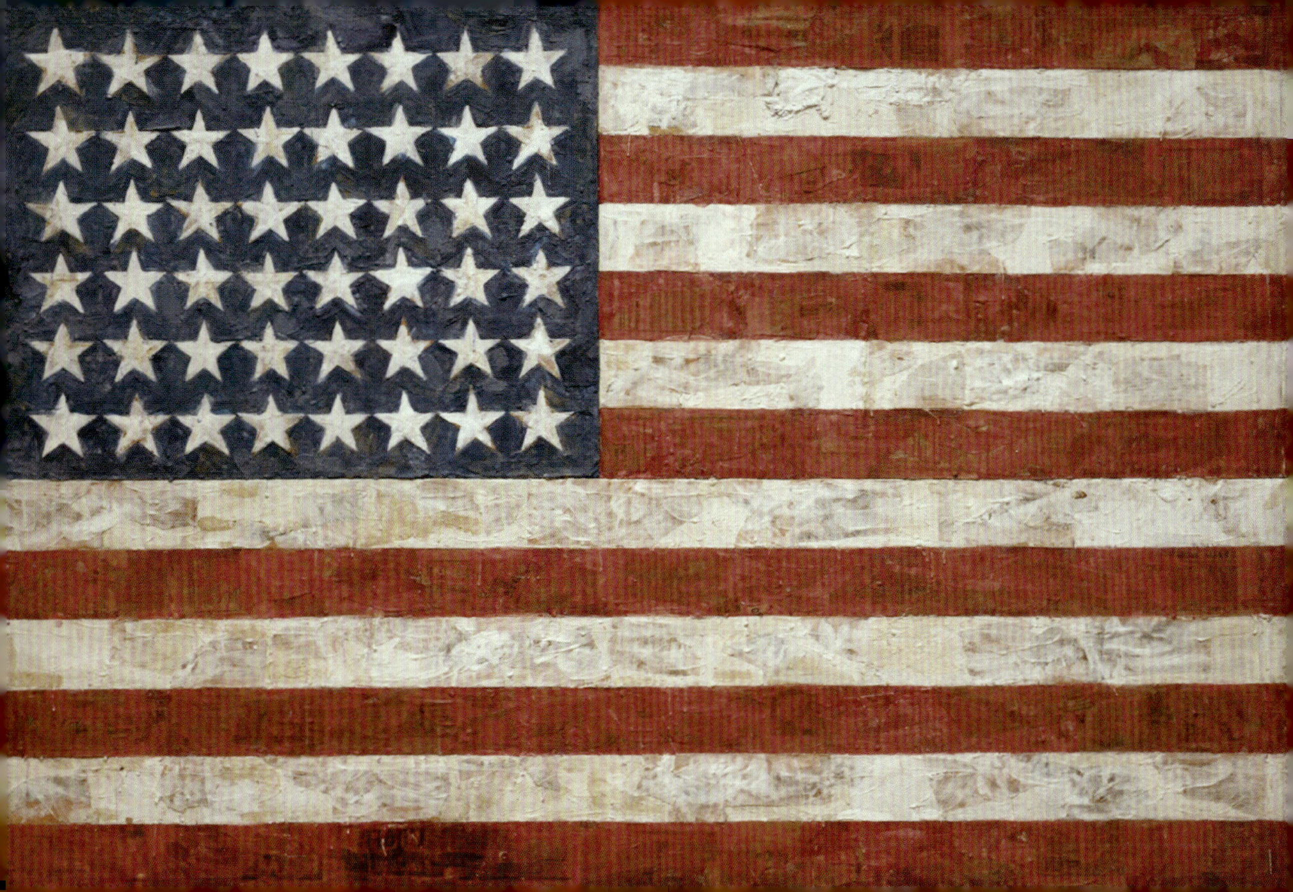

10

Flag

Jasper Johns

1954–5

The dominant style of painting in 1950s New York was Abstract Expressionism, as exemplified by the works of Jackson Pollock, Mark Rothko and Willem de Kooning, which combined personal and subjective human emotions with the formal principles of abstraction. As its name suggests, the movement dismissed figurative realism in painting in favour of a pure abstraction that pointed towards higher, transcendental states. Paint, and its expressive qualities, catalyzed this deeply emotional movement beyond the everyday. Realism was no longer good enough: as Rothko said, 'We worked for years to get rid of all that.' Jasper Johns, one of a number of emerging young Pop artists, sought to challenge Rothko's status quo.

Completed in 1955, and often considered the first Pop Art painting, Johns's encaustic *Flag* was made using hot wax, pigment and newspaper, mounted on three canvases attached to plywood. The painting's heavily textured surface conforms to – or is at least sympathetic with – the conventions of Abstract Expressionism. However, the irreverent depiction of a powerful national symbol that incorporated everyday articles and adverts from the popular press was both new and deeply controversial. Indeed, when the director of New York's Museum of Modern Art wanted to buy it he was justifiably fearful that the public would consider it 'unpatriotic'.

In common with other Pop artists, Johns said that he tended to like things 'that already exist' in the world. With *Flag*, he exploded the myth that artists should always create something new, instead selecting from and interpreting the world around him. During a decade of **Cold War** conflict and communist 51
witch-hunts, the American flag was regularly invoked as a political icon demanding devotional submission. In this context, Johns's playful adaptation of the flag was striking and brave, countering the prevailing political and artistic establishments. As an artist and also a veteran of the Korean War, Johns resisted and refused the symbolic authority of both abstraction and patriotism.

OPPOSITE
Jasper Johns
Flag, 1954–5
ENCAUSTIC, OIL AND COLLAGE ON FABRIC MOUNTED ON PLYWOOD, THREE PANELS

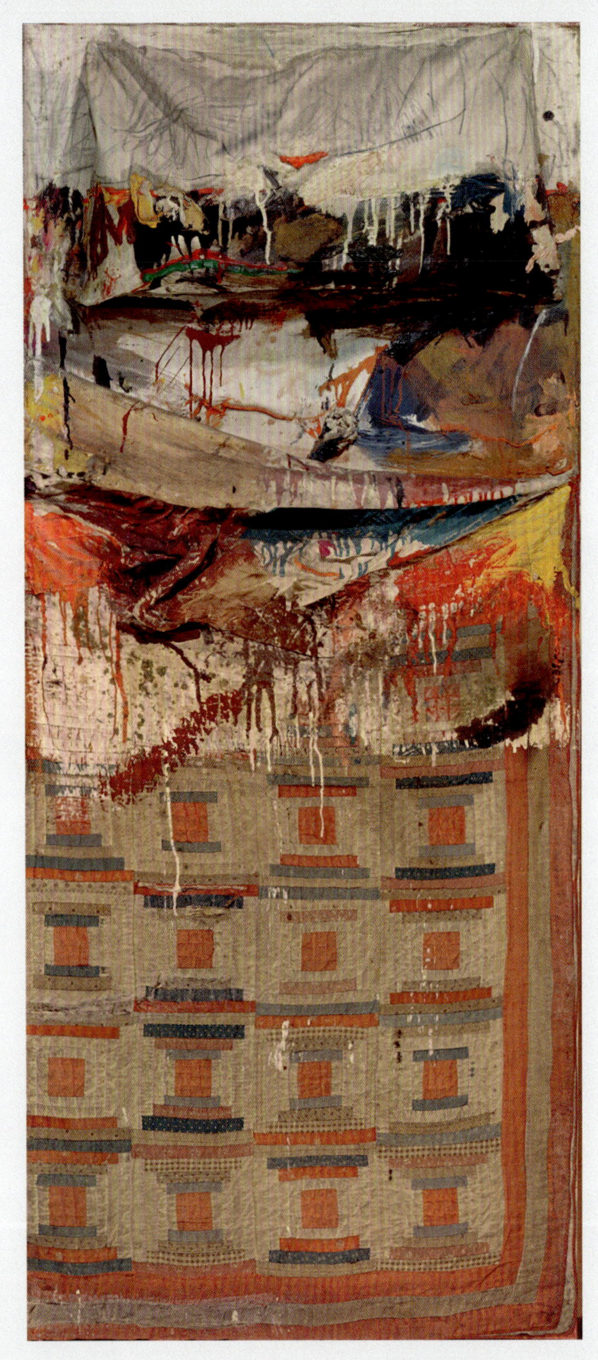

11

Bed

Robert Rauschenberg

1955

As a reflection of his influence, early Pop artist Robert Rauschenberg has been described as 'the American Picasso'. Talking of art and life, he once said, 'I try to act in that gap between the two.' It's no surprise, then, that in 1955 the thirty-year-old began merging paint and canvas with 1 everyday objects. **Marcel Duchamp** had already used newly manufactured items to create 'readymades', but with his Pop 'combines' Rauschenberg began working with discarded objects.

Living in pre-gentrification downtown New York, Rauschenberg couldn't always afford oil paints and canvases. His creative response to poverty was both practical and ingenious, and revealed his lifelong sympathy with physical objects. Learning what he called 'the secret language of junk', he scoured Broadway and local parks for whatever discarded items he could find. The elements of chance and surprise played a significant part in this process and soon became integral to what Rauschenberg called his 'collaboration' with what he found. Liberated from painterly convention, he began incorporating these 'found objects' into his canvases as painted sculptures and sculpted paintings.

Created in the summer of 1955, the most famous of Rauschenberg's combines is *Bed*. He stuck bedclothes – a pillow, a quilt and a bedsheet – on a wooden board and graffitied them with paint and pencil. The paint was relatively cheap and the board was found on the streets, but the bedclothes he later claimed were his own. Seen in this light, *Bed* becomes an intimate, sensual, revealing self-portrait. One early critic thought it looked like a murder scene after the body had been taken away, but Rauschenberg protested that it had a 'friendly' – perhaps even sexual – vitality. Either way, Rauschenberg's collaborative collision of contemporary everyday detritus with traditional (portrait) painting is the first work of sculptural Pop.

OPPOSITE
Robert Rauschenberg
Bed, 1955

OIL AND PENCIL ON PILLOW, QUILT AND SHEET ON WOOD SUPPORTS

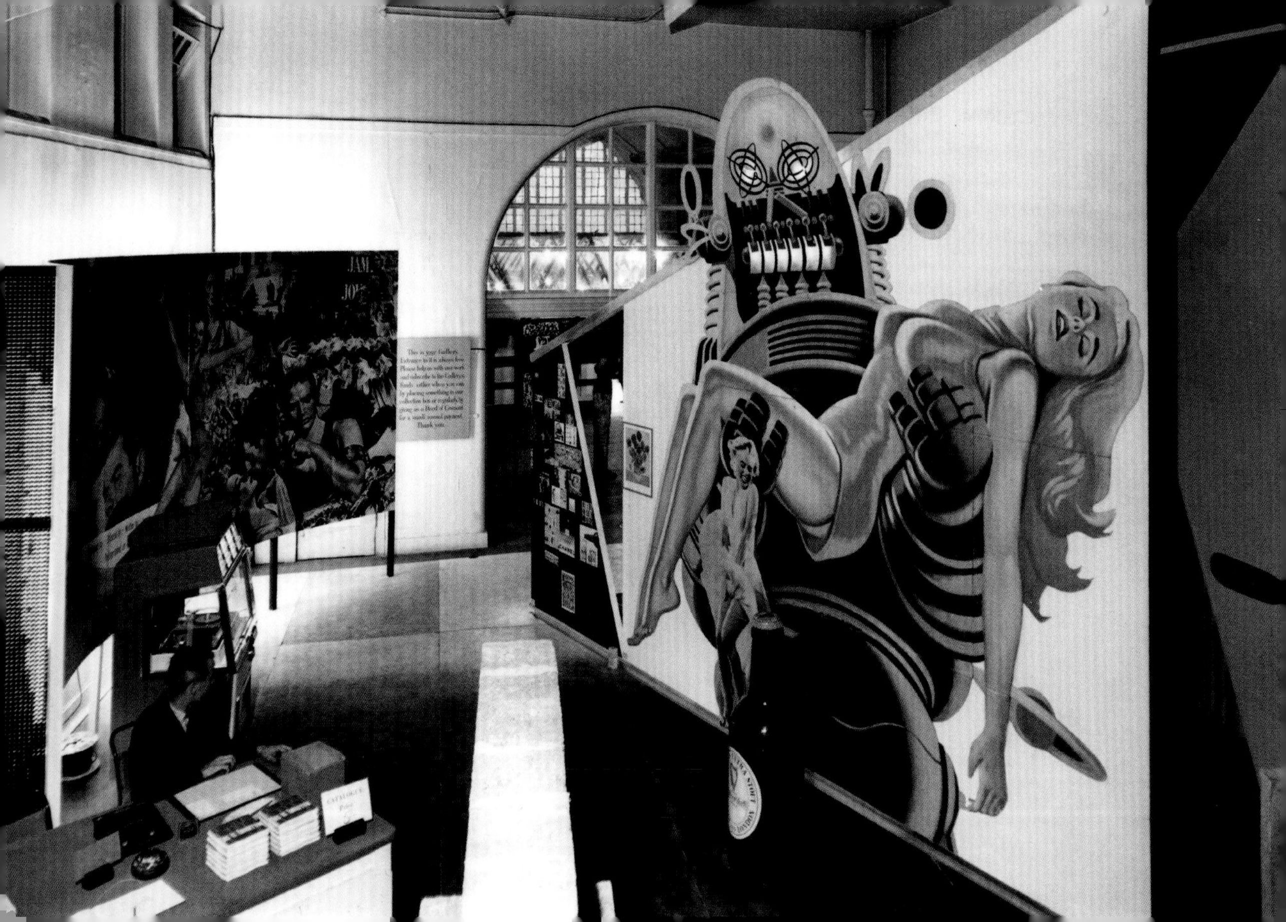

12

This is Tomorrow exhibition

1956

In the summer of 1956, London's Whitechapel Gallery played host to an exhibition of early British Pop artists called *This is Tomorrow*. The title said it all, and the exhibition posters, pasted on walls and hoardings across the city, announced the Pop visuals of a new age. Apparently seen by a thousand people a day during its one-month run, in retrospect *This is Tomorrow* was one
16 of the first Pop **'happenings'**. Opened by an actor dressed as Robby the Robot – a character in the then-recent science-fiction film *Forbidden Planet* – the exhibition was described by design critic Reyner Banham as 'modern art to entertain people, modern art as a game people will want to play'.

Developed as a collaborative project over two years, the show was put together by forty artists, designers and theorists – 'highly independent and free-standing geniuses', according to Banham – some of whom were
6 associated with the **Independent Group**. They were eventually marshalled into twelve groups of three or four, given £50 for materials and instructed to take the wide-ranging theme of 'modern life' as their inspiration. The limited resources available to each group, coupled with the broad theme, produced 12 playfully creative and diverse 'environments' where viewers were 'invited to enter strange houses, corridors and mazes'. Group 6, which included Eduardo Paolozzi, created a shed-like structure full of curious and juxtaposed 'found objects'. The room created by Group 2, whose members included Richard Hamilton and John McHale, was perhaps the most dazzling, however. Theirs was a frantic and mesmerizing ironic Pop collision of Guinness bottles, Hollywood poster pin-ups, art-historical reproductions, a loud jukebox, a 'strawberry perfumed carpet', a
Marilyn Monroe 'readymade' and – 45
only months before the Suez Crisis – a continuously playing film reel of the Royal Navy at sea. Anticipating the ideas and the practices of artists of the next three decades, *This is Tomorrow* was British Pop Art's popular debut.

OPPOSITE
Group 2 exhibit from the *This is Tomorrow* exhibition, Whitechapel Gallery, London, 1956

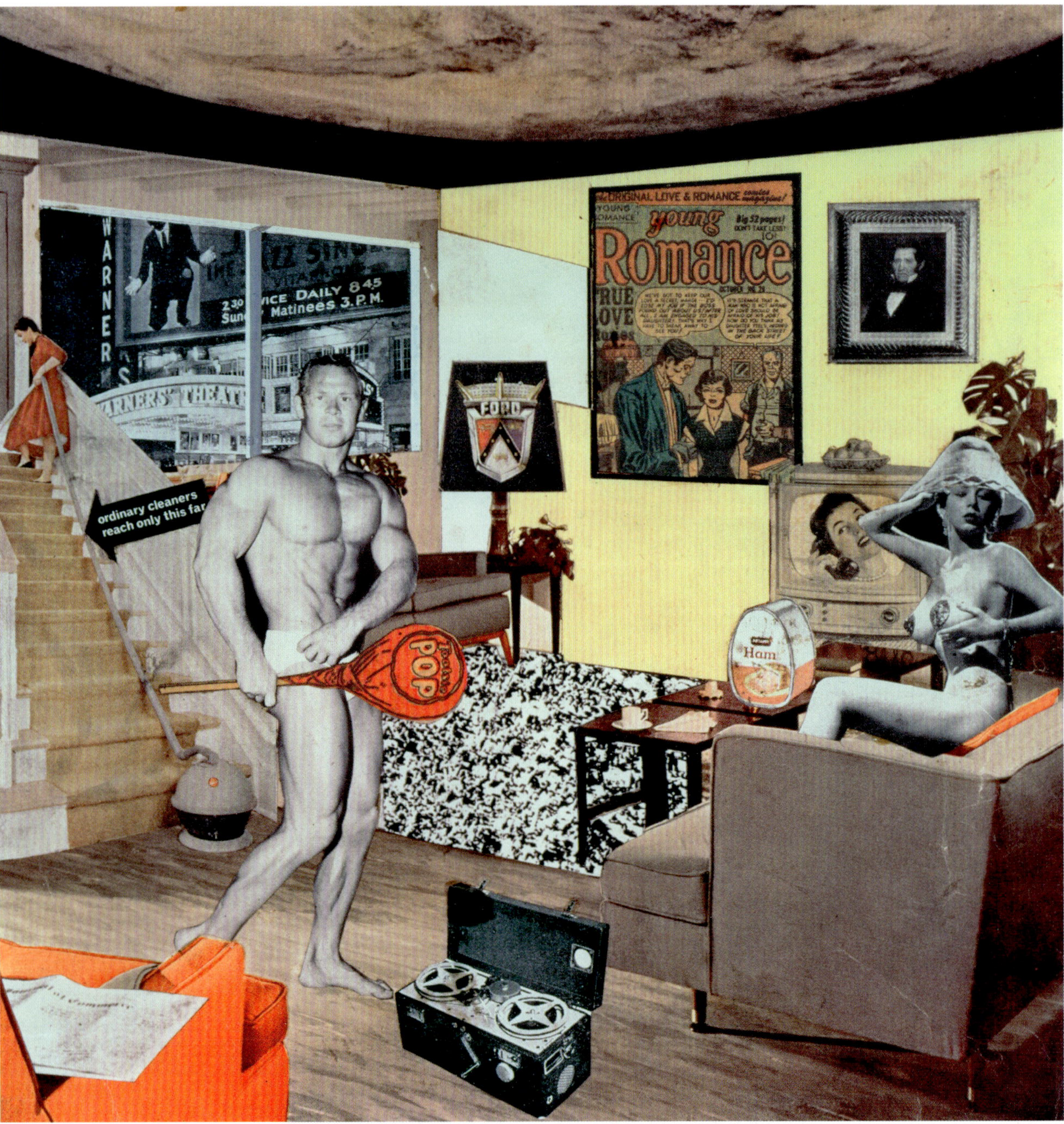

WARNER
DAILY 845
Matinees 3.P.M.
ordinary cleaners
reach only this far
FORD
ORIGINAL LOVE & ROMANCE
Young
Romance
Big 52 pages!
POP
Ham

13

Just what is it that makes today's homes so different, so appealing?

Richard Hamilton

1956

Emblematic of what *Queen* magazine called the 'Age of Boom', Richard Hamilton's 1956 Pop collage *Just what is it that makes today's homes so different, so appealing?* is his most celebrated. Made from material printed in American magazines such as the *Ladies' Home Journal* and partly inspired by the satirical magazine *MAD*, Hamilton created this work for the catalogue of the Whitechapel Gallery's
12 ***This is Tomorrow*** exhibition.

Produced in the space of a morning, the collage shows Hamilton's fascination with the new consumerist aesthetic of the 1950s. In his contemporary Eden, Mr America competitor Irvin 'Zabo' Koszewski takes the part of Adam and brandishes a lollipop emblazoned with the word 'POP'. Hamilton's topless Eve comes, we now know, from a published photograph of the American painter Jo Baer – a model in the early 1950s. Their open-plan sitting room, lifted from an advertisement for floor linoleum, is dominated by an aerial photograph of the Earth. Through the picture window we glimpse Broadway on the opening night of the first sound film in 1927. Prefiguring the work of Roy Lichtenstein, on the main wall Hamilton places, alongside a 19th-century grandee, an advertisement for the 1950s comic strip *Young Romance*.

Although it's unlikely that they were aware of Hamilton's work at the time, American Pop artists were soon using the same iconographic schemes. Many of the ubiquitous icons of consumerism feature prominently in Hamilton's work:
the Stromberg-Carlson box **TV**, the 25
Ford Motor Company logo, Hoover's Constellation vacuum cleaner, even a new cassette recorder, alongside the more prosaic tin of processed ham and the influential *Journal of Commerce*. For all its slick abundance, however, Hamilton's work seems to hint at an underlying anxiety; the room feels as if it might soon close in on its inhabitants, suffocating them with the consumable objects of their desire. British prime minister Harold Macmillan famously declared the following summer that the British people had 'never had it so good', but he also went on to ask, 'Is it too good to last?'

OPPOSITE
Richard Hamilton
Just what is it that makes today's homes so different, so appealing?, 1956

COLLAGE ON PAPER

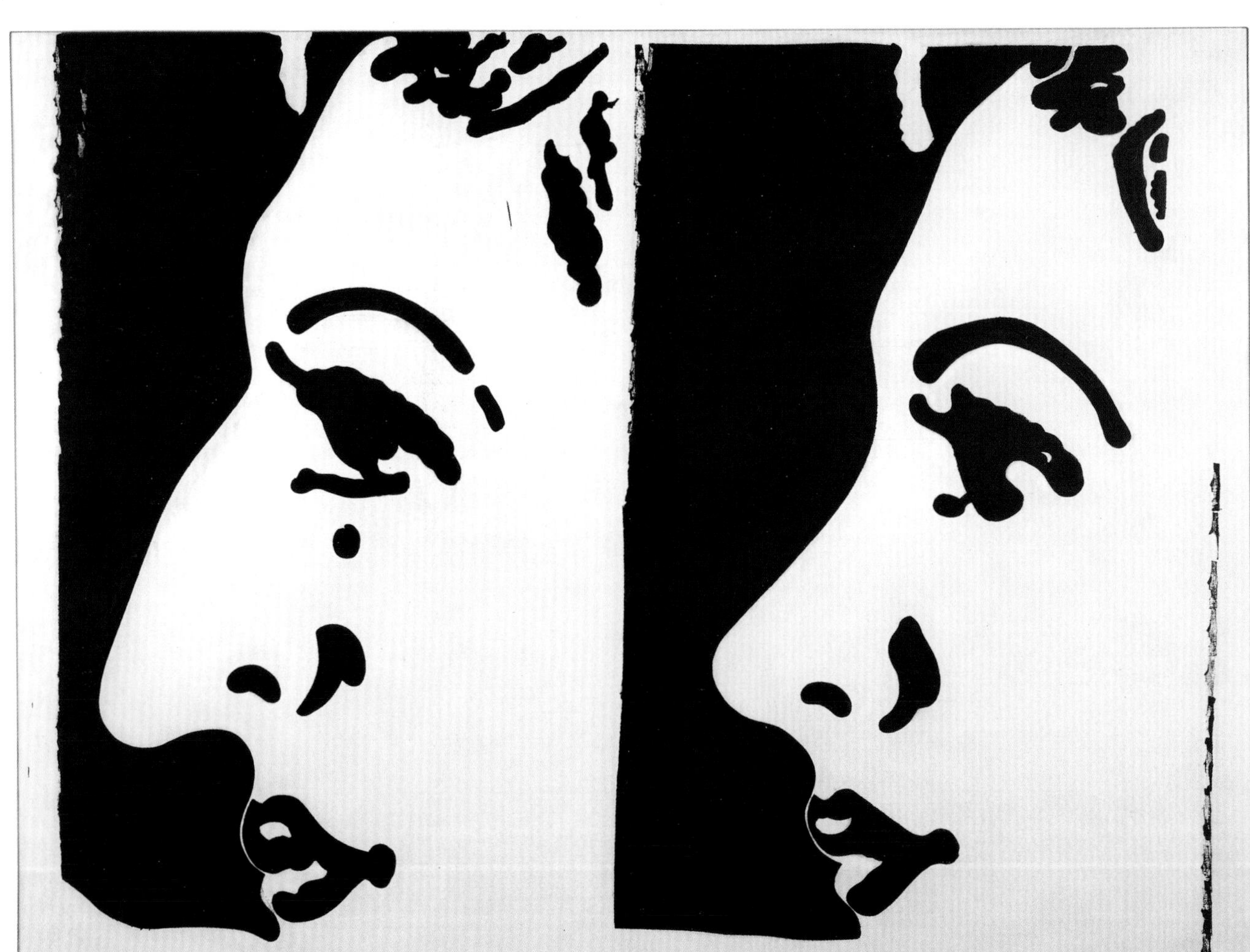

14

Plastic surgery

Pioneered in the early 20th century for injured soldiers returning from the First World War, modern cosmetic plastic surgery is most readily associated with Hollywood celebrities. Golden-age Hollywood icons Mary 45 Pickford, **Marilyn Monroe** and Gary Cooper – believers in the body's ultimate perfectibility – were some of the first to submit to the surgeon's knife. After all, what better way to correct flaws and get themselves lens-ready than cosmetic surgery?

In 1957, on the verge of personal and artistic transformation, 29-year-old commercial illustrator Andrew Warhola (soon to be known as Andy Warhol) had a nose job to correct a nasal skin lesion, though the decision was also no doubt prompted by a desire to perfect the contour of his face. Warhola had never liked his nose and his early student *Nosepicker* paintings from the late 1940s certainly suggest anxiety about its size and shape. In the same way that Monroe defaced photographs of herself she didn't like, Warhol had even improved his passport photo, using a pen to narrow his nose and lower his hairline. Artistically, he was always fascinated by the connection between beauty and pain and transformation, and in 1960–2 he produced a series of images called *Before and After*, inspired by a nose-job advertisement in the *National Enquirer*. Known by his colleagues around this time as Raggedy Andy, and unhappy with the results of his nose job, Warhol would soon begin consciously shaping what would quickly become an iconic public persona, inseparable from dark glasses, white-blond wig and loose clothes, and affecting a defensive, monosyllabic tone of voice.

A willing participant in the evangelical perfection culture he obliquely sought to challenge, Warhol suggests in his 1968 film *Flesh* that real flesh is far less attractive than plastic fantasy. That same year he provocatively claimed, 'I love Hollywood…Everybody's plastic. I want to be plastic.' Poster boy for the American myth of personal transformation – from the mere 'normal' to the profoundly exceptional – Warhol was an observer, hiding behind a constructed plastic persona that became his greatest creation, and would soon become synonymous with Pop Art itself.

OPPOSITE
Andy Warhol
Before and After [3], 1961
CASEIN ON LINEN

POP ART is:

Popular (designed for a mass audience)

Transient (short term solution)

Expendable (easily forgotten)

Low cost

Mass produced

Young (aimed at youth)

Witty

Sexy

Gimmicky

Glamorous

Big business

Hamilton later listed Pop's concerns: 'Man, Woman, Humanity, History, Food, Newspapers, Cinema, TV, Telephone, Comics (picture information), Words (textual information), Tape recording (aural information), Cars, Domestic appliances, Space'

15

The Hamilton treatise

1957

Domestic appliances

Cinema

Woman

Cars

Man

Writing in January 1957 to his friends the British architects Alison and Peter Smithson, Richard Hamilton defined the attributes that were characteristic of Pop Art. For 'Daddy Pop', as Hamilton would later be known, Pop Art was the antithesis of the kind of art loved by high-minded conservative critics. Crucially, it was fun, it was kitschy, it was urbane and it was rebellious.

With an eye to the future, Hamilton wrote that Pop Art was:

—

Popular (designed for a mass audience),
Transient (short term solution),
Expendable (easily forgotten),
Low cost, Mass produced,
Young (aimed at youth), Witty,
Sexy, Gimmicky, Glamorous,
Big business

—

He later listed Pop's concerns:

—

Man
Woman
Humanity
History
Food
Newspapers
Cinema
TV
Telephone
Comics (picture information)
Words (textual information)
Tape recording (aural information)
Cars
Domestic appliances
Space

—

Pop art was accessible and visually stimulating. It was cheap to produce. It was youthful and didn't care for the weight of art history or reverence for it. It was as ephemeral and throwaway as the things that inspired it. It often avoided politics and, rather than disdaining the manufactured and mass-produced, it revelled in the excesses of capitalism. Often, Pop artists weren't interested in changing the world; they just wanted to have fun living in it and interpreting it.

Today, Pop Art still feels recognizable. The digital age has merely proliferated and widened the scope of the mass popular culture that was Pop Art's lifeblood. Living in run-down parts of London, Berlin, Paris and New York, surrounded by junk and finding value in rubbish, with their sometimes-apolitical attitudes and ironic approach to the past, today's hipsters will undoubtedly recognize the aesthetics of decay made fashionable by Pop.

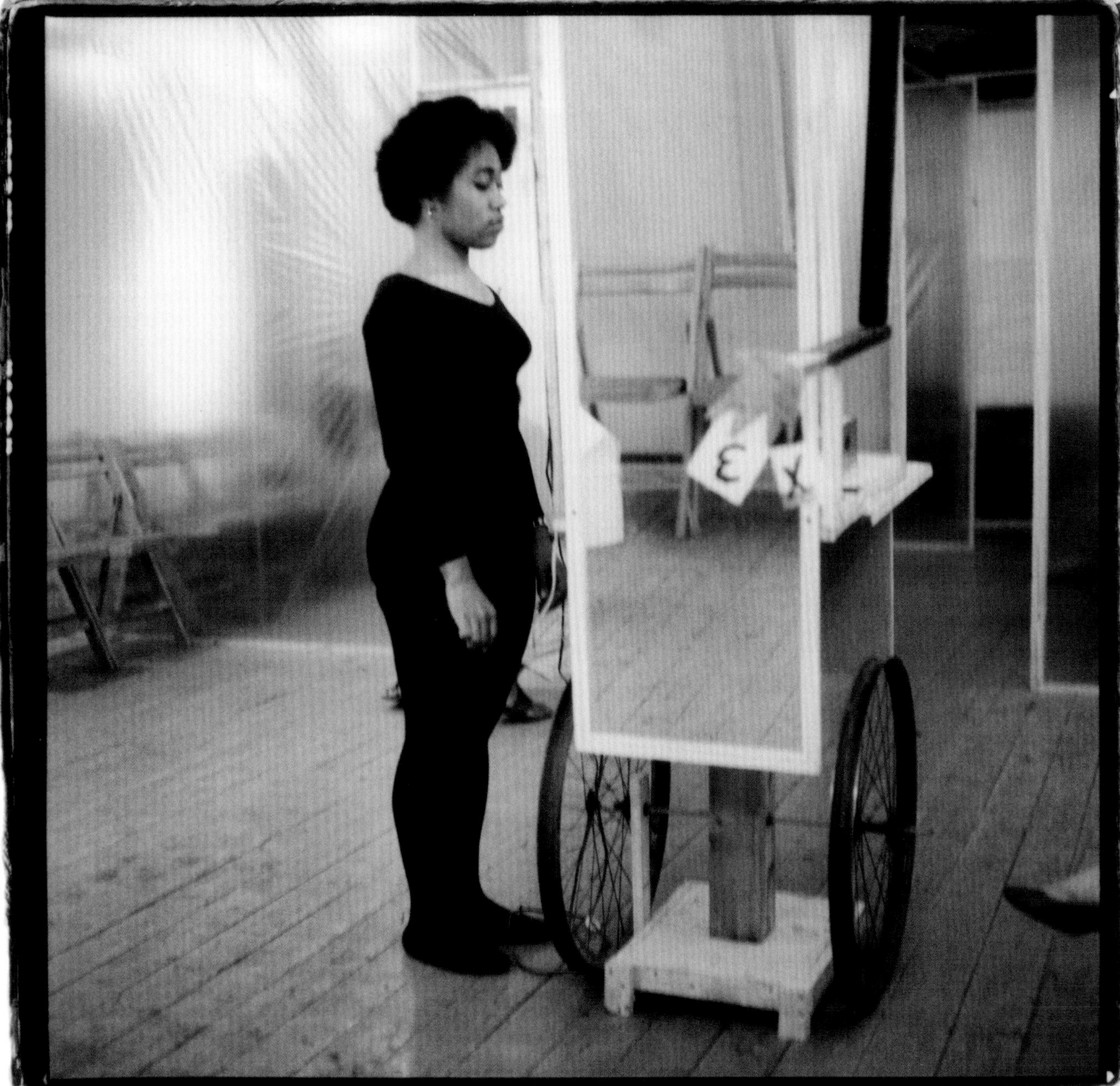

16

The ‘happening’

The ‘happening’ was a term first coined by the American performance artist Allan Kaprow in 1957 at a picnic held at the New Jersey home of Pop artist George Segal. For Kaprow, the happening would be a site-specific multimedia, multi-sensory art installation or living sculptural display – ‘something spontaneous, something that just happens’. Alongside several Pop artists, Kaprow wanted to appropriate familiar spaces, objects, images and sounds and, through the happening, experience them in new ways.

With roots in the Dadaist tradition, Kaprow’s happenings focused on the process of creation rather than on what was being created. For him, a work of art included the artist themselves in an ongoing though timeless and ephemeral process: the happening was the work of art, not the images, sounds or objects that might result from it. Conceived as ‘complete works of art’ – three-dimensional collages, in a way – his events laid bare the creative process and sought to jolt the audience out of their perceived complacency and into active participation. The invitations to his 1959 performance *18 Happenings in 6 Parts*, staged at the newly opened Reuben Gallery in New York, warned attendees that ‘you will become part of the happenings; you will simultaneously experience them’.

The most influential Pop artist to employ the happening was Claes Oldenburg, whose most famous event was the 1961 installation ***The Store***. The creator of several 
happenings in New York and **Los** 
Angeles, Oldenburg even posed as a living sculpture atop a plinth outside the American Embassy in London’s Grosvenor Square. There were other celebrated Pop happenings: for example, Ray Johnson’s New York Correspondence School **‘postal** 
happenings’, Jim Dine’s unnerving installation *Car Crash* (1960), Robert Rauschenberg’s choreographed *Pelican* (1963), staged in a New York TV studio-turned-roller-skating rink, and Stan VanDerBeek’s filmic happening *Movie-Drome* (1965). Because, as Kaprow famously reminded his friend and colleague Roy Lichtenstein, ‘art doesn’t have to look like art’.

OPPOSITE
American performance artist Shirley Prendergast stands next to the *Sandwich Man*, a wheeled sculpture, during preparations for Allan Kaprow’s *18 Happenings in 6 Parts* at the Reuben Gallery, New York City, 2 October 1959

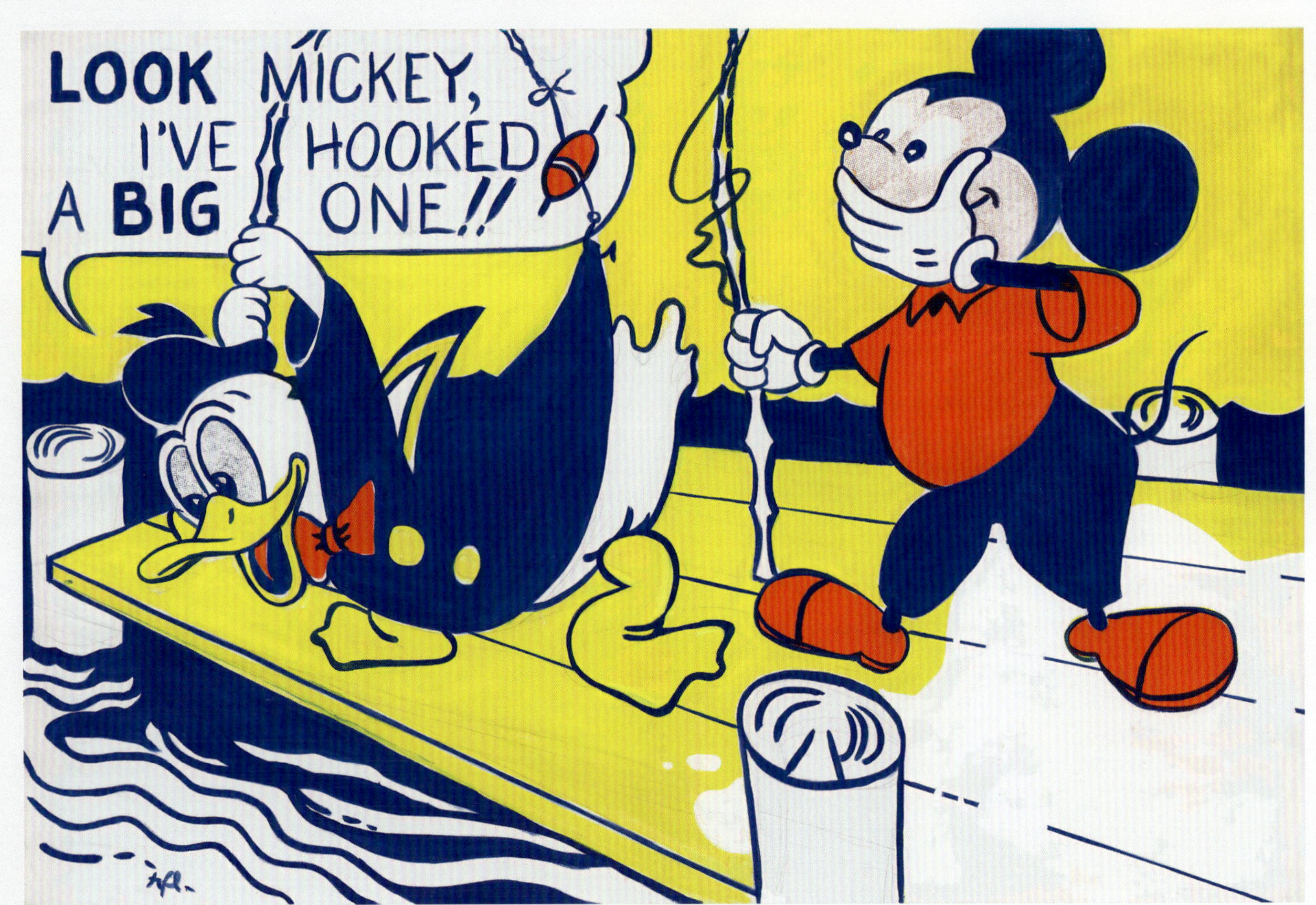
LOOK MICKEY, I'VE HOOKED A BIG ONE!!

17

Disney

Between his teaching duties – commencing in 1958 at the State University of New York Oswego – and family responsibilities in upstate New York, Roy Lichtenstein became the first artist to depict with his own hand the most recognizable of Pop Art motifs: the cartoon character. Executed in 1958, his simple yet assured ink-and-brush study of Donald Duck captures the character's playful personality and marks the start of Lichtenstein's lifelong interest in Disney iconography. Created by a host of Disney illustrators, Donald Duck first appeared in comic print in 1934 and within a decade had become the popular star of well over a hundred Disney animations. He is, like many cartoon characters, an exaggerated, attention-grabbing version of someone you or I might know, making these characters powerful, instantly recognizable avatars.

In common with other Pop artists, Lichtenstein was drawn to whatever had mass appeal. And Donald Duck seemed to be everywhere, licensed for print publication in the United States and across Europe and exported across the world to become one of the most popular and recognizable American mascots of the post-war period. In short, Donald Duck was an ideal subject for the new Pop Art. Besides, at this time Lichtenstein was a young father, married to interior designer Isabel Wilson with two young sons, David and Mitchell. According to Lichtenstein, it was seven-year-old David who, in June 1961, inspired his iconic *Look Mickey* of the same year by pointing to a Disney comic with the challenge, 'I bet you can't paint as good as that!'

Contrary to popular belief, Lichtenstein never produced direct copies or reproductions of **comic-strip images**; 55 57 instead he selected and adapted their most striking motifs or expressive features. In *Look Mickey* – prompted and inspired by an illustration from the 1960 Disney book *Donald Duck Lost and Found* – he retained the exuberant central figures of Mickey Mouse and Donald Duck, but, by simplifying the scene, restraining and heightening his colour palette, reorienting the picture and providing Donald with a speech bubble, he enhanced the exclamatory tone of the original drawing. As these early Lichtenstein works make clear, without Disney and its comic-book aesthetic – perhaps even without the young David Lichtenstein – Pop Art would look very different.

OPPOSITE
Roy Lichtenstein
Look Mickey, 1961
OIL ON CANVAS

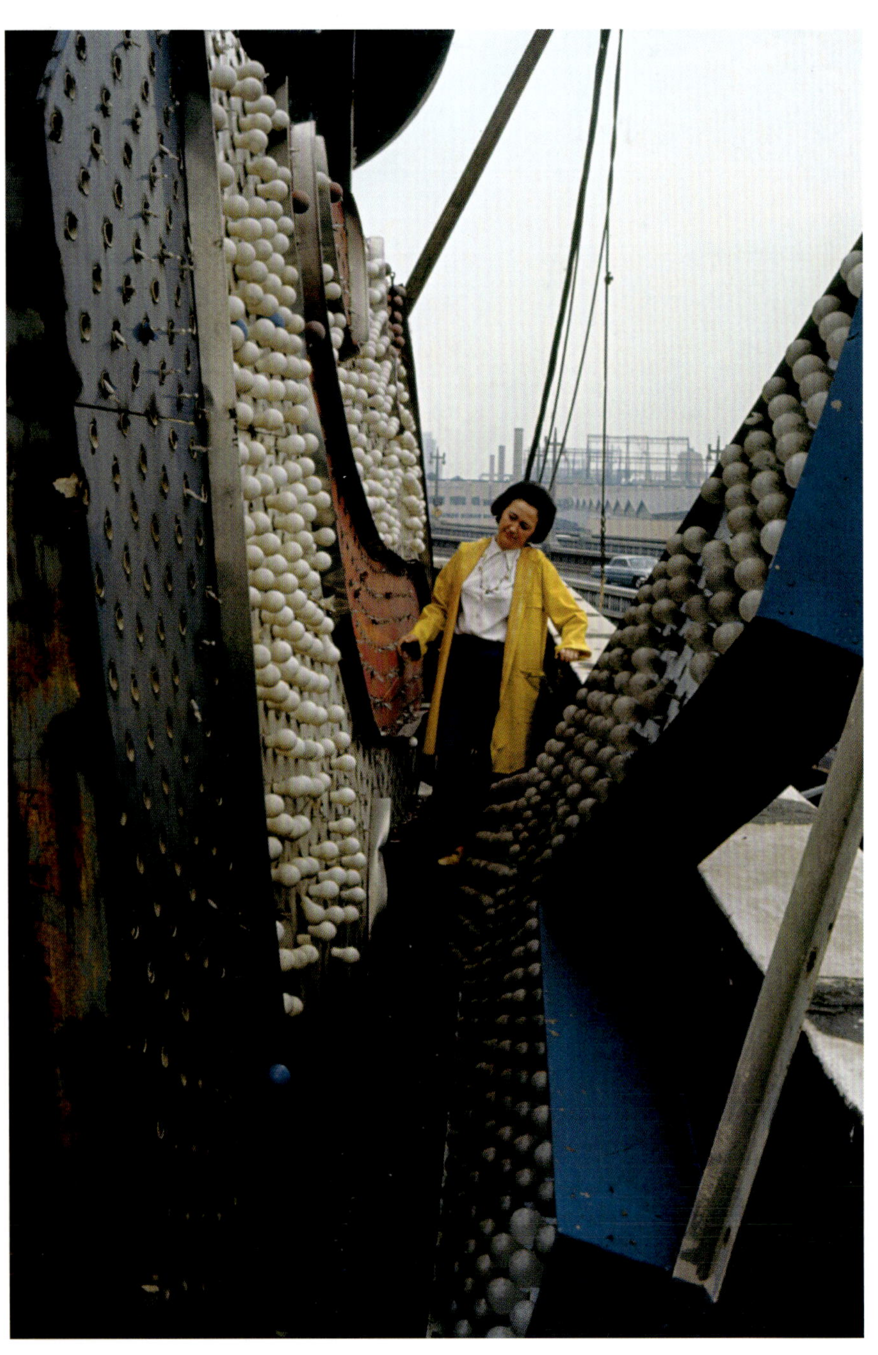

18

Chryssa

A pioneer of Pop sculpture, Greek-born American artist Chryssa Vardea-Mavromichali – known professionally simply as Chryssa – is renowned for her large-scale works of Pop 'assemblage', which make use of industrial materials such as steel, aluminium and neon glass tubing. She came to New York in 1955 and for the next forty years rented a cheap downtown studio that was later described by Pop Art dealer Leo Castelli as 'one of the loveliest in the world'.

Having trained as an artist in Paris
50 and later in **San Francisco**, Chryssa claimed to have always been fascinated by American culture, in which she saw links to her own. The dazzling neon of the advertisements on Broadway and in Times Square provoked what she called her 'visionary state'. The brightly lit streets and, in particular, the gaudiness of Times Square reminded her of the golden Byzantine mosaics and icons familiar to her from her childhood in Greece. The combination of these twin inspirations led to her solo exhibition at the prestigious Guggenheim Museum in New York at the age of only 28.

Lending the signs and symbols of the urban metropolis what she called 'Homeric wisdom', Chryssa explored the mystery and enchantment of the modern city, and the contemporary individual's navigable experience of it, through her Pop assemblages. A pioneer not only as a female Pop artist but also as a maker of large-scale neon-light sculpture, she famously created the monumental *Gates to Times Square* (1966), which was shown for the first time at New York's Pace Gallery. Formed of two huge neon letter A's, it was so large that people could actually walk through it and into a gleaming stainless-steel and Plexiglas box. Just as the natural landscape inspired awe and moved the Romantic artists of the early 19th century, so the modern Pop cityscape spoke to Chryssa of the sublime.

OPPOSITE
Chryssa looks at several disused illuminated signs on a rooftop, New York City, 1965

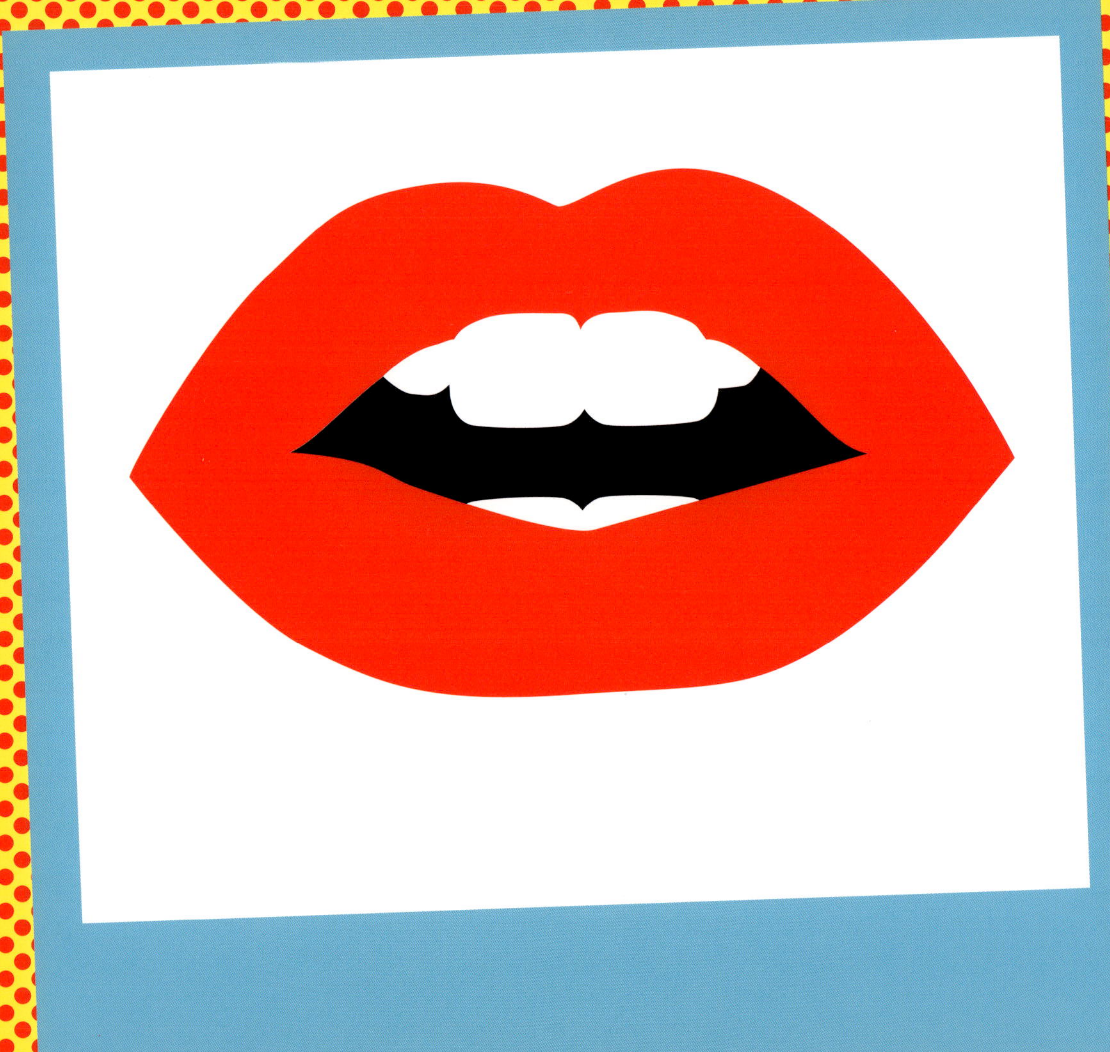

19

Polaroid

Long before the invention of the iPhone, Andy Warhol knew how to capture cool. Buying his first Polaroid camera in 1958, he would soon become famous for photographing the period's key players in culture, sport and high society. In fact, it's difficult to name a personality from the late 1960s, 1970s and 1980s who wasn't photographed by Warhol. Reminiscent of the painted portraits of the past, his Polaroid snapshots captured the 83 glamour of **modern celebrity**.

Polaroid cameras, invented by the American scientist Edwin Land and first marketed in 1948, enabled an affordable photograph to be taken and developed in under a minute. Both instant and disposable, the Polaroid image couldn't be more Pop if it tried and soon became synonymous with Warhol himself. Passing through his studio at the 71 **Factory** in New York, anyone who was anyone eagerly submitted to Warhol's camera and some of these images 36 even became **silkscreen** portraits. Celebrity couples he photographed included the Jaggers and the Lennons; then there were the writers and artists William S. Burroughs, Joseph Beuys and Robert Mapplethorpe, singers Debbie Harry and Diana Ross, designers Yves Saint Laurent and Gianni Versace – not to mention the likes of Farrah Fawcett, Grace Jones, Arnold Schwarzenegger, Muhammad Ali and Joan Collins. Among Warhol's more unlikely subjects were US president Jimmy Carter and the last Empress of Iran, Farah Diba Pahlavi.

Warhol's sitters are, more often than not, seen alone. Like gallery exhibits, they are arranged in self-conscious poses against an austere white background. Their often bare shoulders increase the voyeuristic intimacy of the close-up. The camera is an intrusive, almost confrontational presence – the Pop camera Warhol wanted to become, perhaps, when he famously said, 'I want to be a machine.' The faces of his sitters are bleached by the bright flash but in their eyes what Warhol really captures, as Pop's 'voyeur-in-chief', is both the power and the vulnerability of fame.

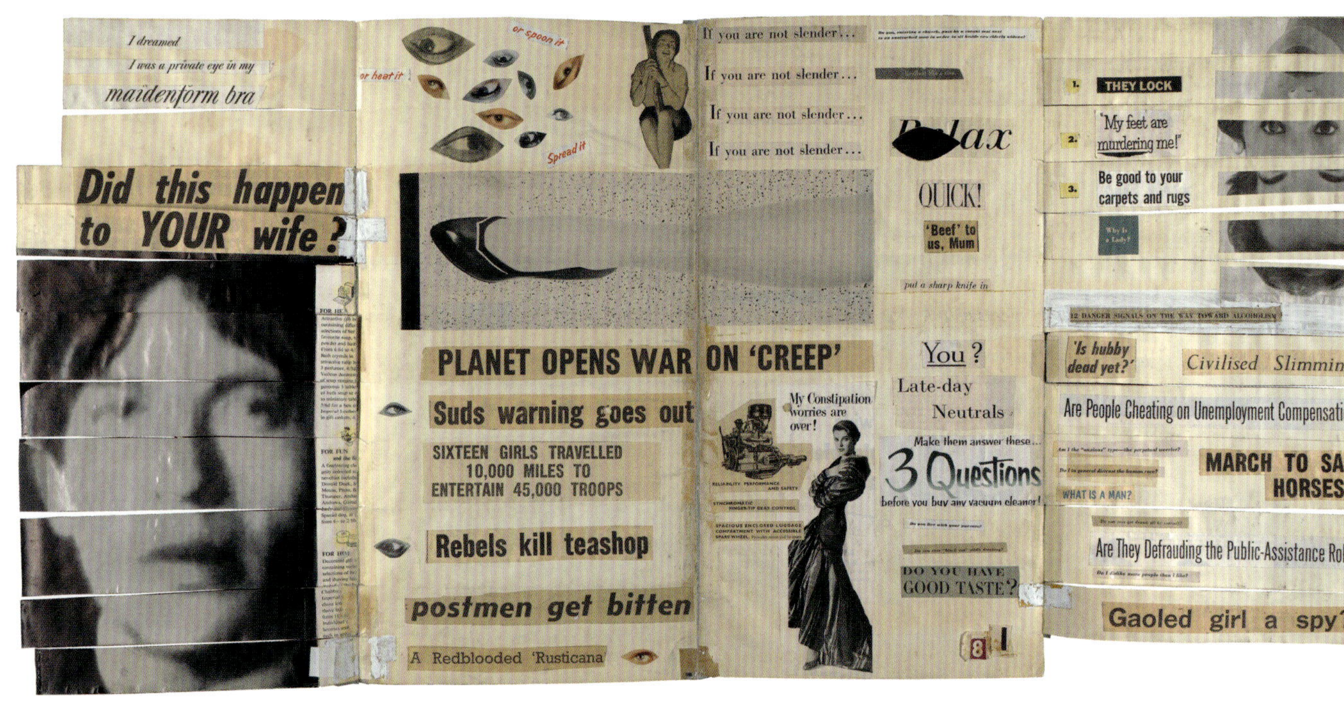

I dreamed
I was a private eye in my
maidenform bra
Did this happen
to YOUR wife?
or spoon it
or heat it
Spread it
PLANET OPENS WAR ON 'CREEP'
Suds warning goes out
SIXTEEN GIRLS TRAVELLED
10,000 MILES TO
ENTERTAIN 45,000 TROOPS
Rebels kill teashop
postmen get bitten
A Redblooded 'Rusticana
If you are not slender...
If you are not slender...
If you are not slender...
If you are not slender...
My Constipation worries are over!
QUICK!
'Beef' to us, Mum
put a sharp knife in
You?
Late-day
Neutrals
Make them answer these...
3 Questions
before you buy any vacuum cleaner!
DO YOU HAVE GOOD TASTE?
1. THEY LOCK
2. 'My feet are murdering me!'
3. Be good to your carpets and rugs
12 DANGER SIGNALS ON THE WAY TOWARD ALCOHOLISM
'Is hubby dead yet?'
Civilised Slimming?
Are People Cheating on Unemployment Compensation?
MARCH TO SAVE HORSES?
WHAT IS A MAN?
Are They Defrauding the Public-Assistance Rolls?
Gaoled girl a spy?

20

‘Pop Art’

1958

It was probably the British collagist John McHale who, at least conversationally, first used the term ‘Pop Art’ to describe the work that he and his fellow London Independents were creating. There are, however, several other British artists and critics of the period, including Frank Cordell and Reyner Banham, who later claimed that they had invented it. Diplomatically, the critic and curator Lawrence Alloway agreed that, between 1955 and 1957,
6 among former **Independent Group**
artists, Pop Art had become a term that ‘acquired currency in conversation’. McHale and Alloway were clearly discussing these developments with their friends. In print at least, though, it was Alloway who, in 1958, first defined what ‘mass popular art’ was and where it came from.

In his article ‘The Arts and the Mass Media’, published in the February 1958 edition of the London magazine *Architectural Design*, Alloway described how ‘mass popular art’ – the kitschy so-called low art of everyday mass media – had superseded the elevated traditions of high art. Later clarifying what he’d written, he said, ‘What I meant by it then is not what it means now. I used the term, and also “Pop Culture”, to refer to the products of the mass media, not to works of art that draw upon popular culture.’ Pop culture, of course, nurses Pop Art.

It is often impossible to locate the precise beginning and end of any artistic movement, particularly a movement like Pop Art, which was both inspired by mass culture and often indistinguishable from it. No artist is immune to popular culture, even if they traditionally disdain it. But during the 20th century, and particularly after the Second World War, Alloway’s ‘mass popular culture’ extended its technological reach further than ever before, proving itself an unavoidable influence on every art movement since.

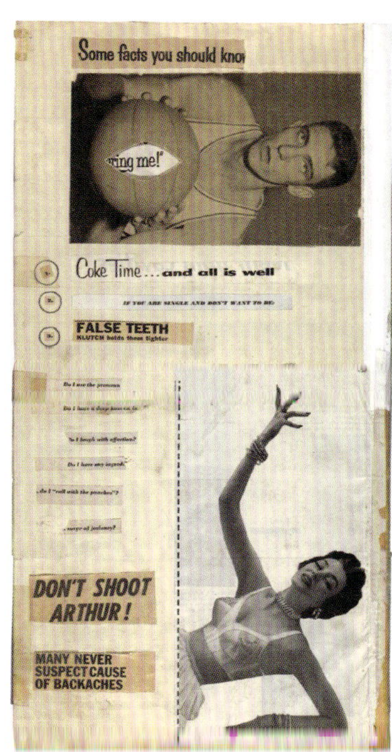

OPPOSITE AND ABOVE
John McHale
From *Why I Took to the Washers in Luxury Flats*, 1954

UNIQUE COLLAGE BOOK

Peak Pop, 1959–68

As the 1960s dawned, Pop Art exploded – not without controversy – onto the New York cultural scene. University art teacher Roy Lichtenstein and commercial shoe illustrator Andy Warhol were independently discovered by New York art dealer **Ivan Karp** 31, their sensational exhibitions becoming controversial **'happenings'** 16 that kicked off an intense five-year outpouring of Pop Art.

Despite critics decrying them as **'New Vulgarians'** 39 and older art-world rivals becoming enflamed with rage at their success (Willem de Kooning called Warhol a 'killer of art' and Mark Rothko called them both **'Popsicles'** 35), Pop Art and Pop artists flourished. Ahead of the curve, their curators and dealers – across Europe and the United States – created a new and extraordinarily lucrative Pop Art market. In response to their times, Pop artists found playful and inventive ways to explore the conflicted world around them.

Pop Art came off the wall with **sculptural paintings by Marjorie Strider** 61 and **installations by Claes Oldenburg** 32. Ray Johnson's **Mail Art** 22 democratized Pop Art just as **Marta Minujín** 78 made it as immersive as possible. **Marisol Escobar** 41 sculpted powerful **wooden figures** 58, while **Corita Kent** [illegible] printed loud political slogans, while [illegible] [illegible] and **Pauline Boty** 72 explored female stereotypes, while Martha Rosler and Allen Jones, in their own ways, highlighted the violence of human relations, both in the home and around the world. As **Rosalyn Drexler made Pop Art out of pulp fiction** 56, ***Interview* magazine** 88 made celebrity achingly mundane, and novelist **J. G. Ballard** 89 made the mundane pretty terrifying. **James Rosenquist painted phallic rockets** 70, while **Tom Wesselmann** 30 and Mel Ramos depicted the soft-core nudes of **Pop porn** 87. **Jann Haworth** 48 made uncanny soft sculpture, while **Dorothy Grebenak** 62 hand-stitched Pop rugs. Creative and long-lasting transatlantic friendships were forged between **David Hockney and R. B. Kitaj** 21 and between **James Rosenquist and Erró** 60. And Andy Warhol – in a 'swinging' decade marred by war, assassinations and **deep anxieties about the atomic bomb** 51 – called death 'the most embarrassing thing that could happen to you', before being shot in a botched **assassination attempt** 82. A defining moment for Pop Art, the 1960s themselves were a period of traumatic ends and new beginnings.

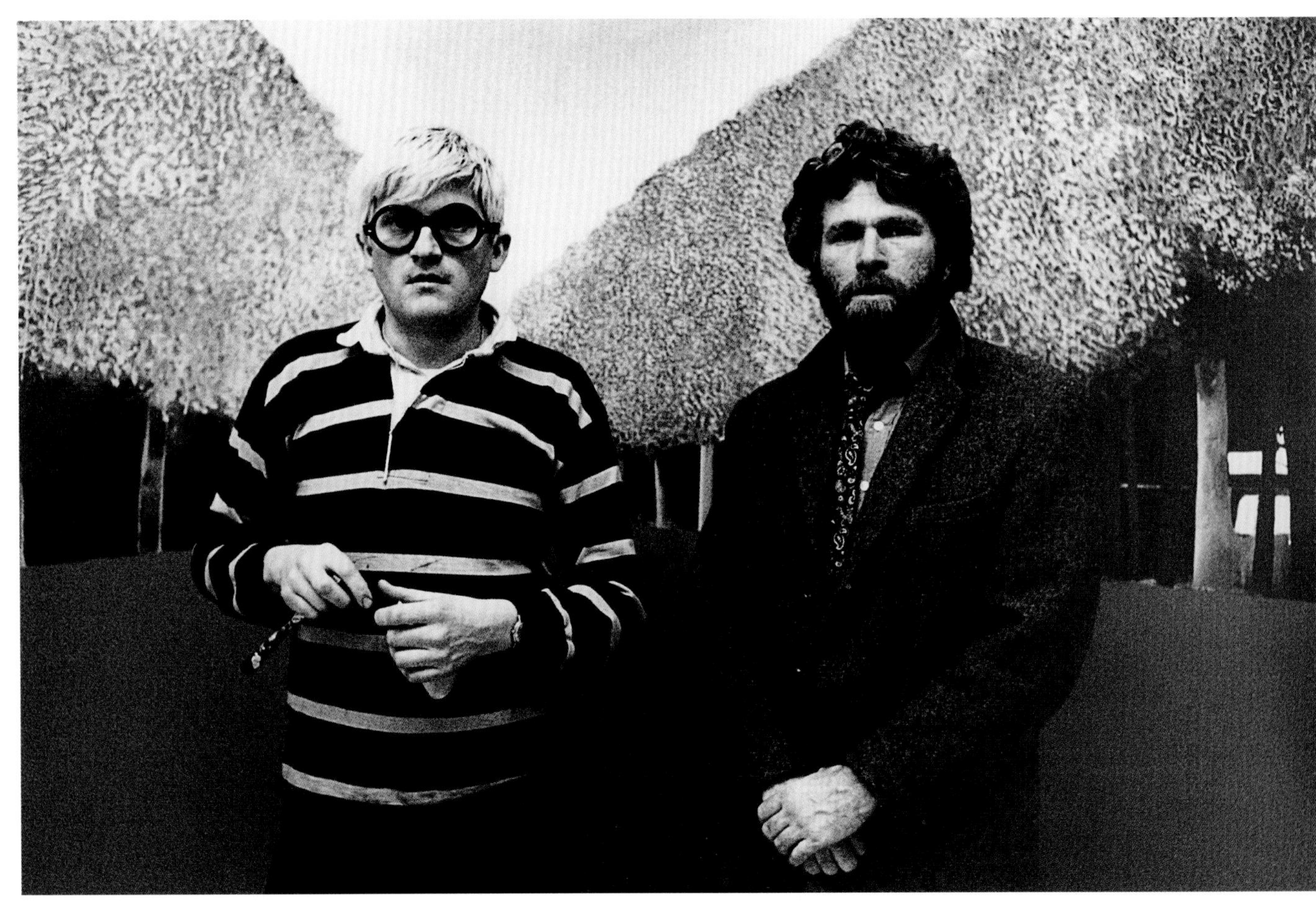

21

R. B. Kitaj meets David Hockney

1959

American Pop artist R. B. 'Ron' Kitaj described British Pop artist David Hockney – best man at his marriage to fellow artist Sandra Fisher – as his oldest friend. Their lasting friendship, which began in 1959 when they met as students at the Royal College of Art in London, was one of the earliest transatlantic Pop alliances.

By 1959, Ohio-born Kitaj – five years older than Hockney – had already studied in New York, Vienna and Oxford, as well as serving in the US Army and the Norwegian merchant navy. Hockney, on the other hand, had only just arrived in London from his native Yorkshire, soon becoming what Kitaj called the 'Bradford Bombshell'. Perhaps surprisingly, they immediately hit it off. Their differences, from one another and from many of the artists around them, created a special bond. If rootedness and homogeneity had played a part in art movements of the past, why couldn't, as Kitaj later argued in his *Diasporist Manifestos* (1989), dispersion and difference now play their own part in the art of today?

In 1961, Hockney and Kitaj showed their early Pop work, alongside that of other students from the RCA, in the *Young Contemporaries* exhibition at the galleries of the Royal Society of British Artists in London. Launching British Pop into the mainstream, the exhibition included works by **Pauline Boty**, Derek Boshier, Peter Blake, Allen Jones, Patrick Caulfield and Peter Phillips. Collectively their art was described by one contemporary critic as a 'sly…bitter-sweet commentary on the reality of things, which might one day evolve into a fully-fledged satire'. 72

Yet Jewish-American Kitaj and Northern working-class Hockney were the self-described 'ambitious exotics' of the RCA group. They encouraged one another to take Pop Art in very personal directions, each reclaiming his respective and diverse history. While Kitaj began exploring Hebrew culture, using it in work that evoked what he called the 'ancient Jewish tradition of commentary', Hockney began exploring gay culture, creating visual images that would stand – according to Kitaj – as 'urgent homosexual messages' of love and hope.

OPPOSITE
David Hockney and R. B. Kitaj, photographed in the 1960s

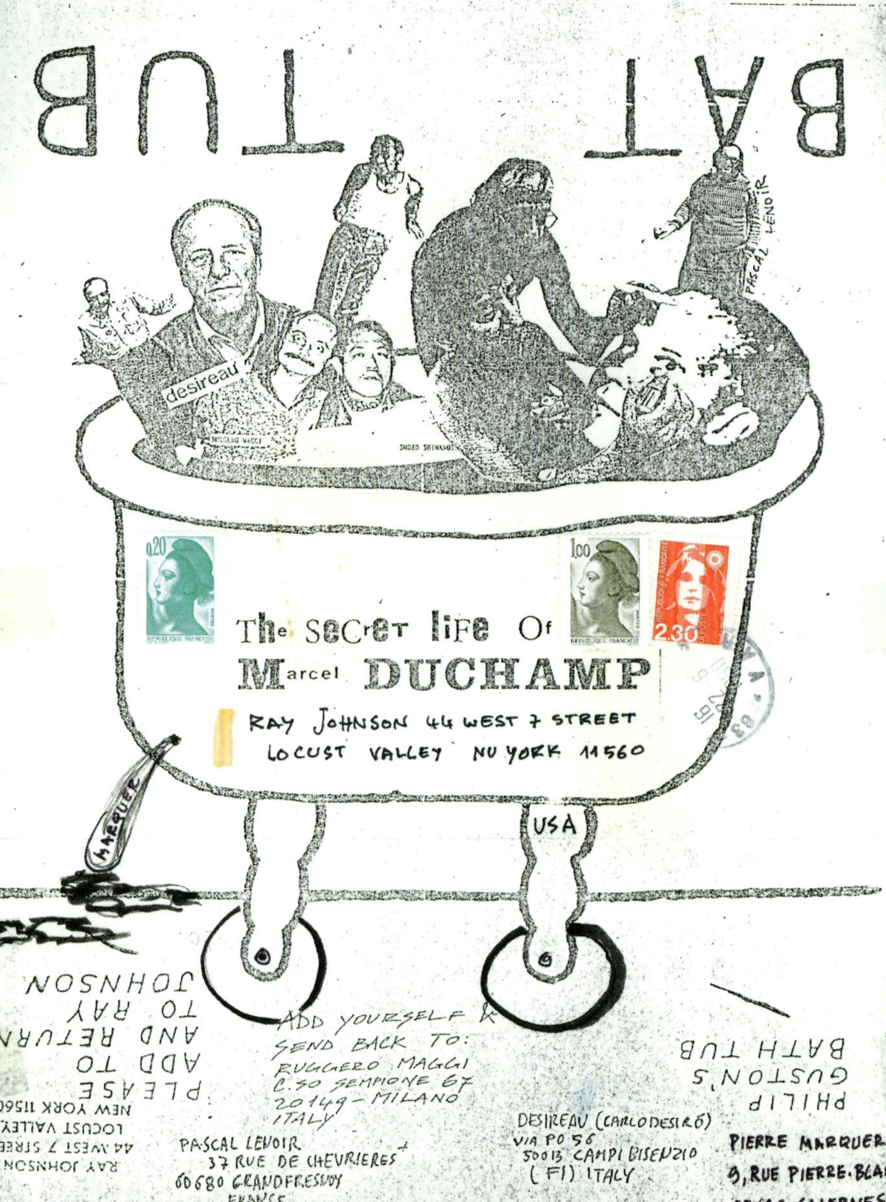

BAT TUB
PASCAL LENOIR
desireau
RUGGERO MAGGI
SHOZO SHIMAMOTO
The secret life Of
Marcel DUCHAMP
RAY JOHNSON 44 WEST 7 STREET
LOCUST VALLEY NU YORK 11560
MARQUER
USA
PLEASE ADD TO AND RETURN TO RAY JOHNSON
RAY JOHNSON 44 WEST 7 STREET LOCUST VALLEY NEW YORK 11560
ADD YOURSELF & SEND BACK TO:
RUGGERO MAGGI
C.SO SEMPIONE 67
20149 - MILANO
ITALY
PHILIP GUSTON'S BATH TUB
PASCAL LENOIR
37 RUE DE CHEVRIERES
60680 GRANDFRESNOY
FRANCE
DESIREAU (CARLO DESIRÒ)
VIA PO 56
50013 CAMPI BISENZIO
(FI) ITALY
PIERRE MARQUER
9, RUE PIERRE-BLANC
83690 SALERNES

22

Mail Art

Once described as New York's 'most famous unknown artist', Ray Johnson was also one of the first American Pop artists. Founder of the Mail Art movement in the 1950s, he and his fellow 'correspondents' showed their work at the 1960 *Gangbang* exhibition, held at the Batman Gallery in San Francisco. As archly noncommittal as ever, fellow commercial artist Andy Warhol once said he'd pay the derisory sum of $10 for anything by Ray Johnson.

An original and inventive variant of Pop, Mail Art soon became known to its adherents as the New York Correspondence School. Johnson's postcards were doodled on, collaged with newspaper and magazine cuttings, and sent through the post to anyone and everyone: friends, artists or members of the public found at random in the local directory. If you received such a postcard, you were obliged to return one – adapting what was sent in your own way. Popular logos, symbols, slogans and images were reclaimed, cut up, rearranged and pasted on postcards and envelopes. Johnson declared, 'I don't make Pop Art, I make Chop Art.' These 'Chop' collages were widely circulated, not just around New York but all over America and as far across the world as the postal services would carry them.

Mail artists rejected the notion that there was an 'end point' to a work of art – that it could or should ever be finished. Their postcard works of art clearly evolved the further they travelled. Stamps accrued over the postcards, often in layers, as they were sent and sent again. The precise angles and positions of these stamps proved a collaboration between artists across great distances. As generous and as inclusive an art as could be, accessible and inexpensive, Mail Art was open to anyone.

OPPOSITE
Ray Johnson
Untitled Mailing (Bat Tub), c. 1983

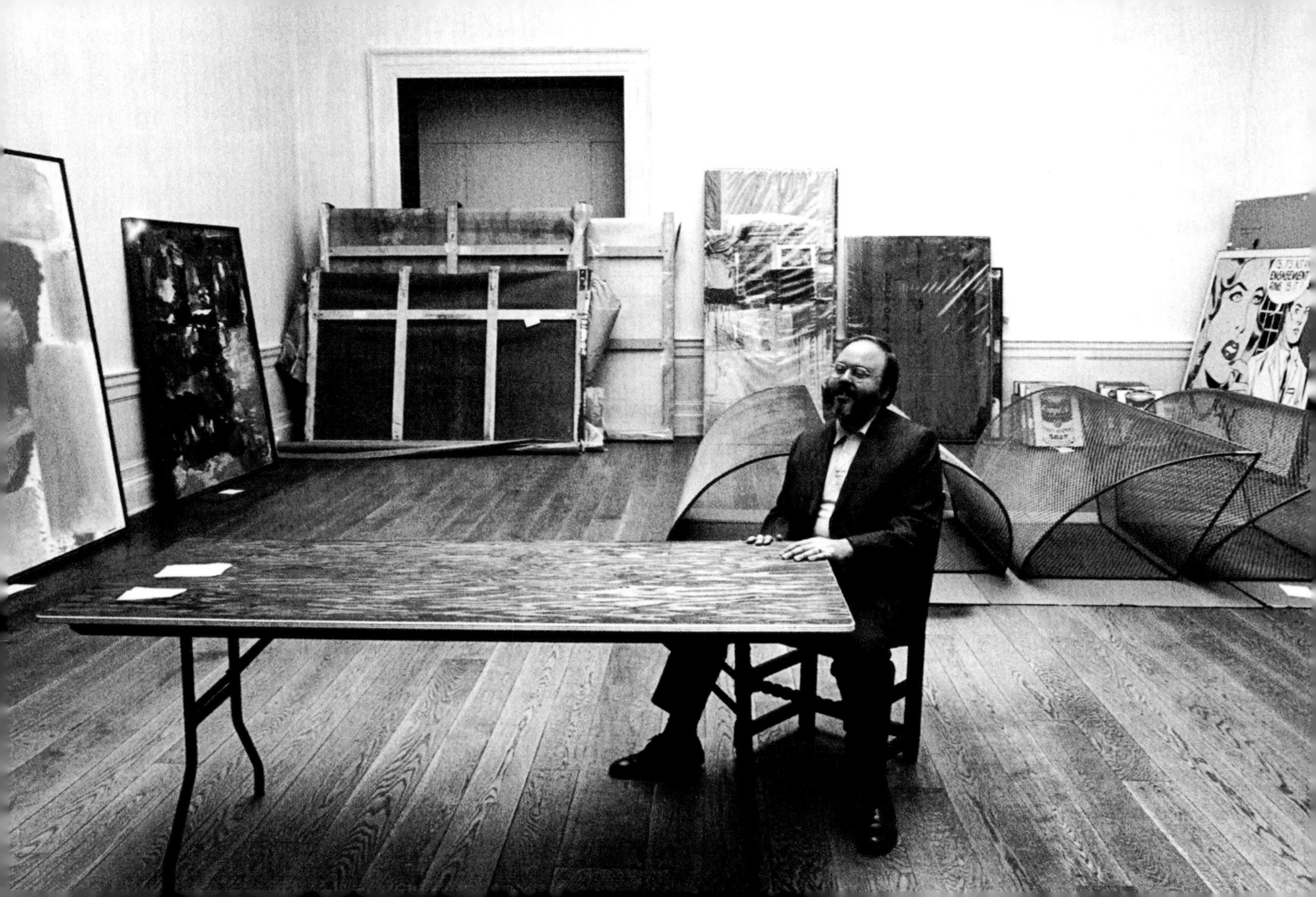
ENGAGEMENT

23

Henry Geldzahler

Henry Geldzahler was a critic, curator, patron and friend to many of the most successful Pop artists. From 1960 until his death in 1994, he bestowed credibility on Pop Art and was in consequence, according to one journalist, 'the most powerful and controversial art curator of the time'. Over the course of the 1960s, he was the centrepiece of an Andy Warhol film and one of Claes Oldenburg's
16 **'happenings'**, he sat for portraits by several Pop artists, including David Hockney, and he was even sculpted
41 by both **Marisol Escobar** and George Segal.

Geldzahler arrived in New York after studying at Yale and Harvard universities and in 1960 became a curatorial assistant at the Metropolitan Museum of Art. An early champion of Pop, he selected Roy Lichtenstein to represent America at the 1966 Venice Biennale and became curator of the Met's new Contemporary Arts department in 1967. Describing the origins of Pop in B-movie terms, he said it was 'like a science fiction movie; young pop artists in different parts of the city, unknown to each other, rising up out of the muck and staggering forward'. Thanks in part to his influential position with the National Endowment for the Arts, from 1966 Geldzahler became a modern-day patron, providing grants to promising young American Pop artists. Like Warhol, he could 'talk the
language of **business** as comfortably 74
as the language of art'. But it wasn't just money that Geldzahler provided: Warhol even claimed, 'Henry gave me all my ideas.'

As New York's Commissioner of Cultural Affairs during the late 1970s and early 1980s – a period of financial bankruptcy which also saw the emergence of AIDS – Geldzahler drove corporate money into art funds and marshalled high profile fundraisers for AIDS research. In the ten years before his death from cancer in 1994, he continued to champion contemporary art, in particular
Neo-Pop artists such as **Keith Haring** 97
and **Jean-Michel Basquiat**. In New 96
York at least, Geldzahler was *the* Pop power broker.

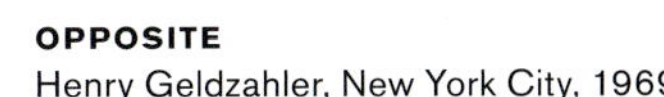

OPPOSITE
Henry Geldzahler, New York City, 1969

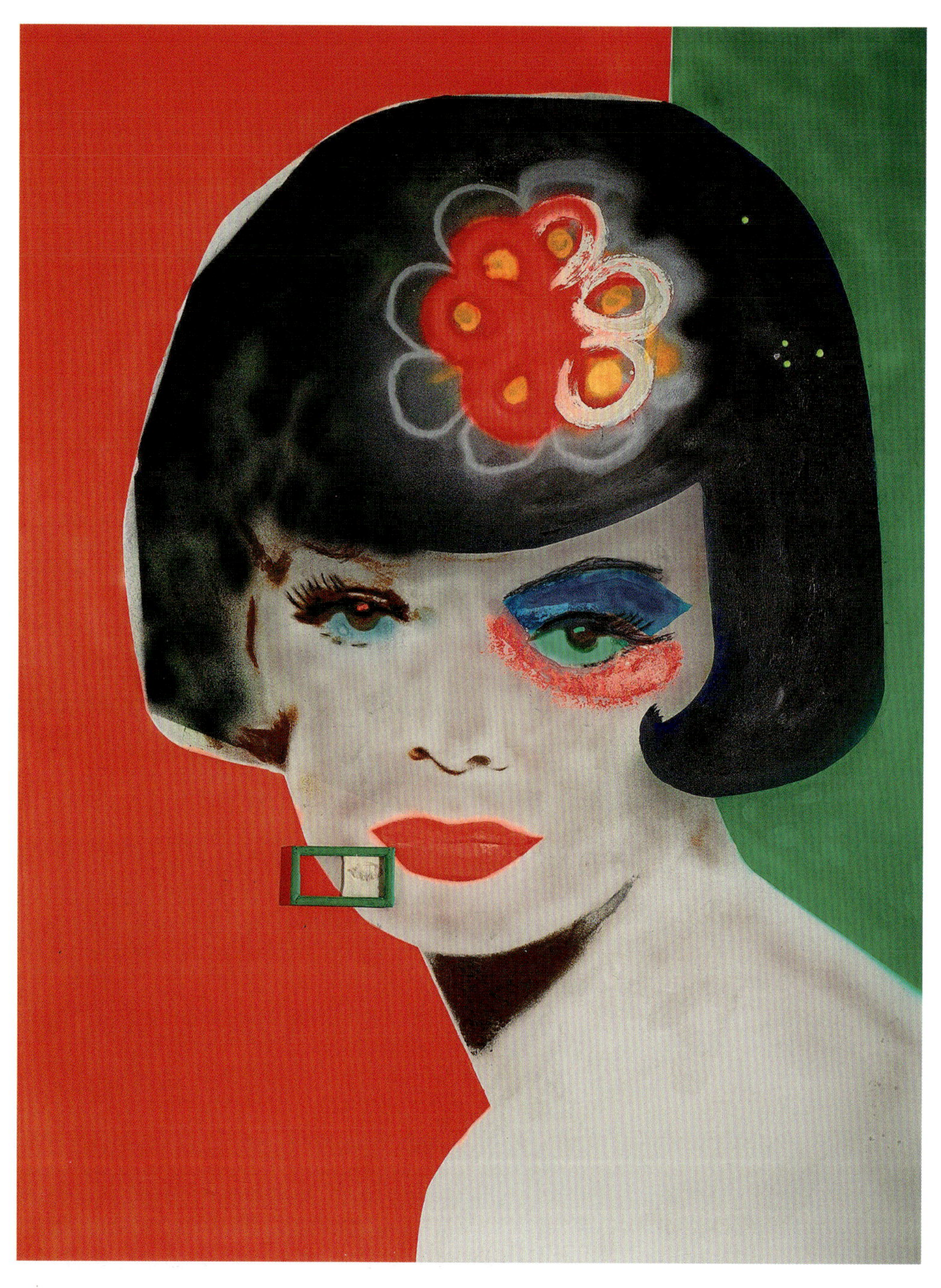

24

Nouveau réalisme

French Pop Art, known as *Nouveau réalisme* or New Realism, was founded in 1960 by Pierre Restany, one of the best-known art critics in France at the time. Published in the same year, his book *Lyrisme et abstraction* advocated that, in the decade ahead, artists should engage with the new consumer culture in a fresh and celebratory way. The result was the New Realist development of *décollage*, the tearing up of mass-media images such as film posters, and assemblage, in which everyday objects were merged in a way similar to Robert Rauschenberg's
11 **'combines'**. Exhibiting in New York, Paris and Milan during the early 1960s, European Pop artists associated with *Nouveau réalisme* – Yves Klein, Martial Raysse, Arman and Jean Tinguely – were encouraged to explore what Restany called 'new approaches in the perception of the real'.

In June 1961, Rauschenberg was one of several American Pop sculptors to show their work alongside that of European artists at the first transatlantic *New Realists* exhibition at Galerie Rive Droite in Paris. But it was the *International Exhibition of*
46 *the New Realists* at the **Sidney Janis** Gallery in New York the following November, curated by Restany, that saw the first large-scale coming together of international Pop Art. Demonstrating commonalities while revealing diversity, Restany hung the work of European *popartistes* including **Öyvind Fahlström**, Peter 29
Blake, Daniel Spoerri, Wolf Vostell and Mimmo Rotella alongside that of Andy Warhol, Roy Lichtenstein, Claes Oldenburg, James Rosenquist, Wayne Thiebaud and **Robert Indiana**. 69

Gallerist Sidney Janis was keen to emphasize the status of the New Realists as 'city-bred' folk artists. The exhibition brochure noted that, living in 'New York, Paris, London, Rome, Stockholm', they found their 'inspiration in urban culture' and were attracted to 'abundant everyday ideas and facts' gathered from 'the street, the store counter, the amusement arcade or the home'. Contemporary American reviews not only highlighted the group's collective interest in the 'supermarket aesthetic' but pointed to its diversity, as sugary American iconography of plenty was contrasted with a 'brooding' European concern with scarcity and 'decay'.

OPPOSITE
Martial Raysse
Last Year in Capri (Exotic Title), 1962
OIL, PAPER COLLAGE, GLYCEROSPRAY AND PAINTED WOODEN FRAME ON BOARD

You're years and dollars ahead with

THE NEW AND MAGNIFICENT CROSLEY

You'll be patting your good judgment on the back for years—if you get Crosley Family Theatre Television now! Crosley is built for the future as well as today. Receivers are tested in a special laboratory against a *perfect* image—one far superior to anything telecast commercially today, thus assuring you of top performance over the years as transmitters are improved and station facilities further perfected. Inside your Crosley are all the most advanced electronic improvements that make the difference between ordinary television and Crosley quality-plus television. Among them are these outstanding features:

Full Room Vision . . . with the new Crosley Wide-Angle Family Theatre Screen.*

New Super-Powered Circuit . . . furnishes the extra power required for clearer, sharper pictures on today's big picture tubes.

New Improved Unituner . . . gives more precise tuning for picture and sound.

New Precision Contrast Control . . . provides the extra contrast and crispness you need for lifelike picture quality. There are no murky gray pictures.

New Patented Built-in Dual Antenna . . . the first entirely automatic, omni-directional built-in dual antenna . . . exclusive with Crosley.

Rich Theatre Tone . . . matched Crosley speaker and audio system provide the full range of sound you are accustomed to hear in the movies.

Twenty beautiful new models . . . these ultramodern receivers, electronically as fine as can be built, housed in cabinets of exquisite taste and beauty, are offered at such modest prices that you are dollars ahead with a Crosley. See them today at your Crosley Dealer's!

*Patent Pending

Crosley Division AVCO Cincinnati 25, Ohio

Better Products for Happier Living

Shelvador® Refrigerators . . . Freezers . . . Sinks . . . Garbage Disposers . . . Radios Electric Ranges . . . Electric Water Heaters . . . Steel Kitchen Cabinets . . . Television

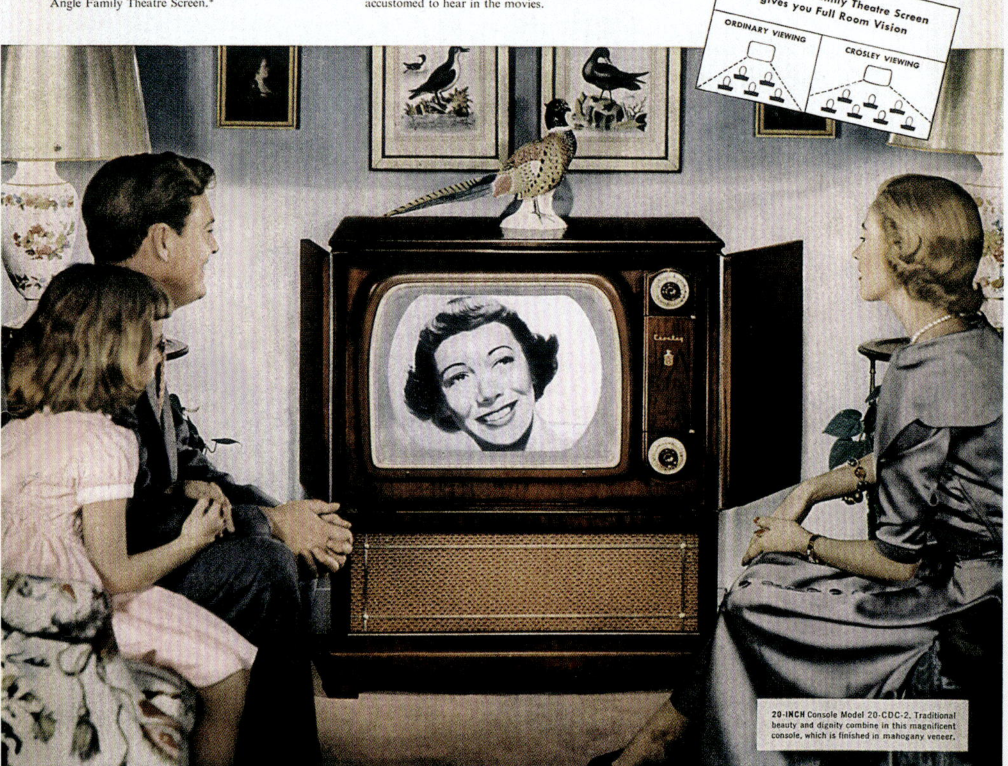

20-INCH Console Model 20-CDC-2. Traditional beauty and dignity combine in this magnificent console, which is finished in mahogany veneer.

CROSLEY
Family Theatre
TELEVISION

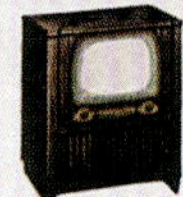

17-INCH Console Model 11-453 is designed to blend admirably with modern or traditional furnishings. Cabinet of rich mahogany veneer. Also offered in blond wood.

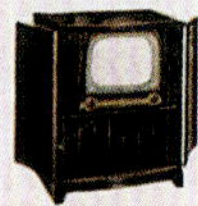

17-INCH Console Model 11-460 has a gorgeous cabinet with bow front in selected mahogany veneer. Doors have rectangular, brushed brass handles. Also in blond wood.

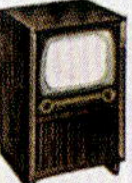

16-INCH Console Model 11-445. The cabinet of this model is supremely simple in design, and finished in glossy, hand-rubbed mahogany veneer. Also in walnut veneer and blond wood.

THE PACE-SETTING DESIGNS ARE COMING FROM CROSLEY!

25

TV

During the 1950s, television extended the reach of celebrity culture and product placement from the cinemas and the streets into the homes of ordinary people. By 1960, television ownership in America had increased by 75 per cent from a decade previously and in Britain nearly two-thirds of the population either owned or rented a TV. While colour broadcasting was launched in America in 1953, in Europe it wasn't introduced until the BBC premiered Wimbledon in colour in 1967.

The American model of commercial television came to Britain in 1955 with the founding of Independent Television (ITV). Challenging the BBC's high-minded influence, ITV sold airtime to an advertising industry that was ready and eager to buy it. In effect, ITV allowed the market to replace the licence fee. Television was what Andy Warhol called 'the new everything' and TV sets quickly became prominent motifs in several Pop images from the 1960s – most famously Warhol's painterly *$199 Television* (1961) and Robert Bechtle's *Zenith* (1968). Edward Kienholz even cast a television in cement for his striking *Cement TV* (1969). While their interests naturally lay in what and who was broadcast, Pop artists also explored the significance that television had in modern life and in the modern home. **Tom Wesselmann's** *Great American Nude #39* (1962), for example, gives the TV set greater prominence than his reclining figure. Pop fantasy quickly replaced physical reality.

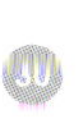

In his 1964 book *Understanding Media*, Canadian philosopher Marshall McLuhan coined the phrase 'the medium is the message' and suggested for the first time that viewers were affected not only by broadcasting content but the very medium that conveys that content – in other words, the television itself. McLuhan explained how TV was rewiring our responses to, and experience of, the world around us. In common with him, Pop artists highlighted the significance of the TV as a powerful icon of modernity.

OPPOSITE
Magazine advertisement for Crosley Television set, 1950s

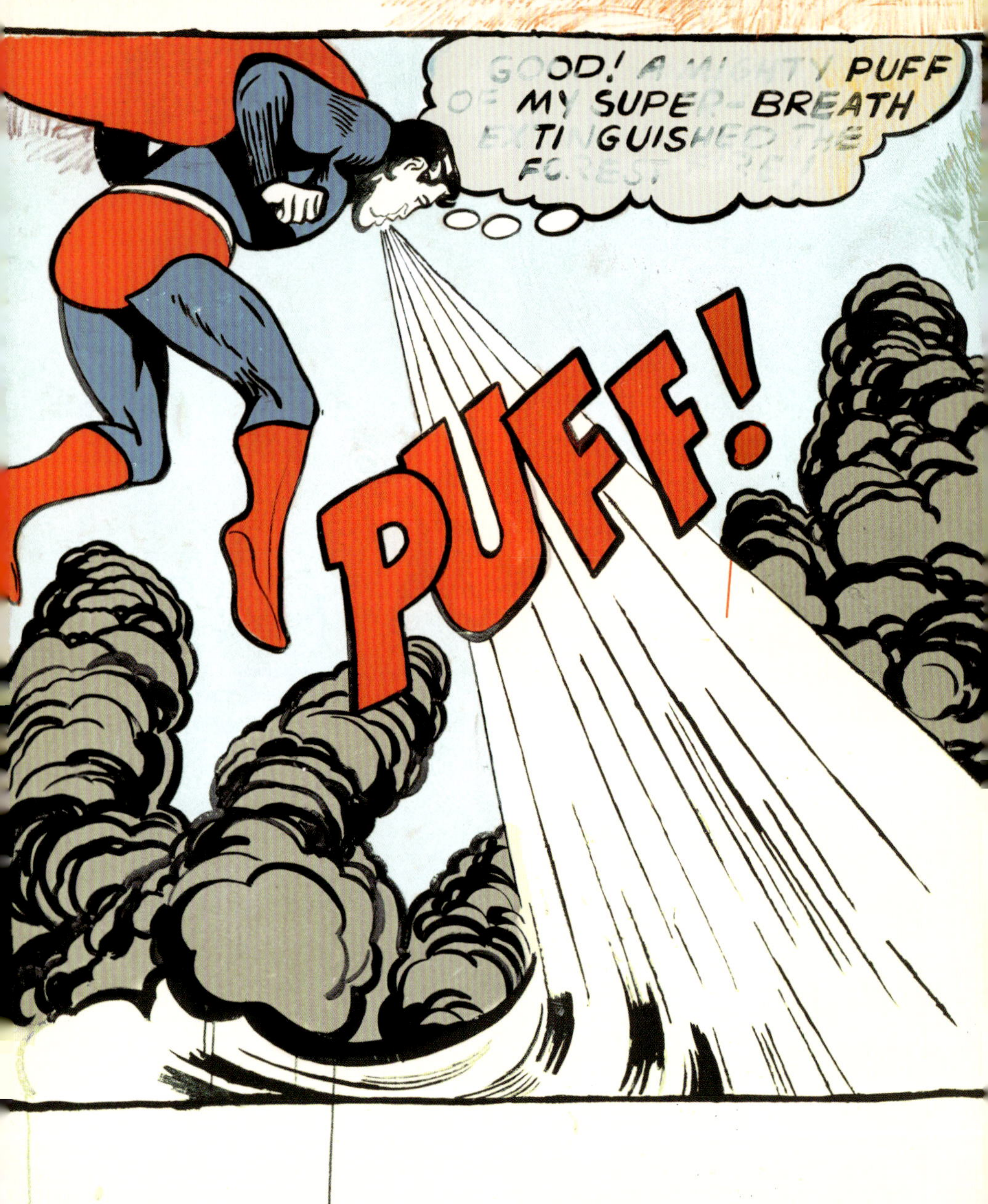
GOOD! A MIGHTY PUFF OF MY SUPER-BREATH EXTINGUISHED THE FOREST
PUFF!

26

Superman

Andy Warhol

1961

Andy Warhol's Pop imagery constitutes
what critic Daniel Wheeler called 'a
collective mirror for contemporary
mass culture', and his *Superman*
canvas is no exception. Exhibited
for the first time in the windows of
5 New York's **Bonwit Teller** department
store on Fifth Avenue in April
1961, *Superman* predates much
7 55 of **Roy Lichtenstein's comic-**
57 **book painting**.

Growing up in America during the golden age of comic books, Warhol was an avid reader of strips that featured crime-fighting superheroes such as Superman, Batman and Captain America. The earliest of these was Superman, the original superhero, first illustrated by Joe Shuster in *Action Comics* in June 1938. In America, Superman quickly became something of a national pin-up. An idealized figure, built like a Greek god, with phenomenal strength used only for good, he is also a corn-fed Middle American boy who saves the world on an almost daily basis. During the 1940s and 1950s, Superman became a cultural icon synonymous with America's fantasy of itself at the centre of the global political stage.

It's easy to forget, however, that Superman was also a refugee with alien blood who is forced to hide his real identity, relocates to the metropolis from the Mid-West and heroically transforms himself. When viewed in this light, it's not difficult to see why millions of Americans identified with him and why Warhol, the self-conscious gay son of Catholic Slovakian immigrants, may have identified with Superman more than most. He famously said, 'If you want to know all about Andy Warhol, just look at the surface of my paintings and films and me, and there I am.' For him, Superman was a deeply resonant motif, and he would later revisit the superhero of his youth in his 1981 comic-book series *Myths*.

OPPOSITE
Andy Warhol
Superman, 1961
SYNTHETIC POLYMER PAINT AND CRAYON ON CANVAS

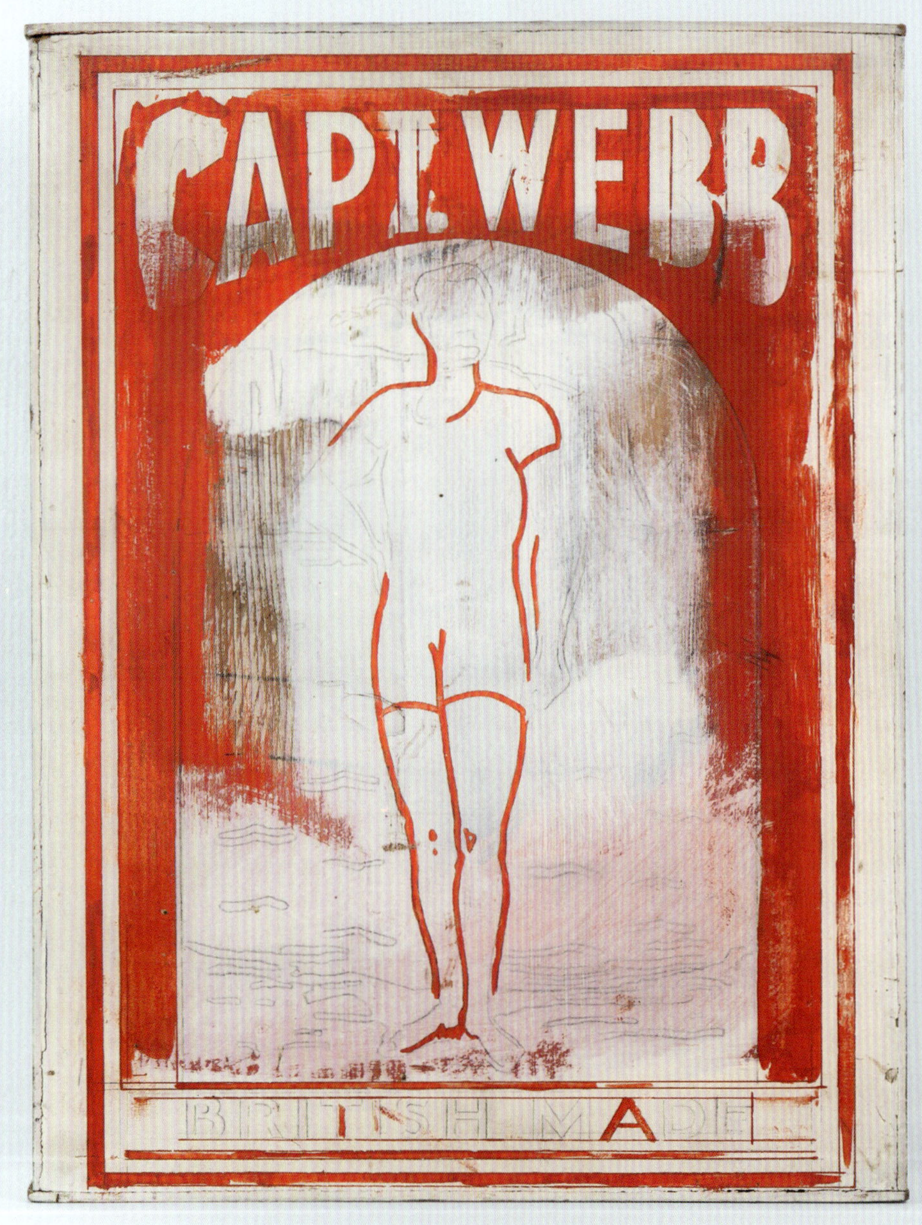
CAPT. WEBB
BRITISH MADE

27

Captain Webb Matchbox

Peter Blake

1961

Alongside Richard Hamilton and Eduardo Paolozzi, Peter Blake – sometimes known as 'the godfather of British Pop Art' – was a founding
6 member of the **Independent Group** in London. In 1961, and three years
63 before Andy Warhol's famous ***Brillo Box***, Blake created his *Captain Webb Matchbox*. It remains the first enlarged imitation of a commercial product as a work of art, and one that encapsulates what Blake himself has described as 'folk Pop'.

Made of wood and painted in a brisk, unfinished style, *Captain Webb Matchbox* was inspired by the well-known British brand of matches with their distinctly patriotic colour palette of red, white and blue. Even in the 1960s, London manufacturers Bryant & May continued to choose as their advertising mascot the Victorian adventurer Captain Matthew Webb. Famously swimming the English Channel in 1875 in under 22 hours, Webb signified 19th-century heroism and a nostalgic 20th-century vision of it. Indeed, Blake once said, 'For me Pop Art is often rooted in nostalgia; the nostalgia of old popular things.' Pleasingly 'unfinished', Blake's Captain Webb is too tired to signify in 1961; slowly disappearing behind white paint, he is identified only by his smudgy red outline.

In the late 1950s, thanks to a Leverhulme Research Award, Blake spent a year travelling around Europe, studying popular culture alongside the established masterpieces of the Renaissance. Avoiding traditional value judgements about art, he could see the connections, the similarities, the parallels. In short, he saw Western visual culture as a connected matrix. A rarity in the Pop Art world, Blake consciously chose to engage in contemporary 'folk' conversations with the past. 'I often appropriate art and quote from it,' he has said. 'You simply can't make art without having that history of art behind you.' For Blake, Pop Art was the new folk vernacular.

OPPOSITE
Peter Blake
Captain Webb Matchbox, 1961
GOUACHE AND PENCIL ON WOOD

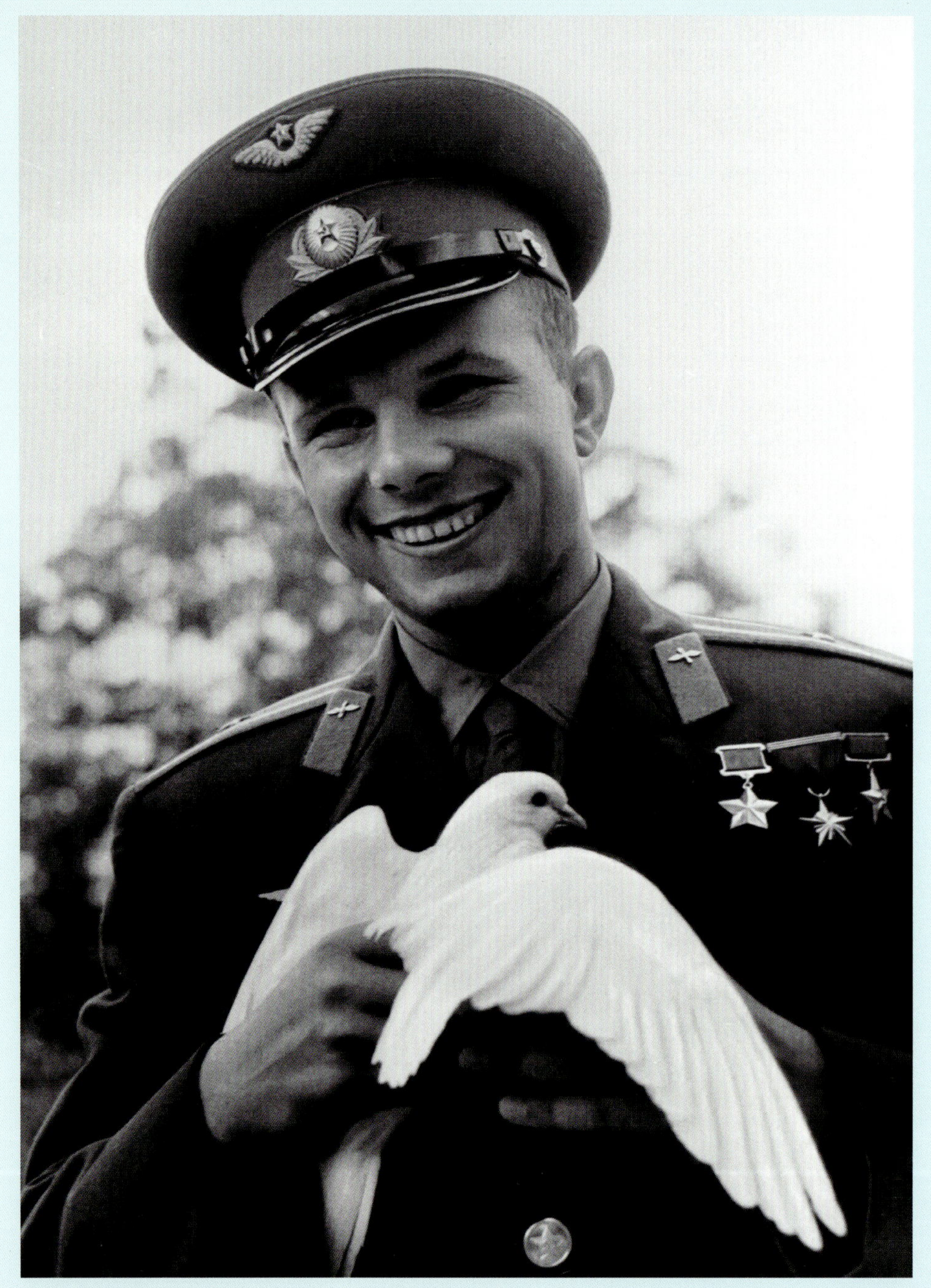

28

The Space Race

81 At the height of the **Cold War**, as the contest for space domination intensified, the United States and the Soviet Union pumped vast sums of money and expertise into their respective national space programmes. In April 1961, and by only three weeks, Soviet cosmonaut Yuri Gagarin beat American astronaut Alan Shepard to be the first man in space.

Just as the London-based Pop artists
had explored the visual fascination
7 with fast-moving **cars** during the
1950s, in the following decade
American Pop artists including Roy
Lichtenstein and James Rosenquist
57 70 made **rockets** a loaded motif, often
accompanied by violent, if highly
stylized, explosions. Indeed, Yuri
Gagarin's famous cry of 'Let's go!'
could easily be found in a Lichtenstein
speech bubble. European Pop Art's
response to the Space Race struck a
subtler, more sceptical note, however.
The title of Derek Boshier's 1962
painting *The Most Handsome Hero
of the Cosmos and Mr Shepherd*
happily plays on the contemporary
trope of good-looking astronauts
cast as real-life superheroes. Yet
Gagarin and 'Shepherd' (whose
name is deliberately and irreverently
misspelled by Boshier) are barely
noticeable in the work, their
tiny figures rooted to the Earth.
Meanwhile, a discarded US flag
is surrounded by what appears
to be dirty clouds of rocket-booster
exhaust fumes.

Back in New York, after attending
one of the photographer Billy
Name's anarchic 'haircutting parties'
(where willing guests would submit
their tresses to the inspiration of
his scissors) in 1963, Andy Warhol
was entranced by Name's interior
decoration – the walls of his
apartment were covered in tin
foil and the furniture sprayed
silver. Soon Warhol would be
commissioning Name (also later
his boyfriend) to decorate his own
apartment in precisely the same
way. This would become known
as Warhol's Silver **Factory**. The 71
space-age future was the American
future – better, brighter and more
exciting than ever – and if the future
was to be silver and spacey, so was
Pop Art's headquarters.

OPPOSITE
Yuri Gagarin, 1961

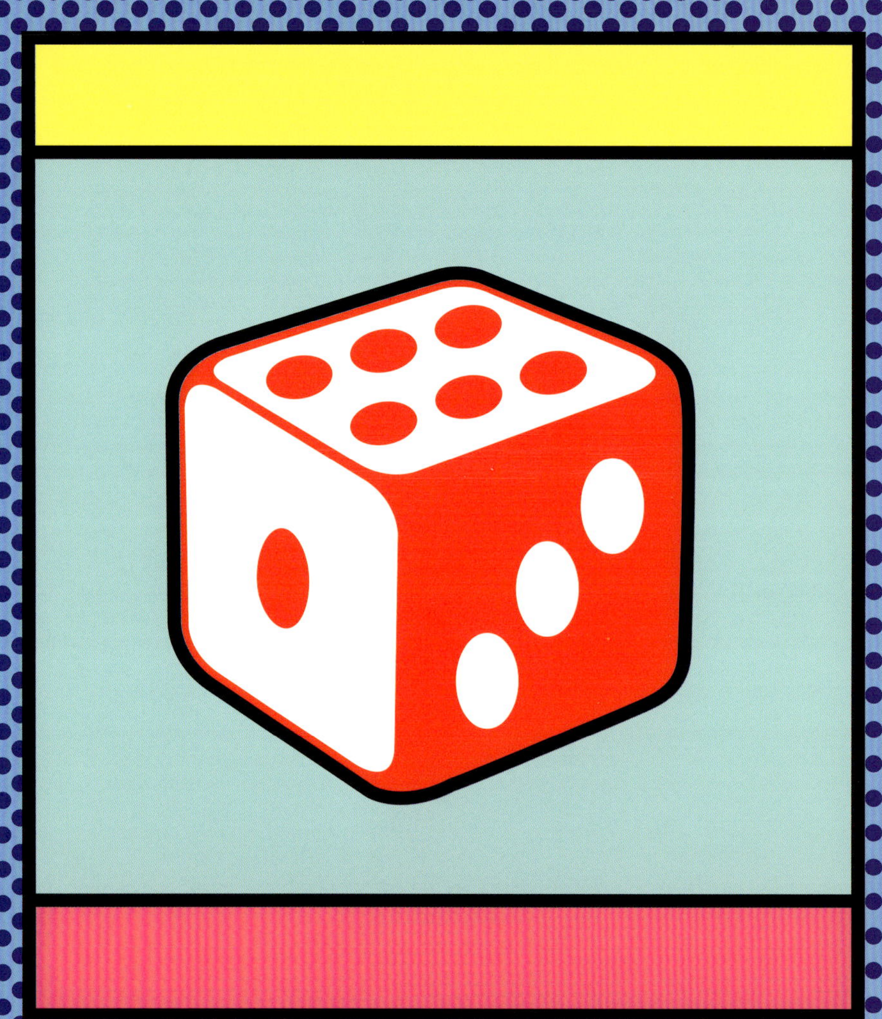

29

Öyvind Fahlström

Described by art historian Tilman Osterwold as the 'most important Pop artist outside America and Britain', Swedish artist Öyvind Fahlström arrived in New York in 1961. He and his wife, fellow Swedish artist Barbro Östlihn, had just spent three years living and working in Paris. Only a year later, his work was chosen by French critic Pierre Restany to be included in
24 the *International Exhibition of the* ***New***
46 ***Realists*** at the **Sidney Janis** Gallery (Östlihn's was not).

A poet, film-maker, composer, sculptor and artist, Fahlström sought to counter what he called the 'terrifying shortness of life' and the 'struggle to experience and create happiness' in a diverse body of work during the 1960s and 1970s. He is perhaps best known for his drawn, painted and collaged works that look like Pop fever dreams, composed of allusions, words and symbols, curious diagrams and little figures.

As something of a cultural outsider who was simultaneously fascinated and appalled by American capitalism, Fahlström was able to make work critical of the reigning ideologies of the times. Like Roy Lichtenstein and Andy Warhol, he often parodied – to a markedly more political effect – the US dollar bill. Free market capitalism transfixed Fahlström. His most intriguing works are a series of Monopoly-inspired board games – for example, *World Trade Monopoly* (1970) – that participants could actually play. He painted hundreds of small magnetic items to be placed on a painted metal board inscribed with his own witty set of Monopoly rules. Monopoly was, as he described
it, '*the* game of capitalism' and **good** 74

business was good Pop Art.

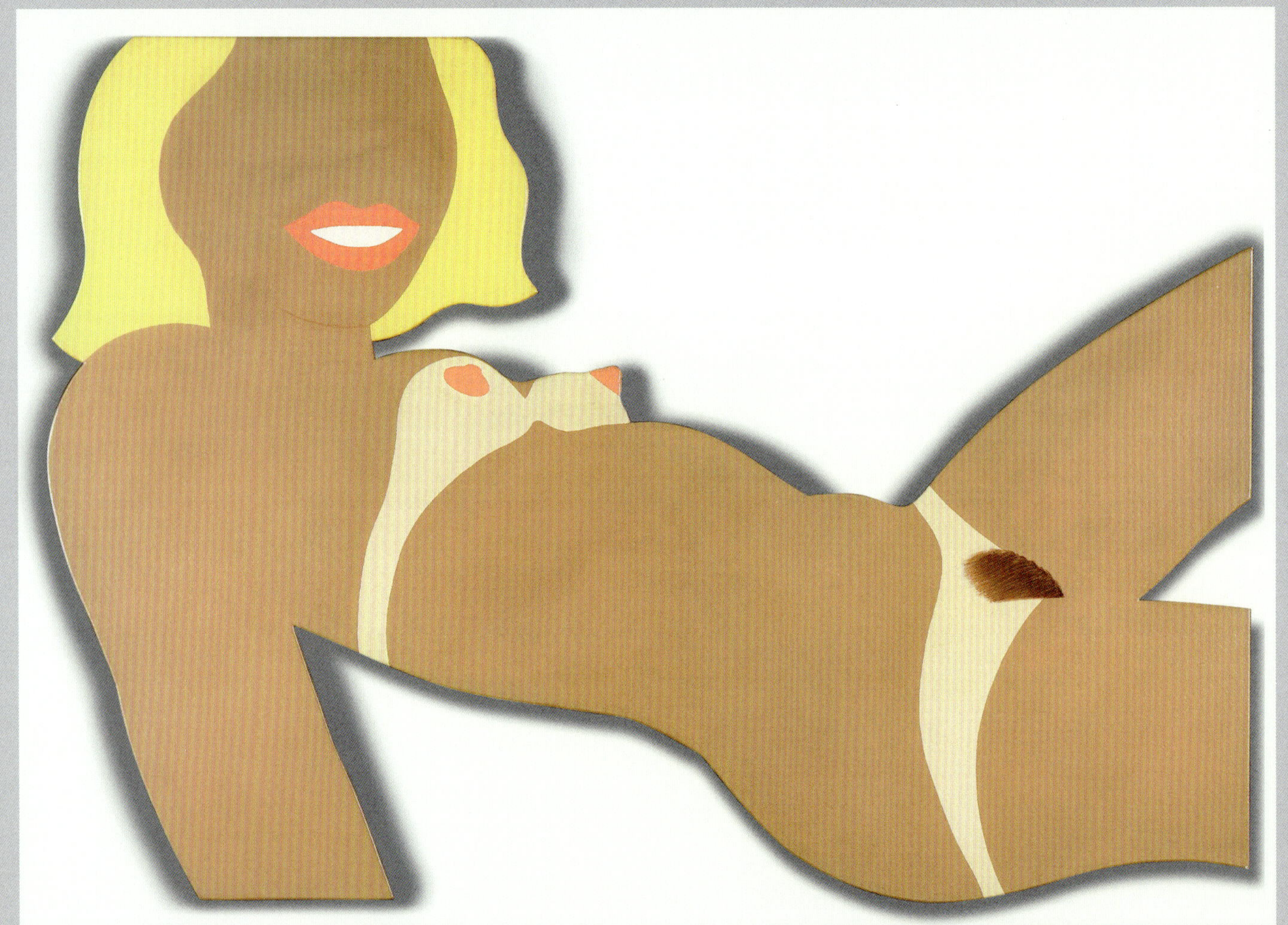

30

Tom Wesselmann

[illegible] **'Big Six'**, as defined by critic Arthur C. Danto in 2009, Tom Wesselmann made luscious still-life paintings characterized by bright, sometimes acidic colours. They depict an abundance of branded items –
34 cigarettes, **Coca-Cola**, milkshakes, beer, white bread, Kellogg's cereal, hot dogs, ketchup and Del Monte tinned fruits. But it's for his series of vibrant *Great American Nudes*, begun in 1961 – and the inspiration for British novelist
89 **J. G. Ballard's** 1968 short story 'The Great American Nude'– that he is best known today.

Updating the Renaissance motif of the reclining female nude, Wesselmann's work responded to the new widespread availability of printed pornographic images. His nudes celebrate the sexual liberations of the [illegible]
[illegible] highlighting modern **pornography's** commodification of the female body. Developing the implications of Richard Hamilton's *$he* from 1958–61, Wesselmann's nudes are faceless and anonymous, often arranged alongside consumer products – as if just as easily bought, discarded and replaced.

[illegible] developed and – no doubt influenced by Pop sculptor Marjorie Strider's **'Bikini Nudes'** – morphed into 61
three-dimensional acrylic-glass mouldings that bulged from the image surface. As recurring Pop porn motifs, erect penises and female breasts even invade, and dominate, his later still-life and landscape work. Sex was everywhere, and Pop Art had to respond.

Inspired by contemporary print and advertising culture, Wesselmann – a former US soldier and psychology graduate – moved to New York in the late 1950s to study at the Cooper Union college. Like many Pop artists, he would begin his career teaching art in local high schools, before having several solo exhibitions in 1961 and featuring in the *International* [illegible] **New Realists** at the [illegible]
Sidney Janis Gallery the following year. [illegible]
Denying 'any kind of group intention', however, Wesselmann claimed to 'dislike labels in general' and renounced his Pop Art membership. Despite this, and therefore with some irony, his images are among the most instantly recognizable of the Pop Art movement.

OPPOSITE
Tom Wesselmann
Great American Nude #62, 1965
LIQUITEX POLYMER PAINT ON PLYWOOD

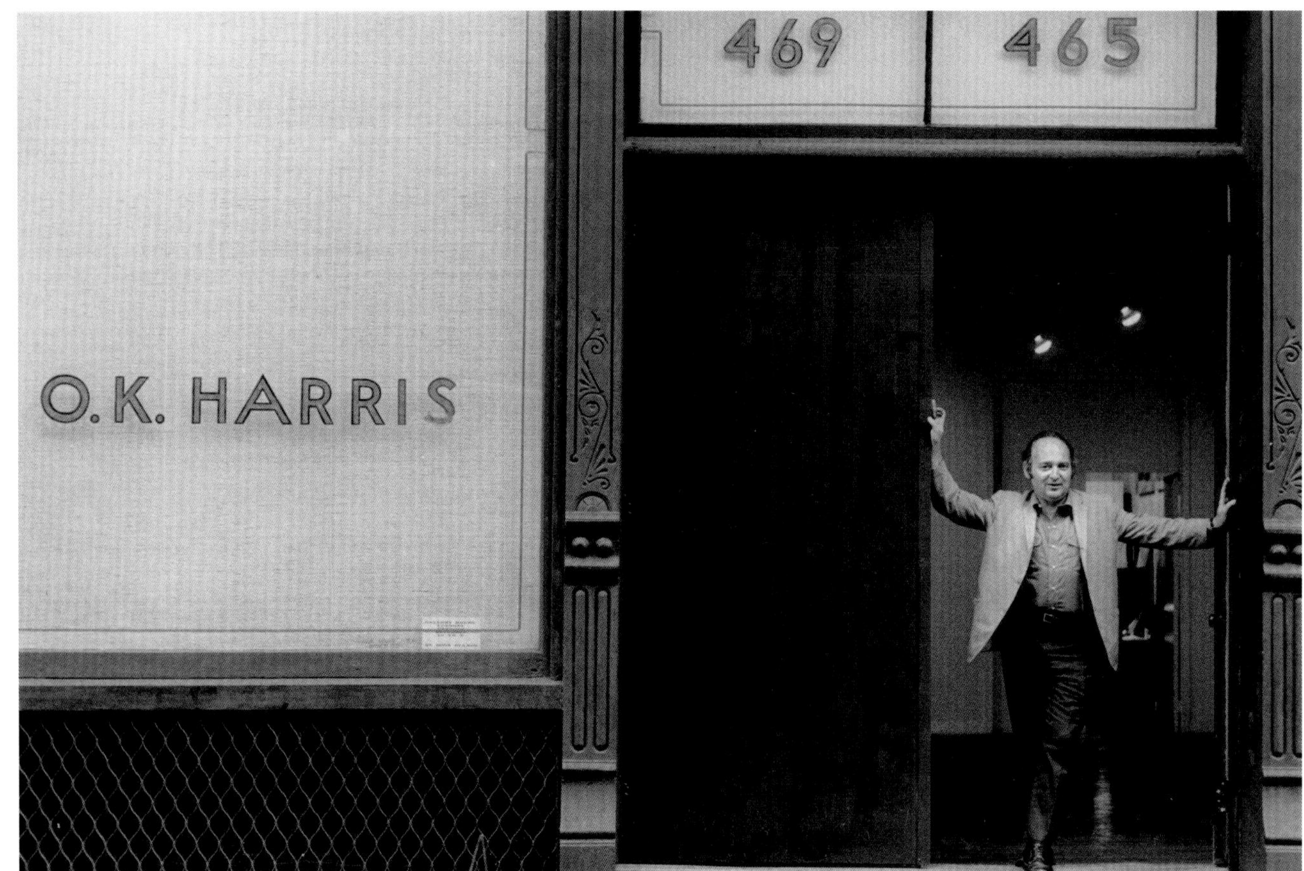
469
465
O.K. HARRIS

31

Ivan Karp

An associate director of the influential Leo Castelli Gallery in New York, Ivan Karp was a pivotal Pop Art patron and dealer. In 1961 he was the first gallerist to recognize and exhibit the mature work of Roy Lichtenstein, and he would go on to foster the careers of Andy Warhol, Claes
30 Oldenburg, **Tom Wesselmann** and Robert Rauschenberg.

On first encountering Lichtenstein's early work in the autumn of 1961, Karp recalled that he was initially uncomfortable, telling the artist, 'You really can't do that, you know.' And yet he marvelled at Lichtenstein's audacious celebration of commercial
17 adverts and **comic-book cartoons**. The five paintings Lichtenstein presented that autumn were, Karp said, 'peculiar and alien and strange'. As it turned out, however, it was precisely for this reason – because they were so 'cold and blank and bold and overwhelming', so 'unsettling' – that Karp immediately decided to buy and exhibit them.

That autumn, Karp made another discovery. Warhol's work had just been included in a group show at the nearby Allan Stone Gallery and, soon after, Warhol visited Karp's Upper East Side gallery. On seeing Lichtenstein's newly installed work, he recoiled in horror. Both artists – completely independently, it seems – were creating very similar kinds of work. Karp needed to see for himself and, when he visited Warhol's powder-blue studio on Lexington Avenue, he was astounded. Clearly something new and fresh – and often baffling – was afoot among young artists.

A former ice-cream salesman and film editor, Karp was, according to his *New York Times* obituary, 'New York's deftest and most enthusiastic salesman of the new art', not only defining the American Pop Art canon
but also creating its **highly lucrative** 74
market. He was described by the *New York Times* as knowing 'as much as, if not more than, anybody else about what's going on in the hidden corners of the art world'. Karp's own maxim was 'No genius should go undiscovered.'

OPPOSITE
Ivan Karp in front of O.K. Harris, the gallery he founded in 1969, August 1979

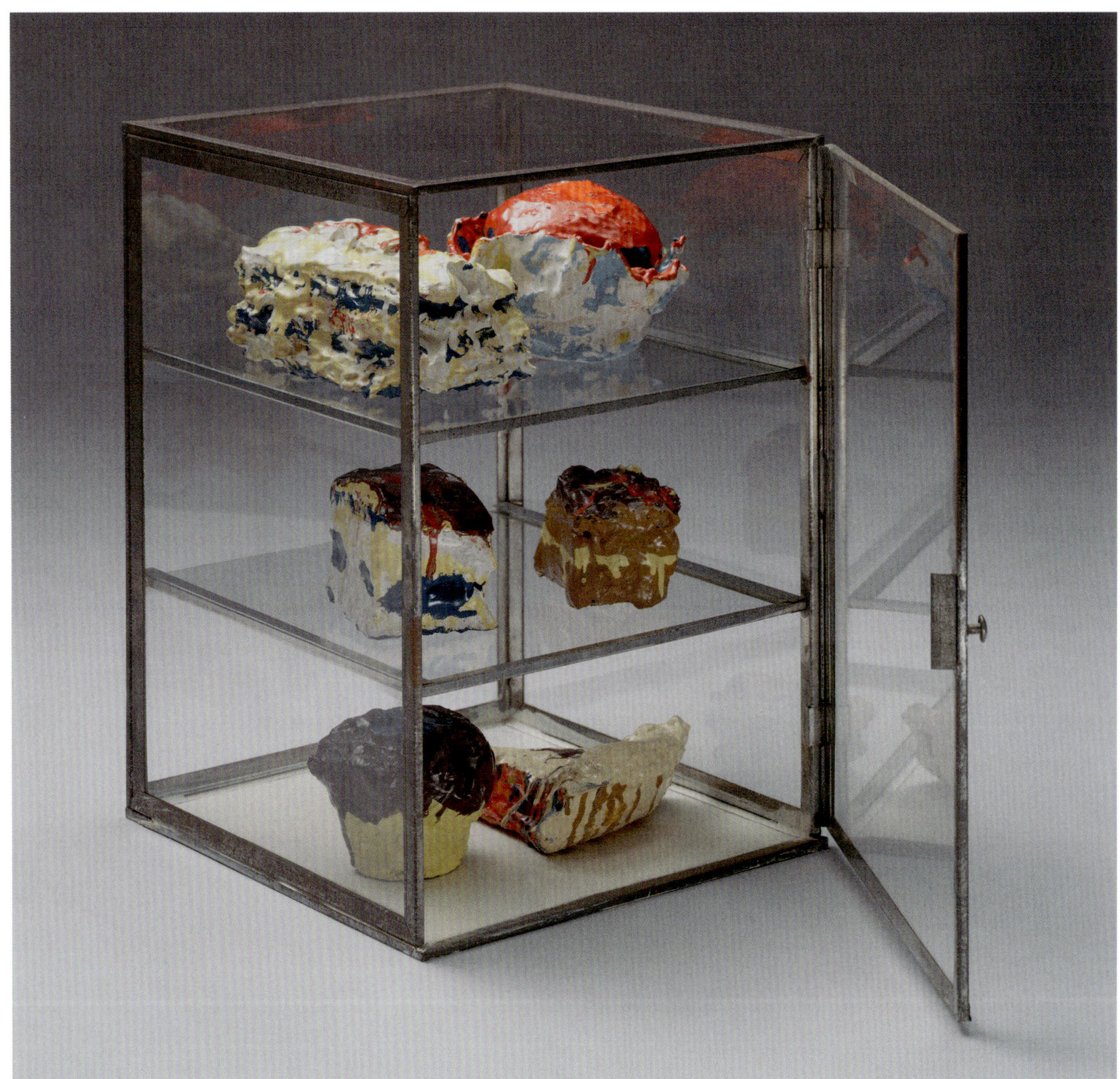

32

The Store

Claes Oldenburg

1961

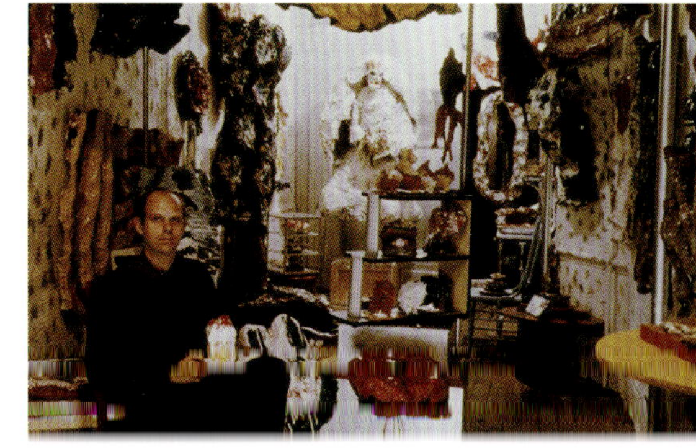

A Pop Art landmark, Claes Oldenburg's sculptural installation *The Store* opened in New York in December 1961. For two months, Oldenburg rented an old shop space on the Lower East Side, designing print advertisements and posters, hanging his own work and manning the till at the front of the shop himself. He created everything on display in a studio at the back of the shop, with newly sculpted goods replacing whatever was sold. And everything was democratically priced between $20 and $500. With *The Store*, Oldenburg wanted to 'violate the whole idea of painting'. In order to explore what he called 'total space', he made from scratch a shop 'environment' that became 'an extension of painting space' and an art event with the feel
16 of an avant-garde **'happening'**.

Ultimately, *The Store* was Oldenburg's inventive way of circumventing the accepted gallery system. Veiled by humour and novelty, it was also a self-conscious critique of consumerism. It directly exposed the romantic fallacy that art resists commodification, so much so that it prompted the rhetorical question: what is an art gallery anyway but a supermarket for the creative industries? To think of galleries in any other way was to ignore the reality of modern capitalism and the reality of Pop Art.

In the lead-up to the opening of *The Store*, Oldenburg's diaries and notebooks attest to his detailed observations of contemporary food, drink, cafés and supermarkets. Using a wide variety of materials, including plaster over wire mesh, he sculpted everything from raw food, processed hamburgers, packaged products, fruits and baked goods to stationery, clothes, shoes, underwear and even cigarettes. Taking inspiration not from gallery curators but from the immigrant shopkeepers of the Lower East Side, Oldenburg displayed his Pop Art in a radically eclectic, ironic and eye-catchingly 'vulgar' way.

ABOVE
Claes Oldenburg
in *The Store*, 1961

OPPOSITE
Claes Oldenburg
Pastry Case, 1961

PAINTED PLASTER SCULPTURES 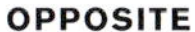
IN GLASS-AND-METAL CASE

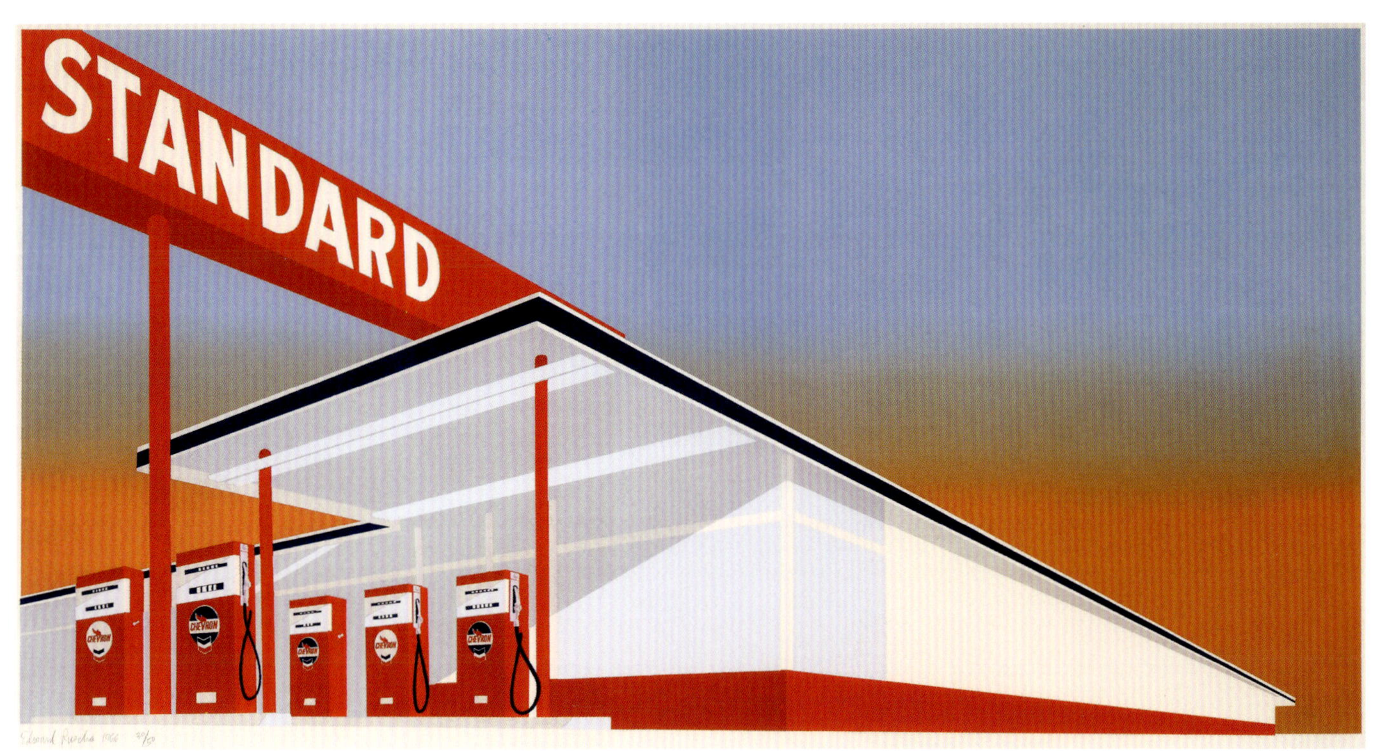
STANDARD

33

Ed Ruscha

Pop Art just wouldn't 'pop' without Hollywood and Ed Ruscha's work is now synonymous with the hauntingly
50 glamorous **Los Angeles** landscape.
Moving from his native Nebraska to Los Angeles in 1956, Ruscha studied at the California Institute of the Arts and went on to work not only as an artist but as a writer and photographer too. Settling in the Los Angeles district of Culver City – the location of many of Hollywood's major studios – Ruscha even turned to film-making himself. His mesmerizing and yet little-known films from the 1970s suggest the potent Pop mythology of concrete-freeway LA and explore the transformative magic of Hollywood.

In 1962, Ruscha created *Large Trademark with Eight Spotlights*, boldly depicting a graphic version of the iconic 20th Century Fox logo. One of his first paintings to include movie motifs, it has become Ruscha's most famous. In common with other Pop artists, he returned throughout his career to trademarks, deftly turning them into works of art that could be traded themselves on the buoyant Pop Art market. If art was, eventually, to become coopted by the advertising industry, why not just start there?

Ruscha's high-impact painting style is also indebted to his early professional life as a layout artist for the Carson/Roberts advertising agency in Los Angeles. Based on his series of photographs of American gas stations published in 1963 as *Twentysix Gasoline Stations*, the following year he painted *Standard Station, Amarillo*, of which the opposite is a later screenprint version.
Employing the **ad-man's** palette of 9
primary colours with black and white, Ruscha exaggerated the perspective to evoke an an iconic advertising billboard. While gas station motifs – and others he employed such as the Hollywood sign and even movie celluloid itself – were expected, and instantly recognizable, quite often the materials he used were not. Ruscha experimented with painting using strange and diverse materials, from gunpowder to chocolate, from blood to fruit juice. After all, as he claimed, 'Art has to be something that makes you scratch your head.'

OPPOSITE
Ed Ruscha
Standard Station, 1966
SCREENPRINT

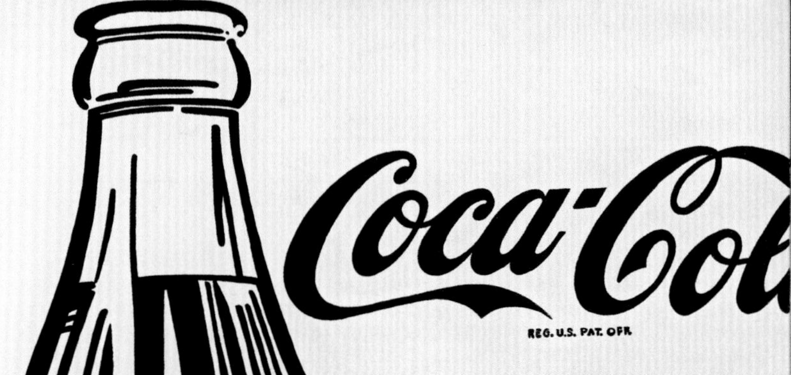
Coca-Cola
REG. U.S. PAT. OFF.

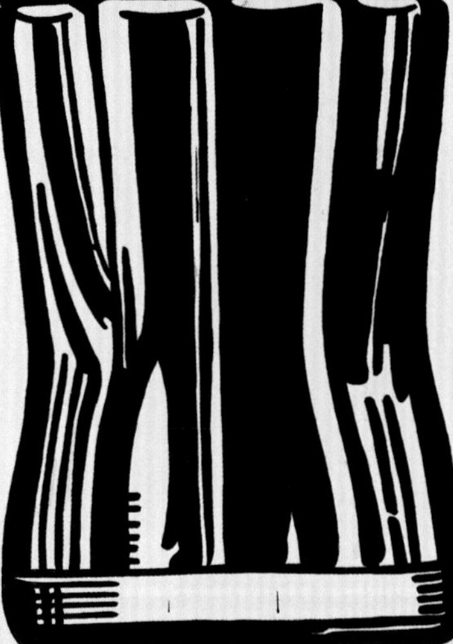
Coca-Cola
TRADE MARK REGISTERED

34

Large Coca-Cola

Andy Warhol

1962

Although not the first of his meditations on the Coca-Cola brand,
36 Andy Warhol's 1962 **silkscreen** series *Large Coca-Cola* is the best known. His Coca-Cola canvases dating from two years earlier look unfinished and display hurried brushstrokes in the 'painterly' style. The silkscreen technique of the *Large Coca-Cola* series however, possesses the sleekness and precision of mass production, hides Warhol's hand and heralds the coming of his later work. In black and white, the image looks like a
25 **TV** still, the bottle's shape suggestive of the human body and its 'large' size suggesting potency. Recognizing the connection between brand, individual desires and the power of advertising, Warhol understood that sex sells.

Despite the launch of branded tin cans in 1955, glass-bottled Coca-Cola retained its iconic popularity. Its fizzy burst of sugar and caffeine, once thought medicinal, was uniquely American. Coca-Cola marketing campaigns from the 1950s and 1960s evoked a stake in youth, glamour and vitality. Robert Rauschenberg was the first artist to recognize this when he embedded three Coke bottles
in the heart of his 1958 **'combine'** 11
sculpture *Coca-Cola Plan*.

Coca-Cola boss Robert Woodruff famously wanted to see his product on sale all over the world and it seemed as if his imperialist dreams were coming true – even if, as Warhol wryly noted, the Abstract Expressionists tried not to notice. Warhol, as we might expect, welcomed Woodruff's evangelism as an expansion of the
American Dream and wrote: 4

—

What's great about this country is that America started the tradition where the richest consumers buy essentially the same things as the poorest. You can be watching TV and see Coca-Cola, and you know that the President drinks Coke, Liz Taylor drinks Coke, and just think, you can drink Coke too. A Coke is a Coke and no amount of money can get you a better Coke than the one the bum on the corner is drinking. All the Cokes are the same and all the Cokes are good. Liz Taylor knows it, the President knows it, the bum knows it, and you know it.

—

OPPOSITE
Andy Warhol
Coca-Cola [3], 1962
CASEIN ON COTTON

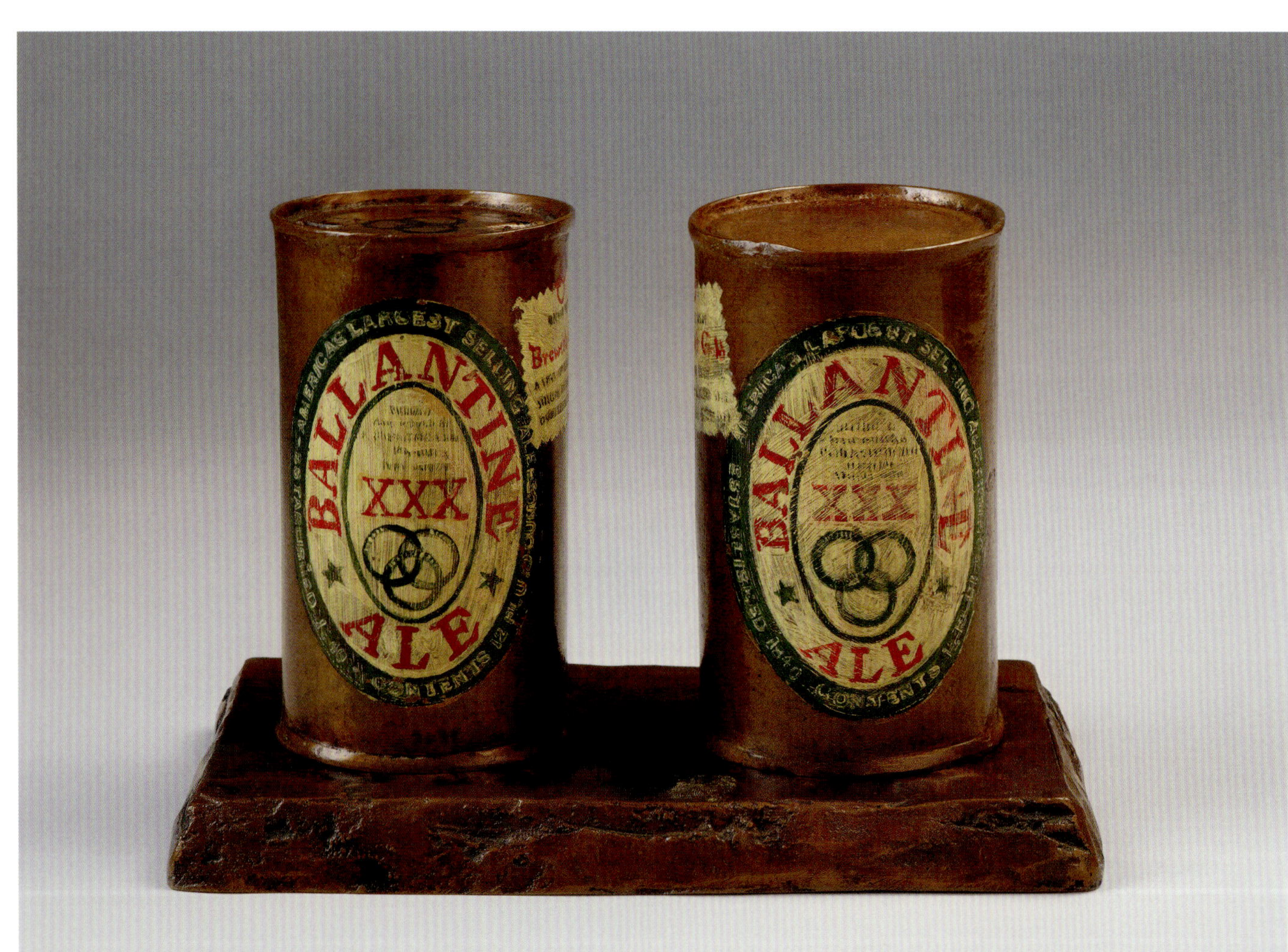
BALLANTINE
XXX
ALE
BALLANTINE
XXX
ALE

35

'Popsicles'

In March 1962 – eight months before the opening of the *International*
24 *Exhibition of the* **New Realists** in New York City – gallery owner
46 **Sidney Janis** hosted an exhibition of work by Abstract Expressionist Willem de Kooning. Somewhat unexpectedly, it was poorly attended and badly reviewed. And for the daughter of fellow Abstract Expressionist Philip Guston, the failure of de Kooning's show indicated that 'Overnight…the art world had changed'. Pop Art was beginning to supersede Abstract Expressionism as the cool new thing and the esoteric, politically left-wing old guard just couldn't stomach its disinterested, deadpan irony. Guston and Mark Rothko were appalled by Sidney Janis's support for the new Pop Art and, along with other Abstract Expressionists, abandoned their contracts with him in collective protest.

De Kooning said of Janis's rival, fellow gallerist and Pop Art supporter Leo Castelli, 'That son of a bitch. You could give him two beer cans and he could sell them.' On hearing this, Pop artist Jasper Johns cheekily cast two bronze Ballantine Ale cans and was soon pleased to confirm for de Kooning that Castelli had in fact managed to sell them. From the perspective of a self-styled outsider and critic of Pop Art, gestures such as this one, artist
Tom Wesselmann noted the 30
following year, represented how 'Some of the worst things about Pop Art have come from its admirers.' Rothko, perhaps the best known of the Abstract Expressionists, is said to have angrily dismissed all of the young Pop artists as 'Popsicles'. It must have been galling for Rothko when the artist Ruth Kligman, last muse of his Abstract Expressionist contemporary Jackson Pollock, became friends with Andy Warhol. She tried to introduce the two, but Rothko dramatically refused even to shake Warhol's hand.

That the ascent of Pop Art in New York wasn't always smooth confirms how entrenched popular support for Abstract Expressionism was. Even two years later, in January 1964, an international feature on Roy Lichtenstein for *Life* magazine posed the question, 'Is He the Worst Artist in the U.S.?' Ever the salesman, Lichtenstein loved it.

OPPOSITE
Jasper Johns
Painted Bronze (Ale Cans), 1960
OIL ON BRONZE

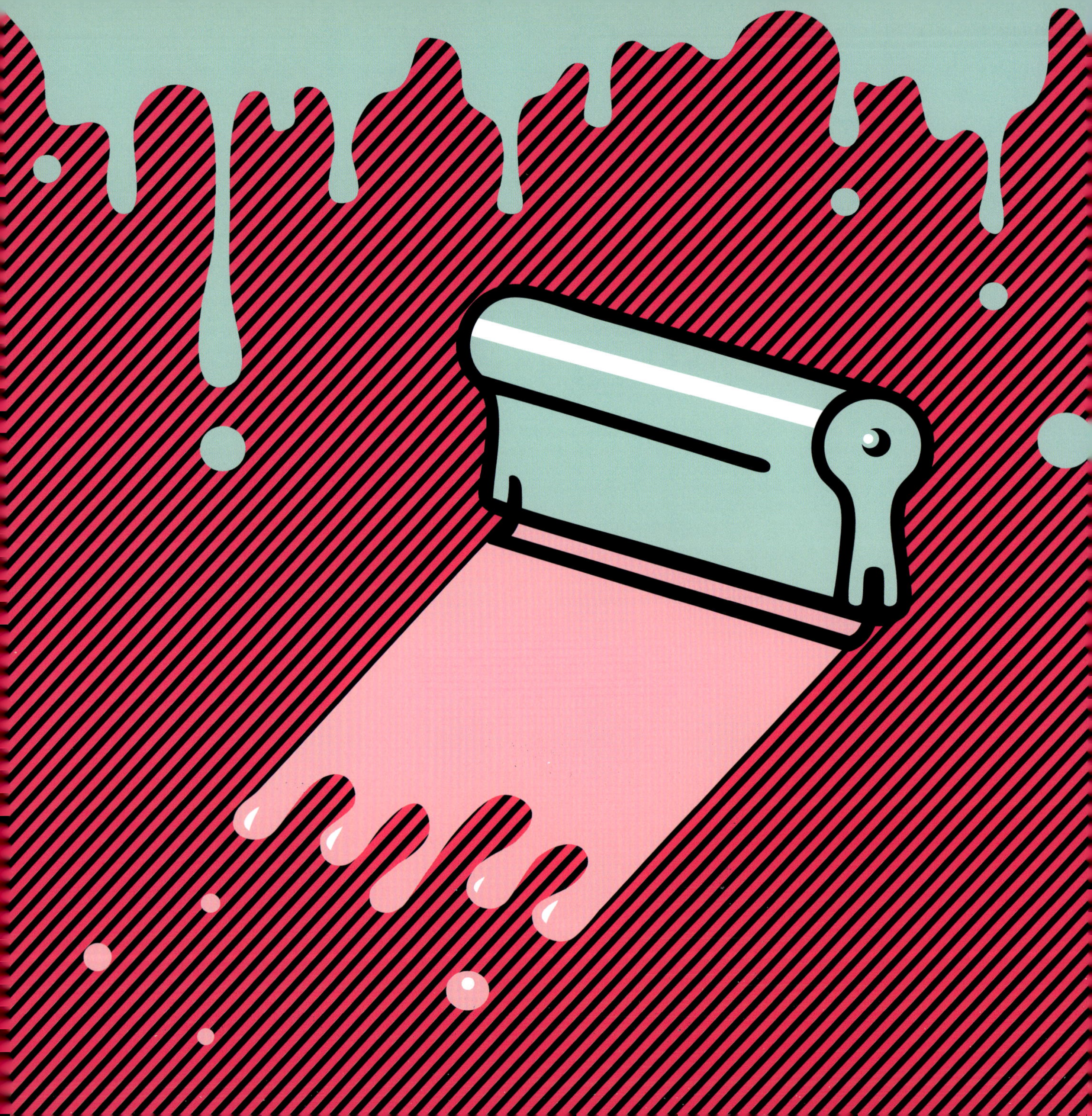

36

Silkscreen

Originally from ancient China, silkscreen printing was first used in the West during the early 20th century. The technique allowed for the easy transfer of an image onto not only paper, fabric and canvas, but also wood, plastic and even glass. Attracted to its versatility, Pop Art innovator Andy Warhol was the first to popularize silkscreen printing during the early 1960s. In many ways, he made it uniquely Pop.

Warhol's silkscreen prints were becoming popular – he could barely keep up with the demand – and despite being obsessed with replicating his work, these too often ended up as one-off designs. In 1963, Warhol told a critic, 'I think somebody should be able to do all my paintings for me.' In response, the New York dealer and gallerist Leo Castelli introduced him to French screen-printing guru Michel Caza. Having spent most of the 1950s working as a printer in Stockholm and Paris, Caza was a silkscreen expert and soon, in a partnership brokered by Castelli, he and Warhol founded the first Pop Art **Factory**. Caza printed 71 hundreds of Warhol's images, many of which were then signed and given as gifts to Warhol's passing admirers.

The main reason why silkscreen printing didn't catch on until after the Second World War was the high cost of the silk used as a mesh through which paint or ink was passed. To some extent, the need for silk rendered the technique elitist. New, affordable fabric meshes were required. British scientists invented polyester fibre in the early 1940s, but it was the American manufacturers DuPont, and later Eastman, who developed commercial polyester fabrics during the 1950s. Far cheaper and much more durable than silk, polyester fabrics looked similar and soon became popular, consumers being more concerned with appearance than feel. Polyester meshes quickly replaced silk meshes in signage and poster production, and Warhol was one of the first artists to notice this. So, his silkscreen prints are not in fact silkscreen prints at all but innovative Pop Art polyester prints.

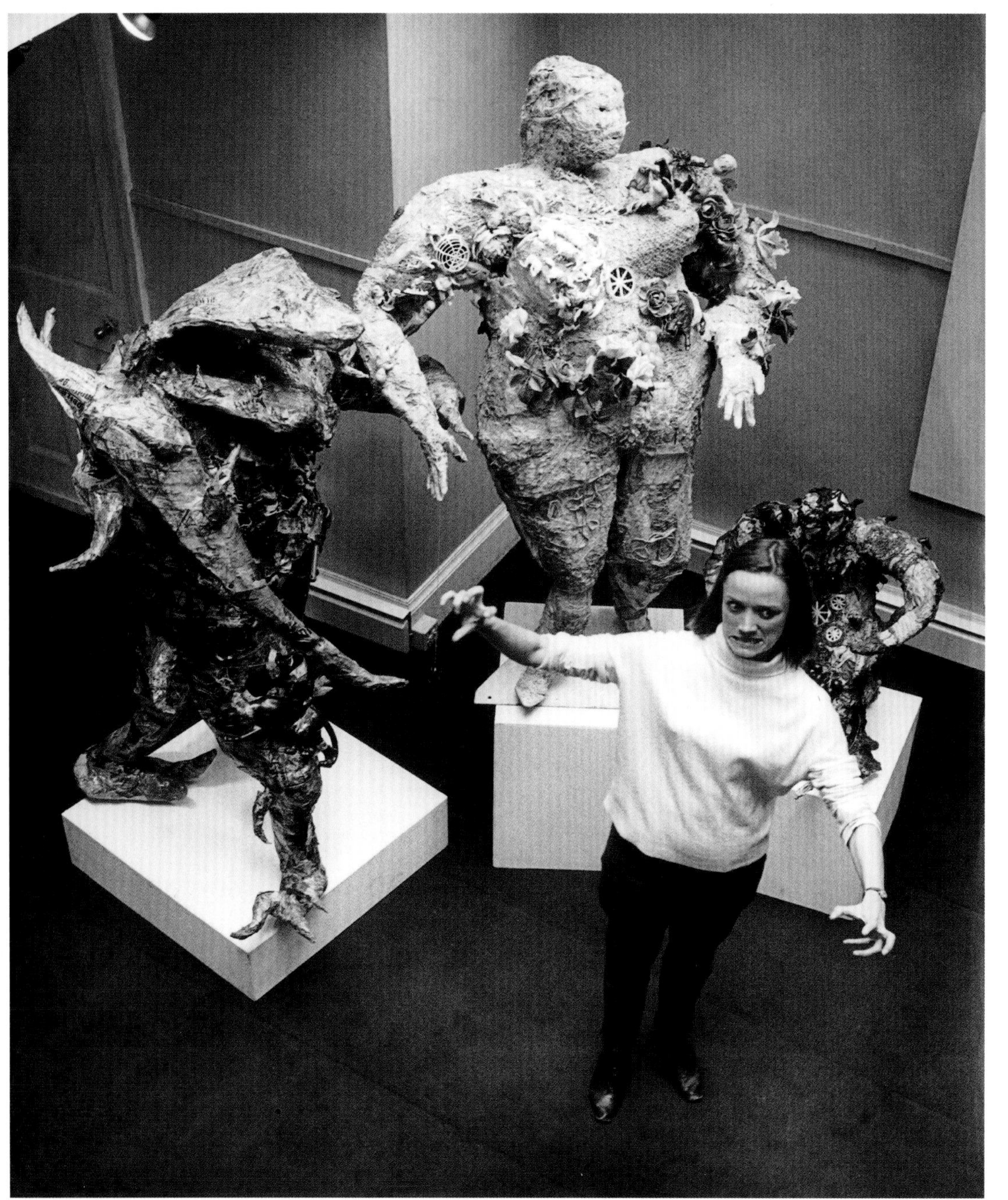

37

Niki de Saint Phalle

As the only female member of the
24 Paris-based **New Realists** group, during the early 1960s the Pop artist Niki de Saint Phalle began creating her influential *Bride* series. Nightmarish, despairing and making use of 'found objects' such as dolls and knives, her 'monstrous' brides reveal her own horror of that contemporary female archetype, no doubt inspired by her unhappy, decade-long marriage to the American novelist Harry Mathews during the 1950s.

A French-born aristocrat and self-taught Pop artist, Saint Phalle was brought up in Connecticut and New York's Upper East Side during the late 1940s. At the age of 18 she became an international fashion model. Although initially drawn to painting in her personal practice, Saint Phalle's first solo exhibition, in 1961 at Galerie J in Paris, consisted of sculptures and assemblages, and later that year her work was included in *The Art of Assemblage* exhibition at the Museum of Modern Art in New York. Friends
1 with **Marcel Duchamp**, Jasper Johns and Robert Rauschenberg, Saint Phalle became the partner and collaborator of another New Realist artist, Jean Tinguely, around this time.

Like that of fellow Pop artist **Marta** 78
Minujín, much of Saint Phalle's work in the early 1960s concerned simultaneous creation and destruction.
Orchestrating unique **'happenings'** 16
in Paris and **Los Angeles**, Saint Phalle 50
created work that was specifically made to be destroyed with guns. Her first public shooting event took place in Paris in February 1961 and over the next few years she staged more, including one at the Malibu beach house of Los Angeles art dealer and Pop champion Virginia Dwan. However, inspired by a friend's pregnancy, Saint Phalle soon began creating her better-known *Nana* series (from the French slang word for a woman). First exhibited at the Alexander Iolas Gallery in Paris in September 1965, these exuberantly colourful and powerfully fecund multimedia sculptures – in contrast to the brides – defined for Saint Phalle a new Pop female archetype.

OPPOSITE
Niki de Saint Phalle with some of her works at Hanover Gallery, London, 1964

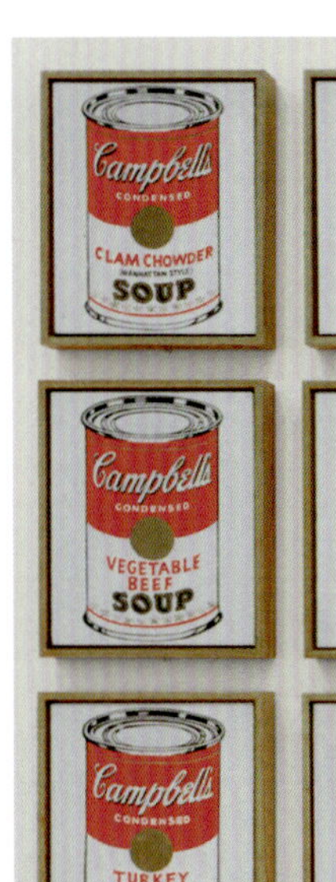
Campbell's
CONDENSED
CLAM CHOWDER
SOUP
Campbell's
CONDENSED
VEGETABLE BEEF
SOUP
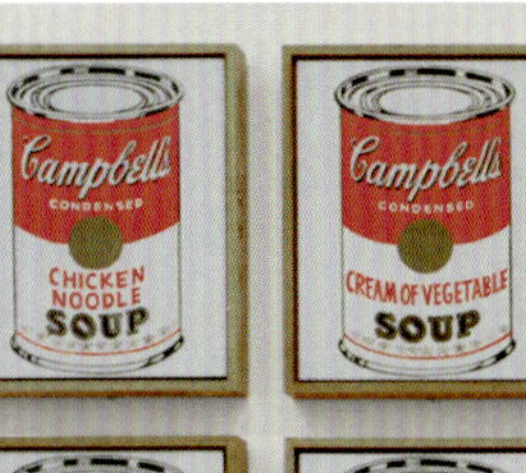
Campbell's
CONDENSED
CHICKEN NOODLE
SOUP
Campbell's
CONDENSED
CREAM OF VEGETABLE
SOUP
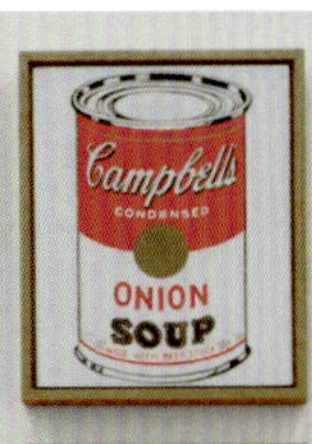
Campbell's
CONDENSED
ONION
SOUP
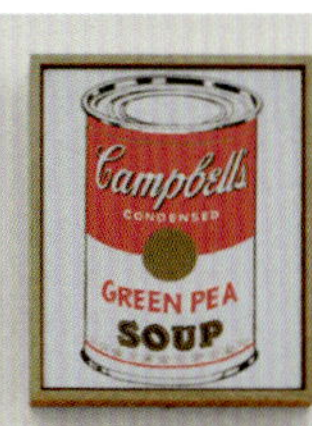
Campbell's
CONDENSED
GREEN PEA
SOUP
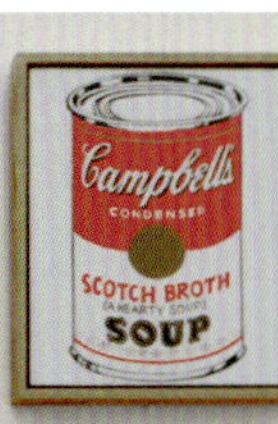
Campbell's
CONDENSED
SCOTCH BROTH
SOUP
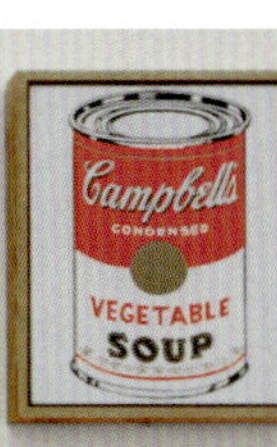
Campbell's
CONDENSED
VEGETABLE
SOUP
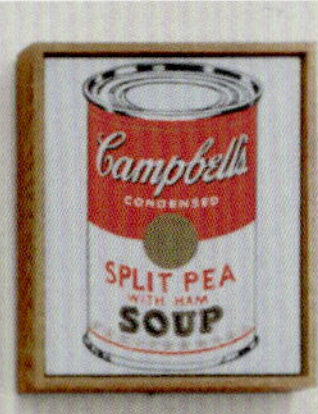
Campbell's
CONDENSED
SPLIT PEA
WITH HAM
SOUP
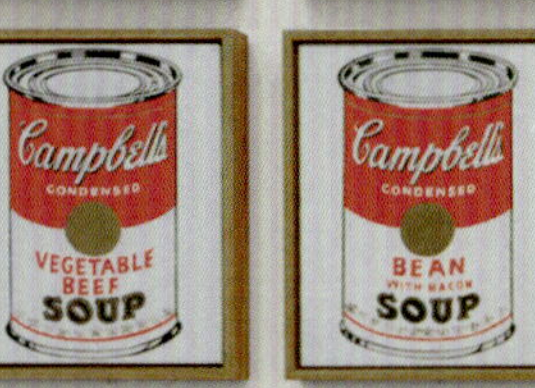
Campbell's
CONDENSED
BEAN
WITH BACON
SOUP
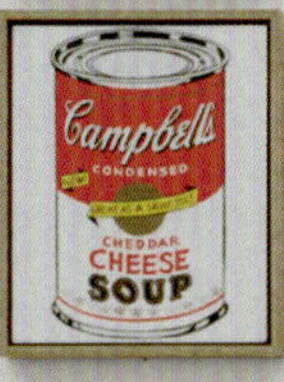
Campbell's
CONDENSED
CHEDDAR CHEESE
SOUP
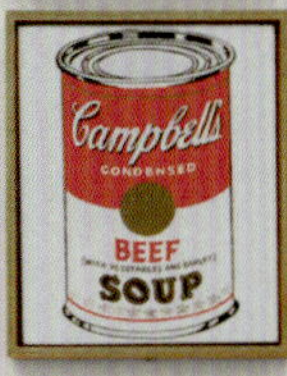
Campbell's
CONDENSED
BEEF
SOUP
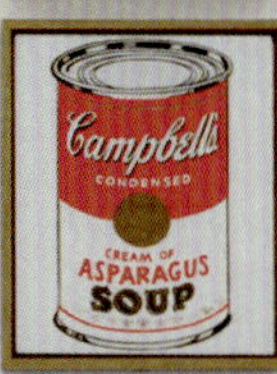
Campbell's
CONDENSED
CREAM OF
ASPARAGUS
SOUP
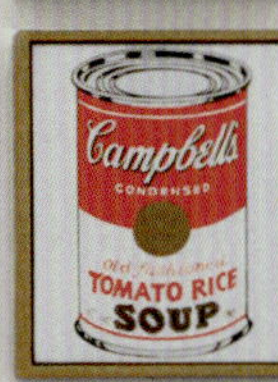
Campbell's
CONDENSED
TOMATO RICE
SOUP
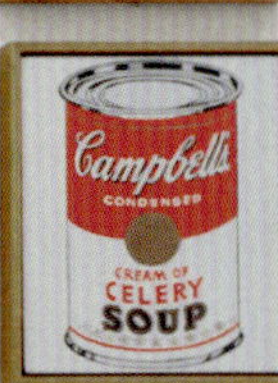
Campbell's
CONDENSED
CREAM OF
CELERY
SOUP
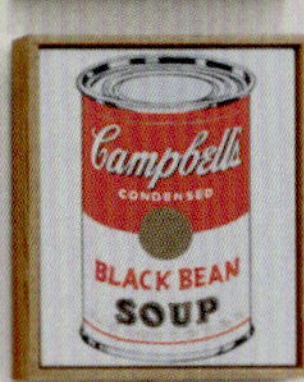
Campbell's
CONDENSED
BLACK BEAN
SOUP
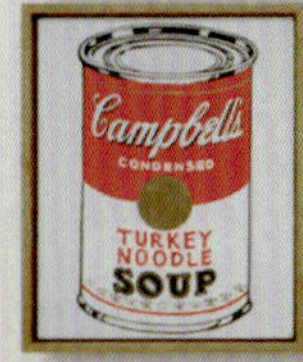
Campbell's
CONDENSED
TURKEY NOODLE
SOUP
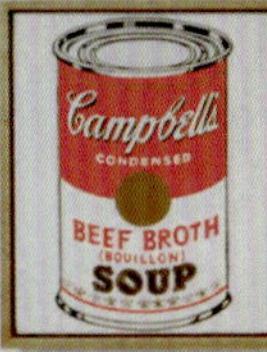
Campbell's
CONDENSED
BEEF BROTH
(BOUILLON)
SOUP
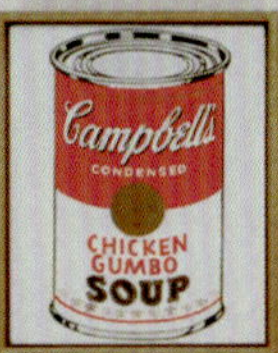
Campbell's
CONDENSED
CHICKEN GUMBO
SOUP
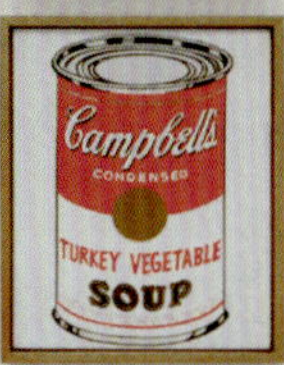
Campbell's
CONDENSED
TURKEY VEGETABLE
SOUP
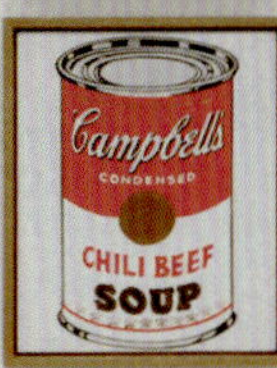
Campbell's
CONDENSED
CHILI BEEF
SOUP
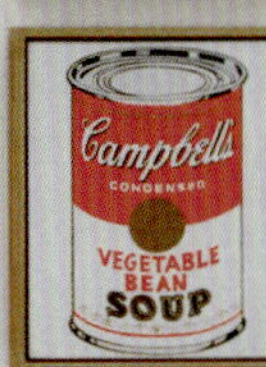
Campbell's
CONDENSED
VEGETABLE BEAN
SOUP
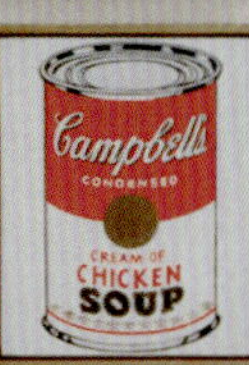
Campbell's
CONDENSED
CREAM OF
CHICKEN
SOUP
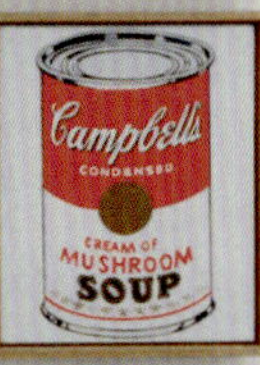
Campbell's
CONDENSED
CREAM OF
MUSHROOM
SOUP
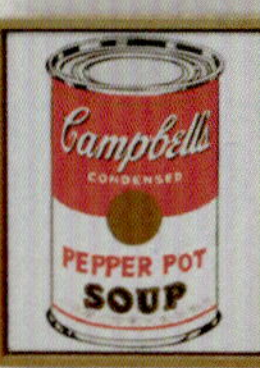
Campbell's
CONDENSED
PEPPER POT
SOUP
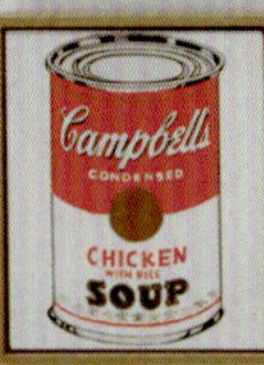
Campbell's
CONDENSED
CHICKEN
WITH RICE
SOUP
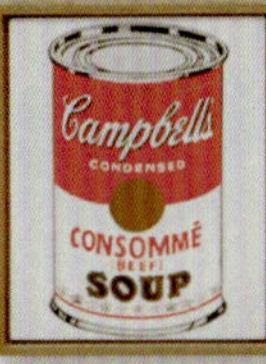
Campbell's
CONDENSED
CONSOMMÉ
BEEF
SOUP
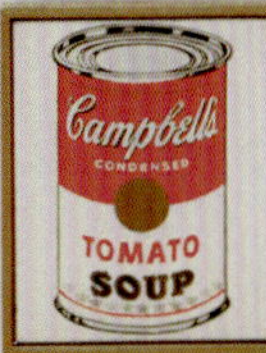
Campbell's
CONDENSED
TOMATO
SOUP
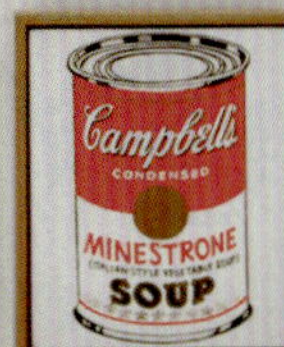
Campbell's
CONDENSED
MINESTRONE
SOUP
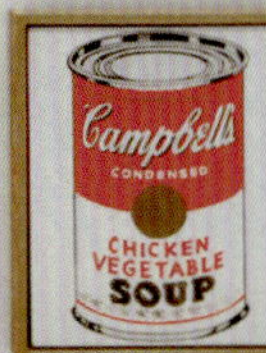
Campbell's
CONDENSED
CHICKEN VEGETABLE
SOUP
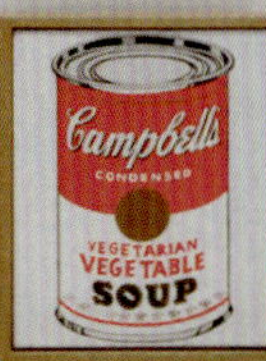
Campbell's
CONDENSED
VEGETARIAN VEGETABLE
SOUP
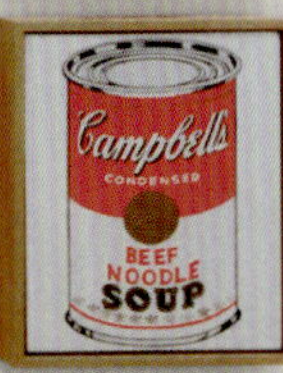
Campbell's
CONDENSED
BEEF NOODLE
SOUP

38

Campbell's Soup Cans

Andy Warhol

1962

Casting around for new subjects, in 1962 Andy Warhol began a series of images based on the then-ubiquitous American soup brand Campbell's. When asked later why he chose that as a subject, Warhol claimed, 'I used to drink it. I used to have the same lunch every day, for twenty years.' After a visit to Warhol's New York City studio
50 in spring 1962, **Los Angeles** art dealer Irving Blum was so impressed by *Campbell's Soup Cans* that he immediately offered Warhol his first solo exhibition, which was held at the Ferus Gallery in Los Angeles.

Warhol's 32 Campbell's soup cans are arranged as if displayed on supermarket shelves. Collectively, they convey – both literally and symbolically – abundance and plenty. The low-cost availability of the Campbell's brand suggests choice for the consumer. Be they rich or poor, all Americans can live easily and conveniently, sustained by Campbell's soup. But Warhol's soup cans also evoke the existential boredom of the supermarket aisles, the numbing sameness of the modern marketplace. Each soup can is different – but this is a standardized kind of difference and the eye registers only the banal repetition of colour and brand name. The viewer scans the available flavours, from clam chowder to beef noodle, just as the shopper would – in interest, boredom or apathy. It doesn't matter which because, Warhol seems to be saying, Campbell's soup simply exists and no judgement is needed. In this way, Warhol's soup cans register a uniquely American moment in history.

The Campbell Soup Company still uses thick black outlines, a striking colour scheme and italicized text in
its branding – just as **Coca-Cola** [illegible]
does. Striped across the tins, a patriotic red-and-white palette evokes the United States flag. These colours are also strangely suggestive of the human mouth – rather like
Tom Wesselmann's sculptural 30
images of scarlet-lipped women and their gleaming white teeth – anticipating the twinned Pop motifs of food and pleasure.

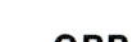

OPPOSITE
Andy Warhol
Campbell's Soup Cans, 1962
ACRYLIC ON CANVAS

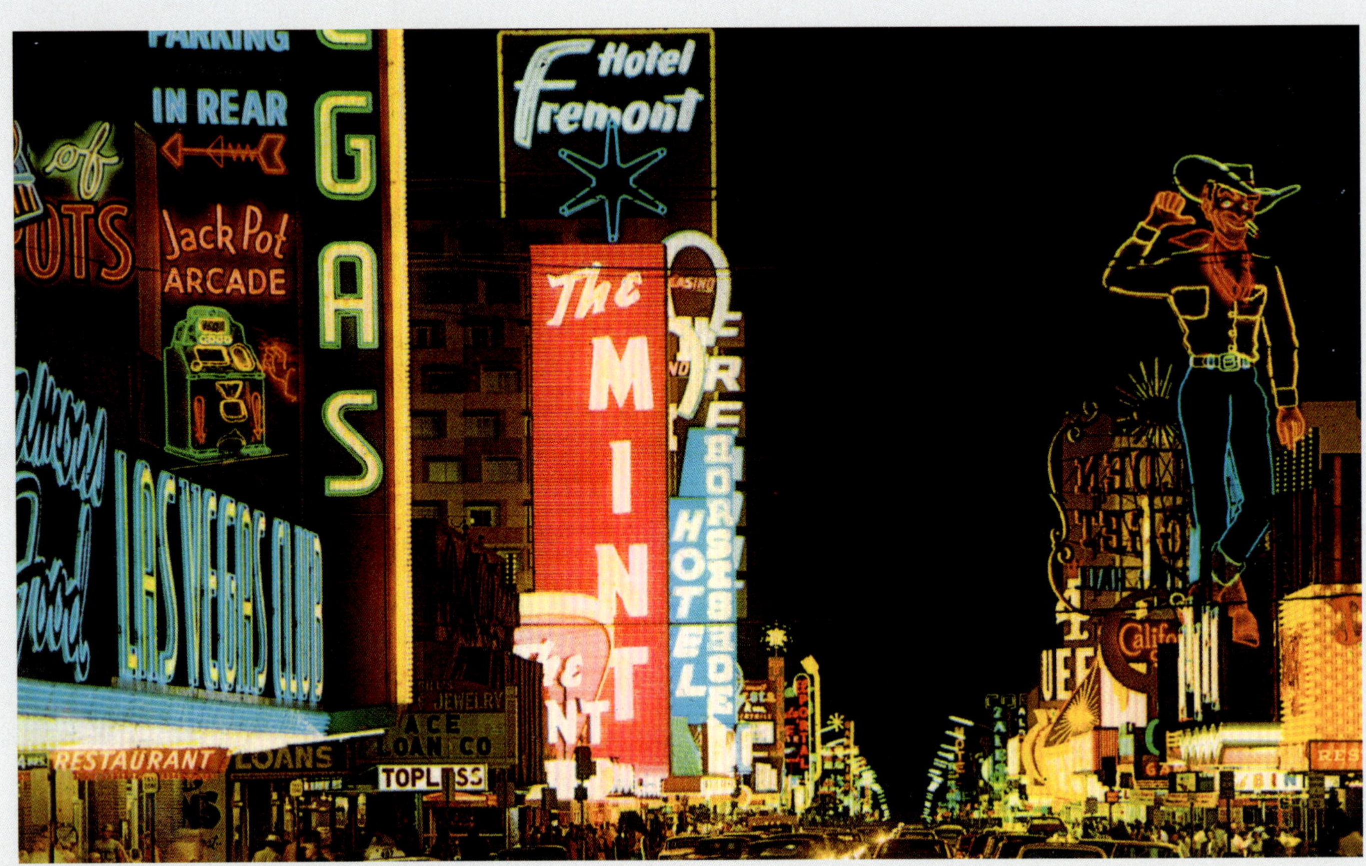

IN REAR
Jack Pot
ARCADE
GAS
Hotel
Fremont
The
MINT
LAS VEGAS CLUB
HOTEL
RESTAURANT
LOANS
JEWELRY
ACE
LOAN CO

39

'New Vulgarians'

In a review of Roy Lichtenstein's solo exhibition at the Leo Castelli Gallery in New York in the spring of 1962, critic Max Kozloff declared Lichtenstein to be one of the 'New Vulgarians'. These barbaric figures were, for Kozloff, destroying what constituted 'good art'. Pop Art had arrived and Pop artists were, instantly, notorious celebrities.

In an *Art International* article, Kozloff claimed that Pop Art wasn't just bad art but a hard 'slap in the face'; an insult to the art establishment and an assault on everyone, 'philistines and cognoscenti' alike. He saw cherished art galleries 'invaded by the pin-headed and contemptible style of gum chewers, bobby soxers and, worse, delinquents'. In a sense, he was right, because 1962 turned out to be a busy year for Pop artists, not to mention a shock for the many critics. As well as Lichtenstein's debut in February, there was a spring feature called 'The Slice of Cake School' in *Time* magazine and the opening of the *International*

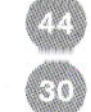

24 *Exhibition of the* ***New Realists***
46 at the **Sidney Janis** Gallery.
44 **Eleanor Ward** also gave
30 **Tom Wesselmann** his first solo exhibition that same month, followed

by **Robert Indiana's** in October 69
and, in November, Warhol's first solo exhibition in New York. And that spring, as if calculated to exasperate the critics, Ray Johnson, known for his radical Pop Art

'happenings', staged an ironic 16
'Nothing' in an empty gallery space. When attendees enquired, 'What's happening?' Johnson replied with gusto, 'Nothing!'

Pop Art was the first movement to possess what we might nowadays call a postmodern sensibility. Pop artists rejected the traditions of high art and exploded the Romantic notion of the artist as hero. Pop artists weren't heroes, they were celebrities. Observing this valorization of the 'vulgar', architects Robert Venturi, Denise Scott Brown and Steven Izenour spend time studying the garish appeal of Las Vegas. Published in 1972, their book *Learning from Las Vegas* – taken alongside Reyner Banham's *Los Angeles* (published in 1971) – expounded on the outlandish beauty of these film-set cities and, together with the Pop Art aesthetic, proved a direct influence on the new postmodernism.

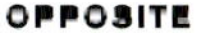

OPPOSITE
Neon signs in Fremont Street, Las Vegas, 1968

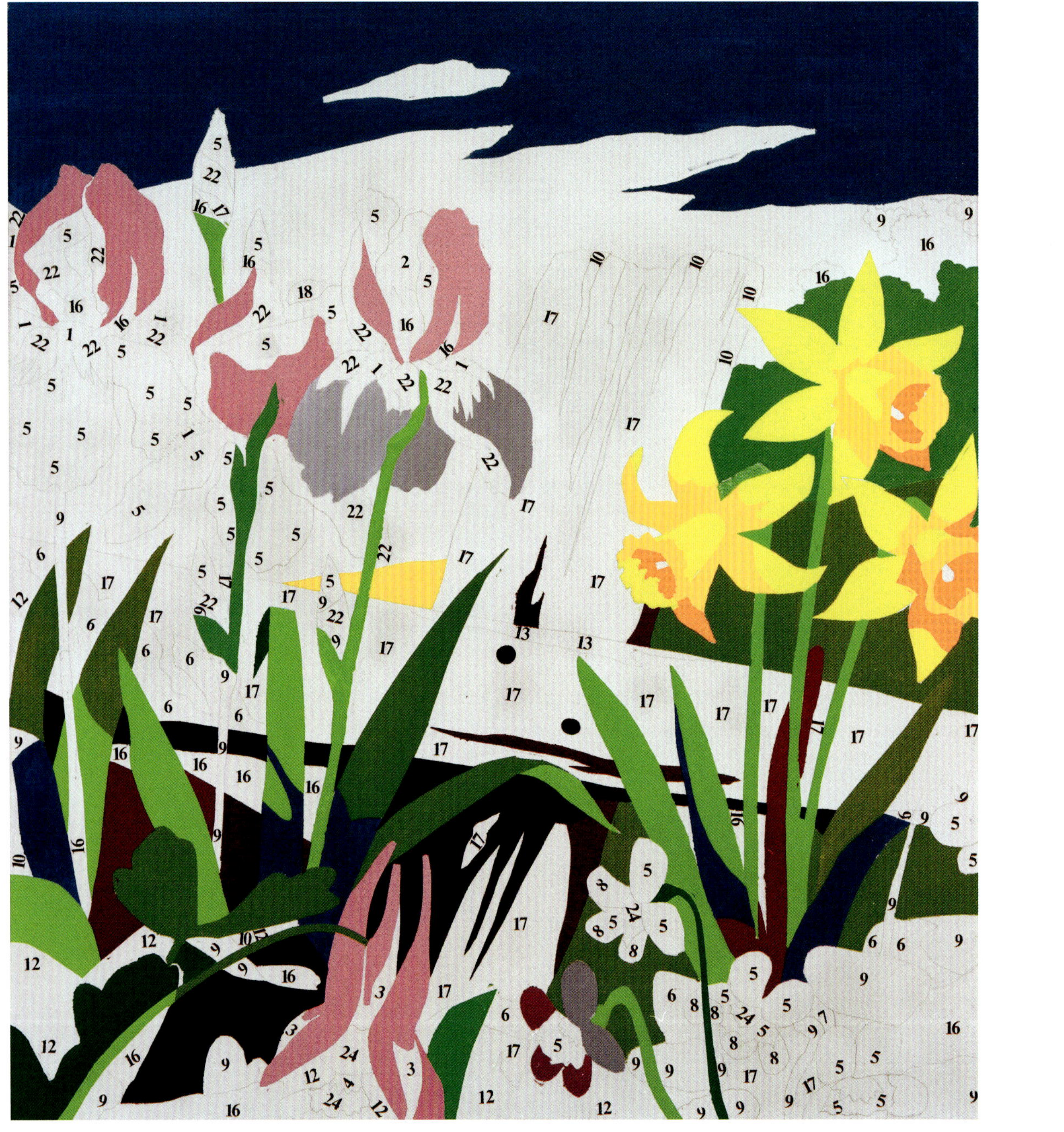

40

Do It Yourself

Andy Warhol

1962

Seeking to distance his work from that of Roy Lichtenstein, and in search of popular new visual distractions, in 1962 Andy Warhol began developing five parodic paintings known as his *Do It Yourself* series, the very concept of do-it-yourself neatly encapsulating the Pop Art philosophy.

Despite, or even because of, their associations with childhood, suburban boredom and old age, Warhol loved do-it-yourself painting or 'painting by numbers' sets. Cheap, ephemeral and essentially undemanding, these gave everyone the opportunity to create a 'perfect' work of art. Heralding what one horrified critic called the 'end of painting', Warhol's [illegible] and Sailboats retain their colour-key numbering and, in consequence, deliberately appear half-finished. The paintings are revealed to be mathematical exercises in efficient, mechanical precision. And yet, disruptively, Warhol refuses to follow his own colour key. After all, how else would we see the hand of the artist and know these to be works of art?

The consumer culture of the 1950s had popularized the term 'do-it-yourself' so widely that, by the early 1960s, it already conjured images of suburban home improvement. Easily assembled furniture, for example, allowed husbands the fantasy of being well-trained craftsman – pioneers, even, 'building' their own homes. The vogue for instant food, made widely popular by the 1950 publication of *Betty Crocker's Picture Cook Book*, allowed housewives the illusion of being expert cooks. During that same decade, colourful mass market 'painting by numbers' [illegible] by Detroit industrial designer Dan Robbins. Anyone, whether an aspiring amateur or a recognized professional, could now create, or recreate, a masterpiece and feel like a great artist. That anyone could do it, so easily and so instantly, and discard it too without a care, felt to Warhol both distinctly American and distinctly Pop.

OPPOSITE
Andy Warhol
Do It Yourself (Flowers), 1962

ACRYLIC AND SCREEN PRINT ON CANVAS

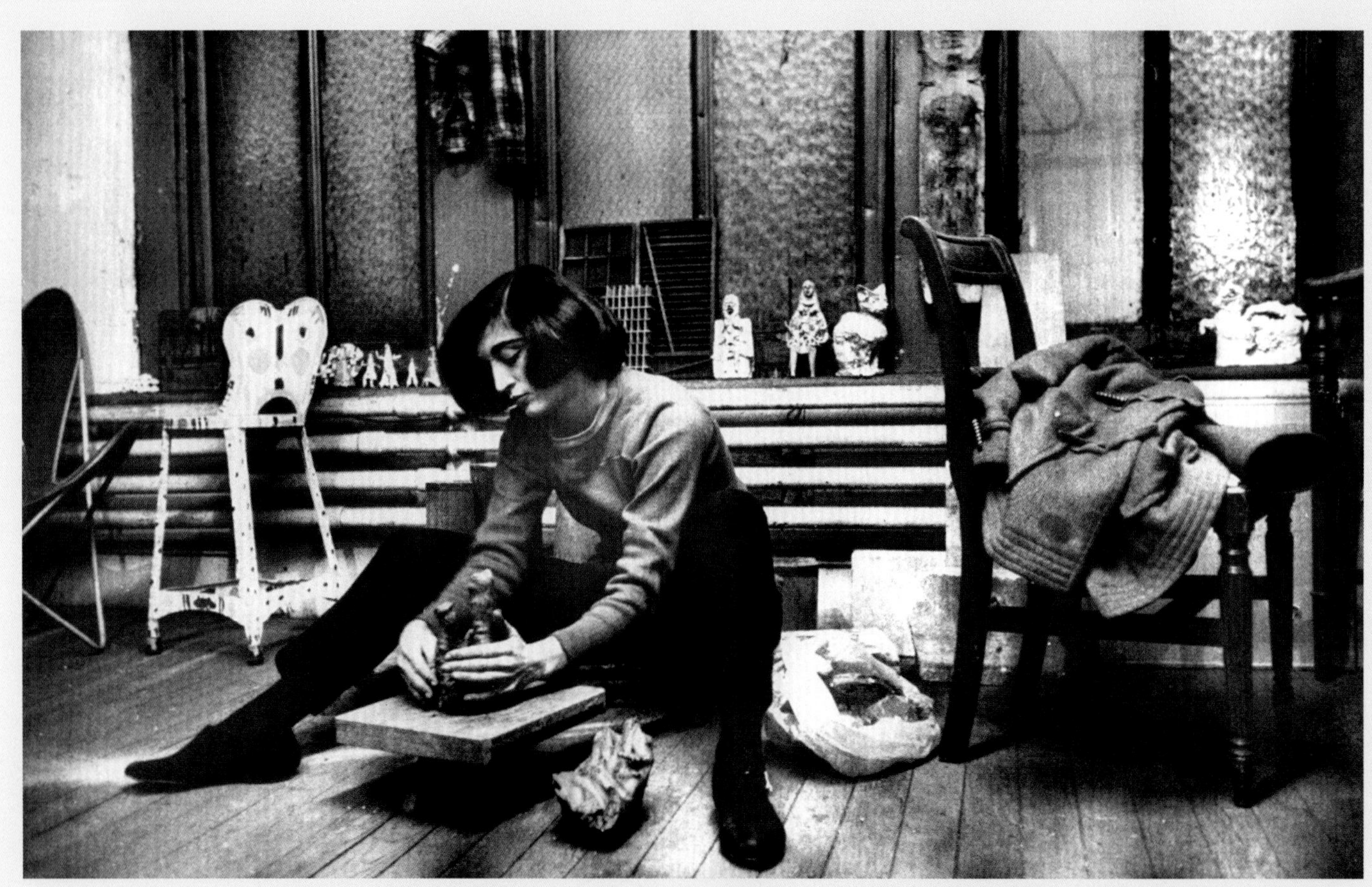

41

Marisol

Referred to as the 'Latin Garbo', radical Pop sculptor Marisol Escobar – professionally often known simply as Marisol – enjoyed her first solo
44 exhibition in May 1962 at **Eleanor Ward's** Stable Gallery in New York. Later featured in the *International*
24 *Exhibition of the* ***New Realists*** at
46 the nearby **Sidney Janis** Gallery, she was listed as one of *Life* magazine's 'Red Hot 100'.

As a Hispanic woman, Marisol didn't always receive the recognition she deserved, and when she did, it was too often the result of being perceived as, in the words of her friend Andy Warhol, 'the first girl artist with glamor'. She later said, 'In the 60s, the men [artists] did not feel threatened by me', thinking 'I was cute and spooky... they didn't take my art so seriously'. Nevertheless, Marisol's work was eagerly profiled by the *New York Times* in 1965 and her solo exhibition the following year at the Sidney Janis Gallery was famously reported to have had three thousand people queuing outside on the opening day.

Born in Paris to Venezuelan parents, Marisol had a determinedly artistic childhood. Studying in both Europe and America, she began her career with a 1957 exhibition at the Leo Castelli Gallery in New York. Her satirical **wooden sculptures**, often 58
featuring famous figures arranged in family groups, always emphasized the figurative over the abstract. While we can't be sure that Marisol ever read it, her group sculptures *Women and Dog* (1963–4) and *La Visita* (1964) were produced a year after the publication of Betty Friedan's groundbreaking 1963 book *The Feminine Mystique*. Friedan's argument that men have manufactured 'feminine mystique' as a form of social and sexual control is powerfully reflected in Marisol's work: her female figures feel somehow awkward and imprisoned. An undeniable Pop radical, Marisol's sculpture was, as she said, a 'funny kind of rebellion'.

OPPOSITE
Marisol Escobar, 1957

FINAL★★ 5¢

New York Mirror

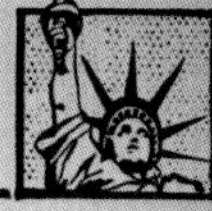

WEATHER: Fair with little change in temperature.

Vol. 37, No 296

MONDAY, JUNE 4, 1962

C

129 DIE

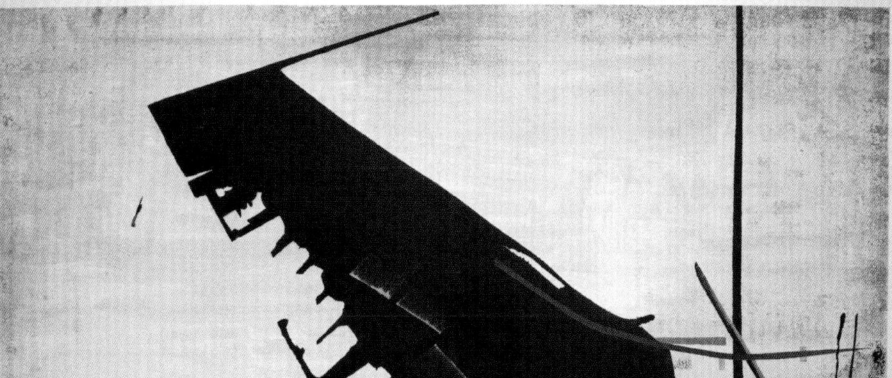

(UPI RADIOTELEphoto)

IN JET!

42

129 Die in Jet (Plane Crash)

Andy Warhol

1962

Over breakfast one morning in early
23 June 1962, **Henry Geldzahler** – then working at the Metropolitan Museum of Art – warned Andy Warhol against self-satisfaction at having secured his first solo exhibition, suggesting, 'Enough life. It's time for a little death.' In other words, Geldzahler thought that Warhol should be addressing
26 darker subjects, because his **cartoon**
34 **characters** and **Coke bottles** would soon become tired. Throwing Warhol that morning's *New York Mirror*, he encouraged him to paint what was going on in the world: 'tragedy, agony and disaster'.

The headline screamed '129 Die in Jet!' A state-of-the-art American aircraft bound for Atlanta had the previous day crashed on take-off at Paris's Orly Airport. Only launched in 1958, Boeing's 707 transatlantic flights were still new, expensive, fast and glamorous – and this particular flight was full of wealthy American socialites and art patrons. The sensational reporting of the Orly crash and the shocking deaths was reminiscent of the 1912 press coverage of the sinking of the *Titanic*. Then, too, over a hundred American passengers died, 71 of whom had been travelling first class.

Responding to Geldzahler's prompt, Warhol returned to his studio with the *Mirror* and began his disturbing
***Death and Disaster* series**, the 77
first of which was his painted canvas *129 Die in Jet (Plane Crash)*. Stripping the original front page of its photo tagline, he otherwise faithfully reproduced the headline and photograph of the wreckage, even down to the ink creases on the page. Warhol soon found himself increasingly drawn to images of violent death, particularly when the victims were glamorous and wealthy. For one's death to be announced – just like one's love affairs – in exclamatory headlines was surely the apex of Pop fame. Warhol clearly understood the compelling voyeurism of disaster photo-reportage. Representing a great event of collective trauma, Warhol's first *Death and Disaster* image also heralds a very modern form of traditional history painting.

OPPOSITE
Andy Warhol
129 Die in Jet (Plane Crash), 1962
ACRYLIC ON CANVAS

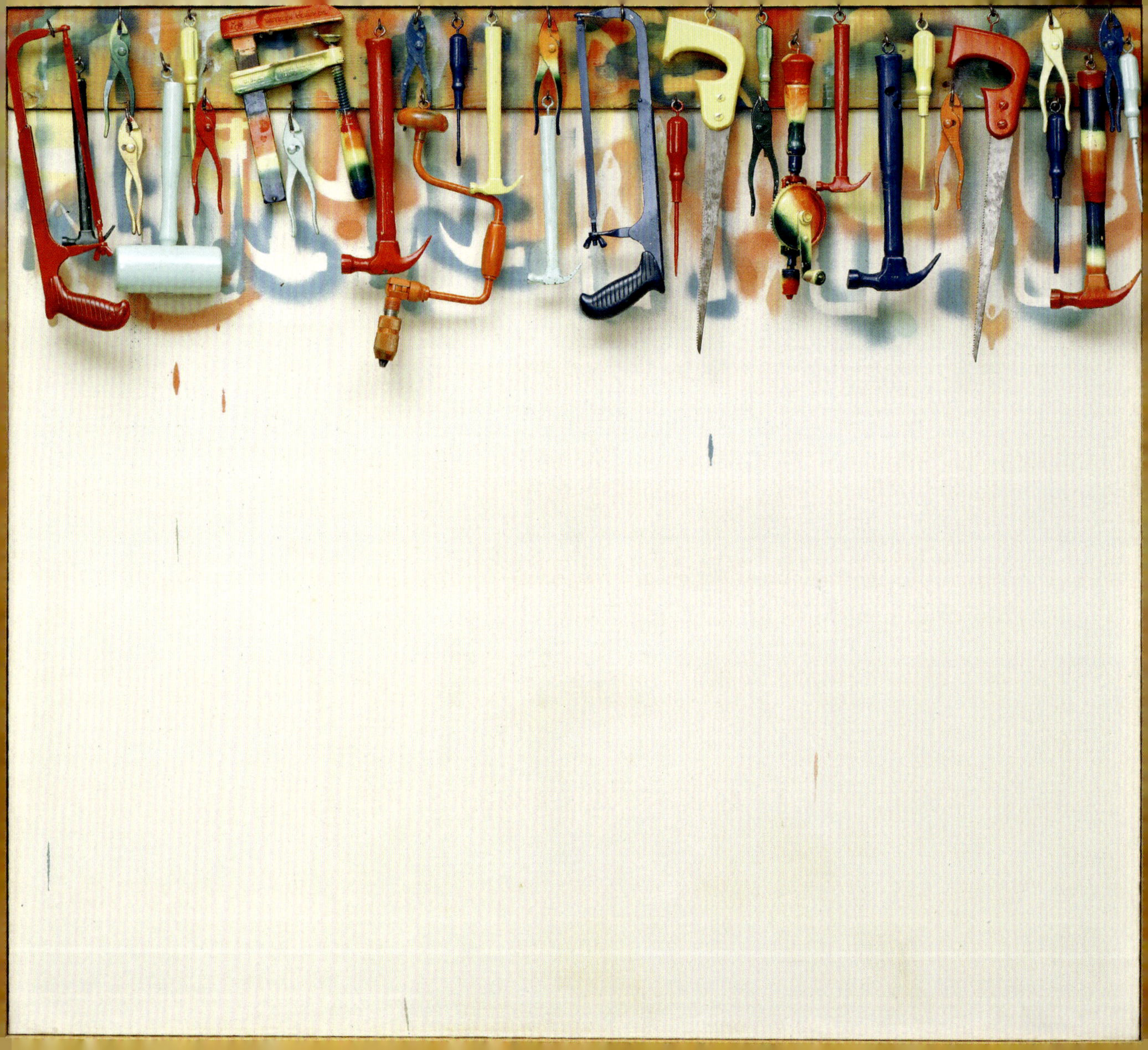

43

Jim Dine

Although Jim Dine featured in curator Walter Hopps's *New Painting of Common Objects* exhibition
50 at Pasadena Art Museum in **Los Angeles** in the early autumn of 1962, the Pop artist's fame has dimmed somewhat in recent years. This may in part be explained by the honesty and simplicity of an approach that emphasized his skills as a draughtsman. Generally eschewing the consumer products of the 1960s home, Ohio-born Dine often drew his inspiration instead from the less aspirational and more practical Pop objects of everyday life.

Expressing his typically down-to-earth Midwestern interest in the mass-produced tools of working-class labour, Dine produced a ground-breaking 1960 Pop performance called *The Smiling Workman* that was one of the first **'happenings'** in New York. Throughout the early 1960s, Dine's diverse work was exhibited in Paris, Rome, Brussels and Cologne, and was included in the influential exhibitions *New Forms, New Media* at the Martha Jackson Gallery in New York and *Six Painters and the Object* at both New York's Guggenheim Museum and the Los Angeles County Museum of Art. Dine also famously exhibited at controversial British art dealer Robert Fraser's Mayfair gallery in London, just around the corner from the American Embassy in Grosvenor Square, in the summer of 1965 and the autumn of 1966. The 1966 exhibition, which comprised 21 often abstract drawings of both male and female genitalia (some of which were larger than life-size) and one collage featuring the word 'Cunt', was raided by the Police and Fraser was found guilty of staging an 'indecent exhibition' under an obscure 19th-century British law. He was fined a total of seventy guineas. Nevertheless, that year Dine made plans to relocate full-time to London, where he stayed until 1971.

Dine's best known work, however, is his series *Tools* (1973), donated to the Tate in London in 1980. Depicting ten conventional metal tools – screwdriver, scissors, pliers, fork, spoon etc. – in ten separate lithographs, Dine brings a delicate Pop beauty to the practical and the prosaic.

OPPOSITE
Jim Dine
Five Feet of Colorful Tools, 1962
OIL ON UNPRIMED CANVAS SURMOUNTED BY A BOARD ON WHICH PAINTED TOOLS HANG FROM HOOKS

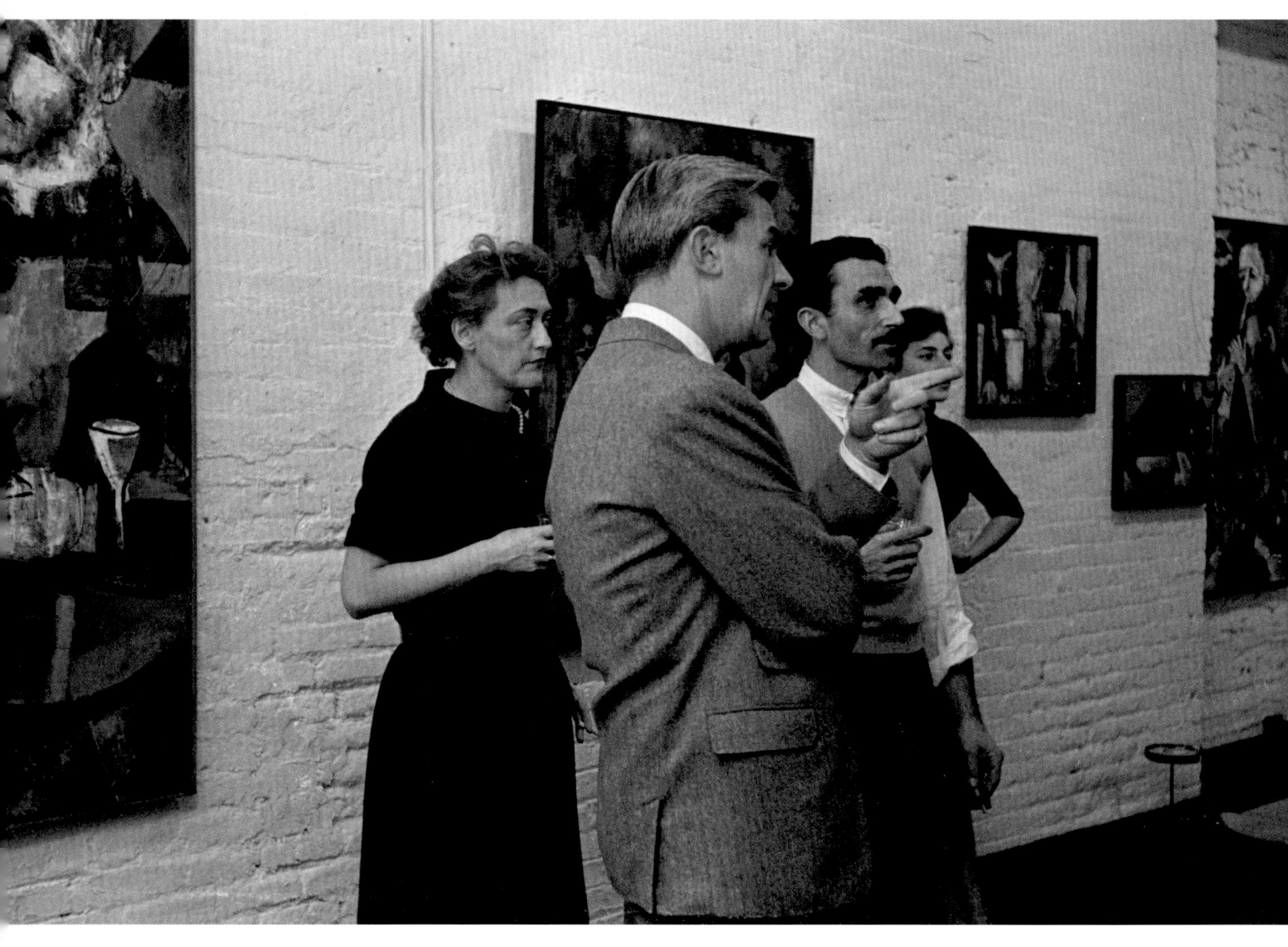

44

Eleanor Ward

41 With what Pop artist **Marisol Escobar** called her 'sense of theatre', New York gallerist Eleanor Ward became the greatest female champion of Pop Art during the early 1960s. Founder of the Stable Gallery, it was Ward who 'discovered' Pop artists Robert Rauschenberg,
30 Marisol, **Tom Wesselmann** and
69 **Robert Indiana**, and in November 1962, she supported Andy Warhol with his first solo exhibition in New York.

After working in advertising for Paris fashion designer Christian Dior, Pennsylvania-born Ward returned to America in 1952 and opened the Stable Gallery in midtown New York the following year. Returning that spring from six months travelling in Europe with his partner the abstract artist Cy Twombly, Rauschenberg took a summer job as a cleaner at the gallery. Ward soon befriended him and gave the two young men a joint exhibition that September. Over the next ten years Ward became known for her yearly exhibitions, the 'Stable Annuals', and was introduced by a friend to Warhol in the summer of 1962. 'I immediately liked Andy as a person,' she remembered, and after seeing his work declared it 'an incredible collection, I was absolutely riveted'.

Fresh from a solo exhibition
in **Los Angeles** that summer, 50 
Warhol debuted in New York
with his ***Do It Yourself*** series, 40 
Campbell's Soup Cans and 38
portraits of **Marilyn Monroe**, 45 
Elizabeth Taylor and Elvis Presley. Press reception was mixed, but *Art International* reviewer Michael Fried called Warhol's 'brilliant' work both 'moving' and 'spectacular'. Fried recognized Warhol's 'instinct for vulgarity' and his 'feeling for what is truly human and pathetic' in the 'exemplary myths of our time'. Yet he signalled what feels in retrospect like a quaintly cautious note: 'I am not at all sure that even the best of Warhol's work can much outlast the journalism on which it is forced to depend.'

OPPOSITE
Eleanor Ward (left) at the Stable Gallery in New York City, 1954

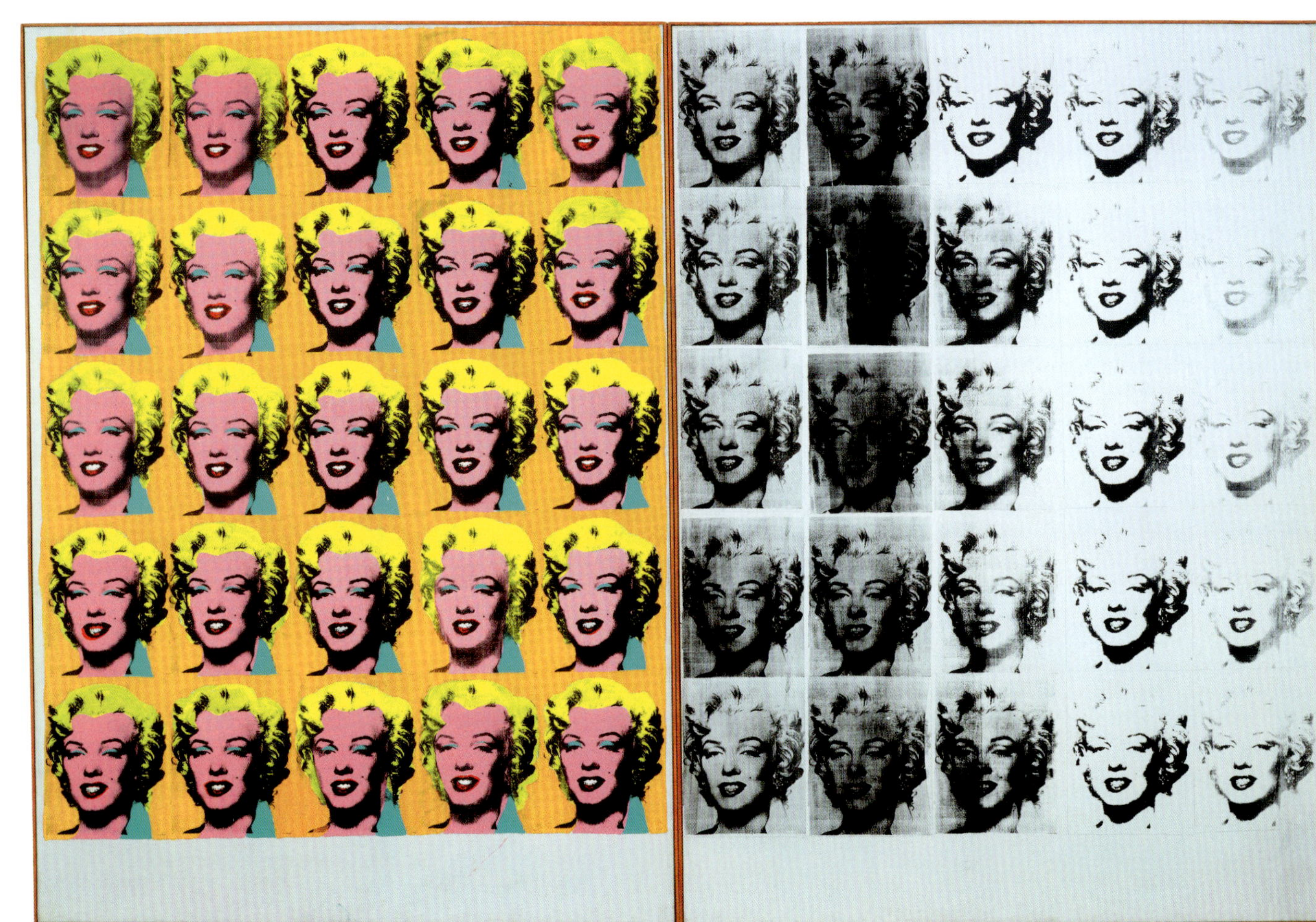

45

Marilyn Diptych

Andy Warhol

1962

Hollywood icon Marilyn Monroe became a Pop Art obsession, her image ubiquitous in the work of artists on both sides of the Atlantic. Monroe died only four days after the closure of Andy Warhol's ground-breaking
50 exhibition in **Los Angeles**, the day before his 34th birthday. One of over twenty Marilyn images produced by Warhol, *Marilyn Diptych* – first exhibited in November 1962 at the
44 **Stable Gallery** in New York – marked both her demise and his ascent.

Although Monroe was characterized as the dumb and ultimately tragic blonde, her breakout role was as a dangerous femme fatale in the 1953 film *Niagara*. Drawing upon a cropped *Niagara* publicity photo, Warhol's memorial combined the uniform colours of contemporary advertising with the textures and subtle variations of traditional
36 **silkscreen** printing. Buried beneath an armorial make-up of electric yellow, green and pink, Monroe appears as much a manufactured
34 brand or commodity as **Coca-Cola** or **Campbell's soup**. Placing her 38
image within a double-panelled diptych frame, traditionally associated with Christian altarpieces, Warhol also emphasizes her cultural power: in the post-war period, the cultural significance of Hollywood celebrities became as potent as that of Catholic saints in Renaissance Italy.

Reading the work from top left to bottom right, however, we witness the arc of Monroe's career from colourful brilliance to weary distress. The repeated image not only suggests Monroe's cultural power but also how compulsive glamour and excess may have contributed to her death. **Fame** 83
is seductive but its nausea-inducing repetition will quite literally here almost eradicate its subject. In her last, unfinished film, *Something's Got to Give*, 36-year-old Monroe played a forgotten woman, forced to impersonate someone else, and only two days before she died she lamented to *Life* magazine that 'fame is fickle'. Warhol implicates all of us in her demise.

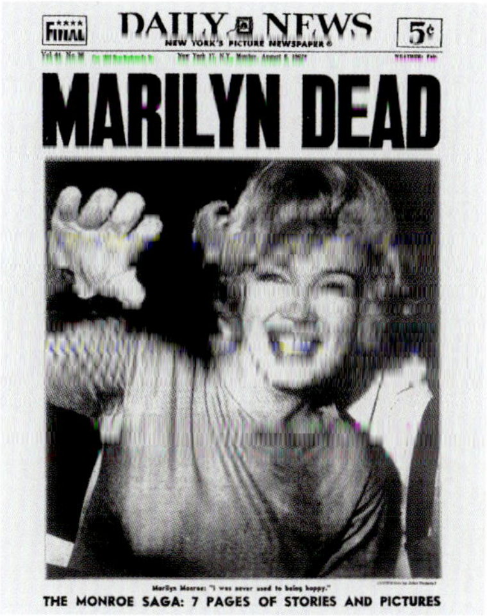

ABOVE
Daily News front cover, 6 August 1962

OPPOSITE
Andy Warhol
Marilyn Diptych, 1962
ACRYLIC ON CANVAS

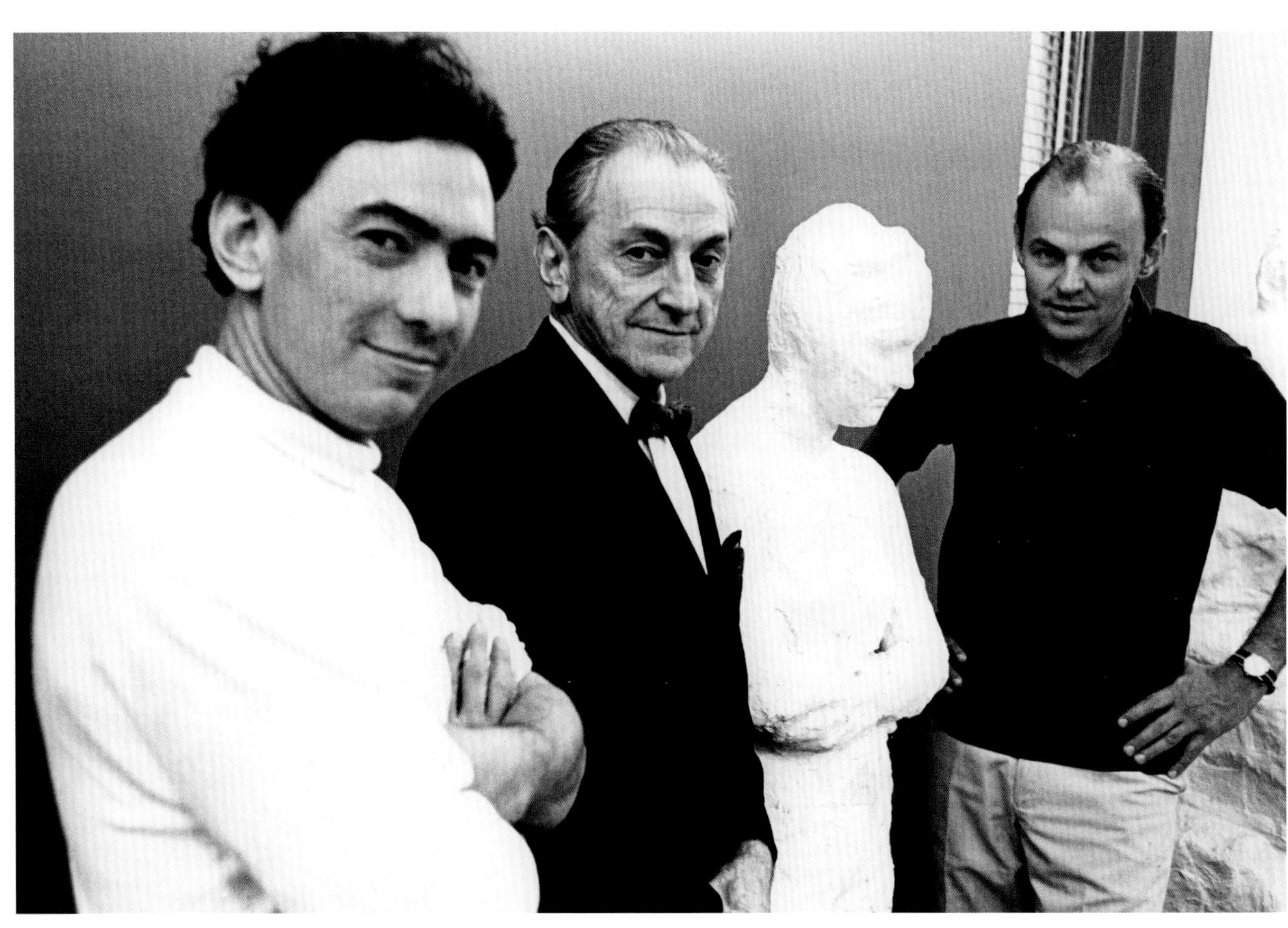

46

Sidney Janis

As described by Alfred H. Barr, the founding director of New York's Museum of Modern Art, Pop gallerist Sidney Janis was 'the most brilliant new dealer, in terms of business acumen, to have appeared in New York since the war'. Despite believing his talents lay in promoting known artists rather than finding new ones, Janis became 'a trend-spotter and a taste-maker' who exhibited the 24 ground-breaking **New Realists** at his midtown gallery in November 1962. Influential critic Clement Greenberg credited Janis with fostering an atmosphere in which American artists could thrive and praised him for valuing American art as highly as everyone else seemed to value European art.

A former ballroom dancer and Naval Reserve officer in the 1920s Janis established the successful two-pocketed, short-sleeved M'Lord men's shirts label. He and his wife, Harriet, began annual trips to Paris, where they became familiar with European modernism. Janis soon started his own private art collection and, in the 1930s, bought his first work by abstract artist Piet Mondrian. In 1939, Janis wound up the shirt-making business to write, in collaboration with Harriet, several books on Pablo Picasso, Surrealism and American folk art. He even became great friends with *enfant terrible* **Marcel Duchamp**. 1

In 1948, as an enjoyable early retirement scheme at the age of 52, Janis opened his gallery with an exhibition by the French abstract artist Fernand Léger. He soon became an early champion of Abstract Expressionism and was one of the first to exhibit the work of Jackson Pollock. As he had represented the most famous Abstract Expressionists, Janis's turn to Pop Art in 1960 horrified many. He went on to represent, among others, Claes Oldenburg, **Tom Wesselmann** 30 and **Marisol Escobar**. By 1967, his 41 legacy was secure. Janis was asked to pose – alongside his prized Mondrian – for the Pop sculptor George Segal. And that year he donated to MoMA an 'unequalled' collection of over a hundred modernist masterpieces.

OPPOSITE
Sidney Janis (centre) with his sons Carroll (left) and Conrad Janis, along with a sculpture by George Segal at the Sidney Janis Gallery, New York City, 1966

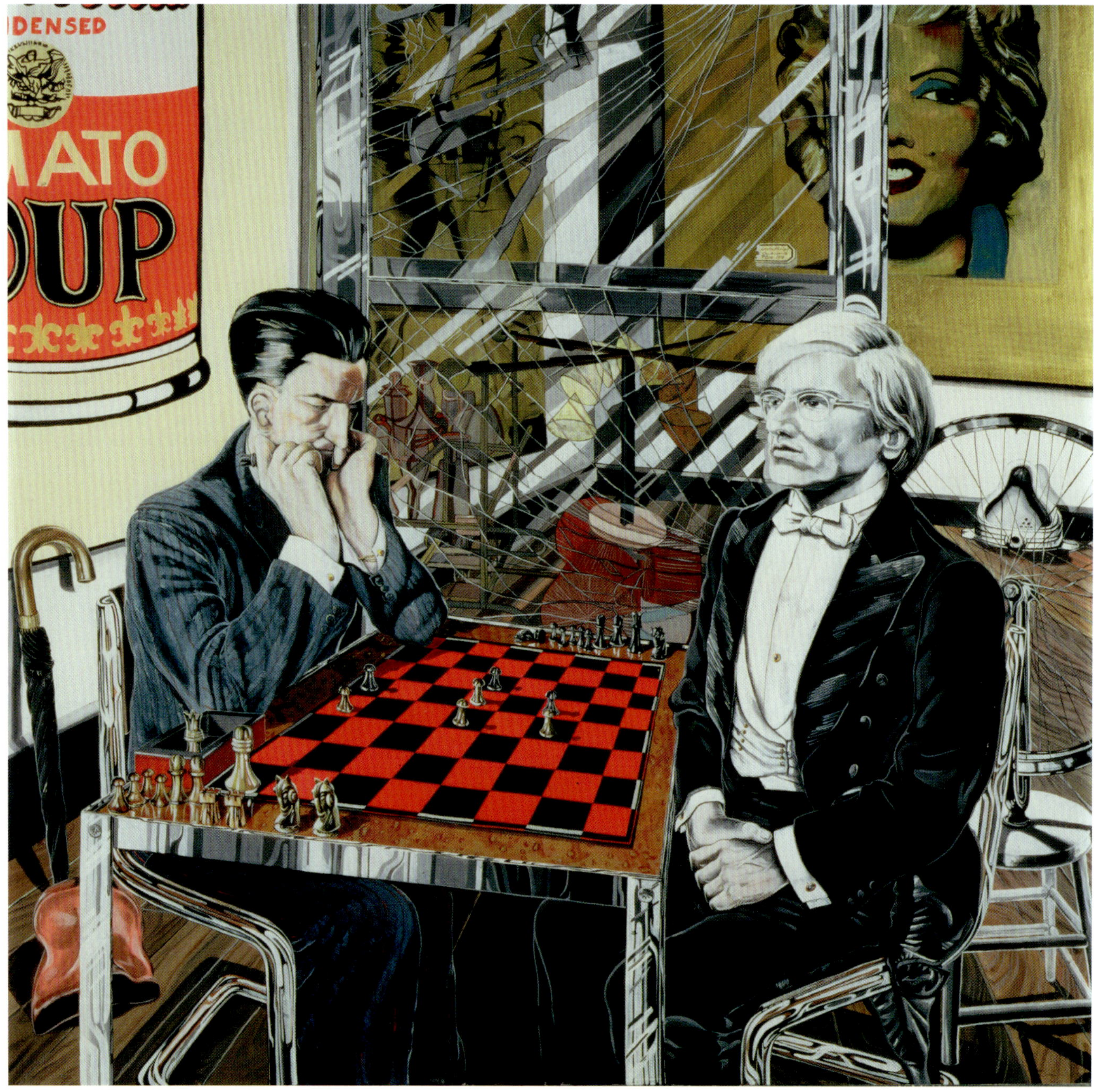

DENSED
MATO
OUP

47

MoMA symposium

1962

Purchasing their $3 tickets in the auditorium of New York's Museum of Modern Art on a cold December evening in 1962 were 75-year-old
1 **Marcel Duchamp** and 34-year-old Andy Warhol. Although they wouldn't meet properly for another four years, that evening they were both expectant members of the audience at the first – and most provocative – Pop Art symposium.

Chaired by MoMA curator Peter Selz, the symposium panel consisted of five key figures from the New York art world. The only woman was 34-year-old art historian and former critic for the *New York Times* Dore Ashton, a well-known champion of the Abstract Expressionists, in particular Mark Rothko and Philip Guston. Ashton was joined by 57-year-old poet Stanley Kunitz, a friend of both Rothko and Guston who would later twice become the US Poet Laureate; 42-year-old Russian-born avant-garde art historian Leo Steinberg; 27-year-old Pop Art lover and assistant curator at the Metropolitan Museum of Art **Henry Geldzahler**; and 34-year-old art critic and defender of high culture Hilton Kramer. 

While focusing their discussions on the aesthetics of American Pop Art, the group were encouraged by Selz to analyze Pop Art's 'value as a meaningful comment on contemporary life as well as the problematic relationship of art to mass culture'. Following a presentation of recent Pop Art, including some of Warhol's own work, the panellists took to their discussion with gusto. Broadly, those in favour of Pop Art (Steinberg and Geldzahler) were outnumbered by those against it (Ashton, Kunitz and Kramer). But the fact that the MoMA saw the need to host this particular symposium, and that these high-profile critics were asked to come together to have their say, demonstrates that by 1962 Pop Art had become the most polarizing development in the New York art world since Peggy Guggenheim had opened her controversial *Art of This Century* exhibition, twenty years before, in October 1942.

OPPOSITE
Philip Core
The Chance Meeting on an Operating Table of a Sewing Machine and an Umbrella: Andy Warhol and Marcel Duchamp, 1978
OIL, ACRYLIC AND GOUACHE ON BOARD

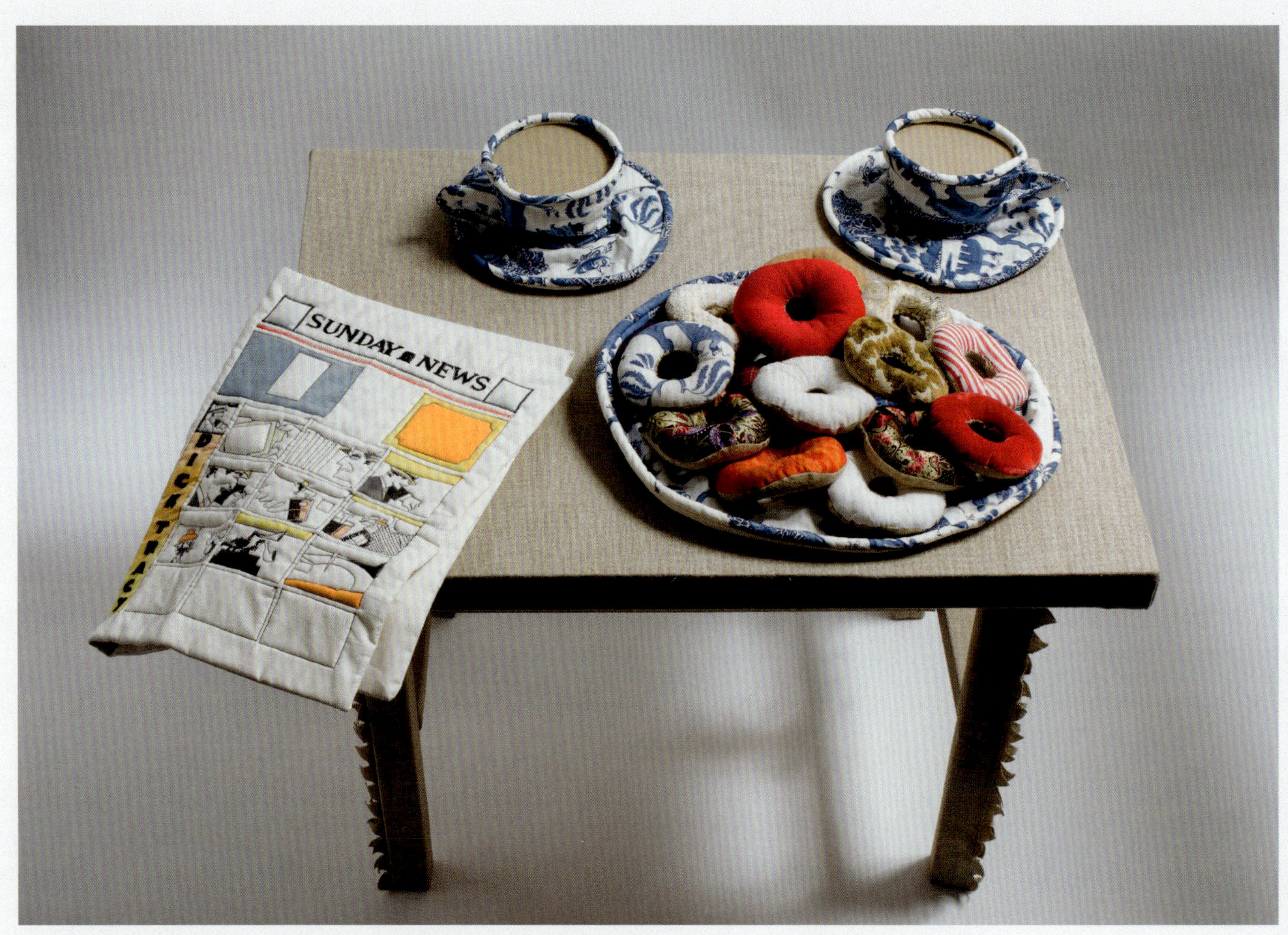
SUNDAY NEWS
DICK TRACY

48

Jann Haworth

American Pop sculptor Jann Haworth – best known for her later collaborative design for The Beatles' *Sgt. Pepper's Lonely Hearts Club Band* album cover – was a radical pioneer of soft sculpture. In 1963, the year she married British Pop artist Peter Blake, her work debuted in the *Four Young Artists* exhibition at the Institute of Contemporary Arts in London.

Having moved to London from her 50 native **Los Angeles** in 1961, Haworth entered the Slade School of Art, where – thanks to what she called its pleasing 'fustiness' – she became a Pop rebel. As a child she had been taught by her artist mother how to sew and stuff dolls; now she began constructing radical soft sculptures of ordinary objects and archetypal figures. Her father, a Hollywood art director, had famously 45 worked on **Marilyn Monroe's** 1959 hit *Some Like It Hot*. 'The concept of the stand-in, the fake, the dummy, the latex model as surrogates for the real, came from being with my father' on set, she reflected.

Creating somewhat disturbing 'dummy sculptures' of Hollywood stars including Mae West and Shirley Temple, Haworth became one of only two prominent female Pop artists working in London during the early 1960s, the other being **Pauline Boty**. As a result, they were, 72 with sad inevitability and despite the fact that they worked in entirely different media, popularly cast as rivals by their male colleagues. Whatever the truth of their personal feelings for one another, or the reality of their professional rivalry, Haworth and Boty were both unique and revolutionary artists. That they were cast as rivals at all speaks volumes about the misogyny of the period.

OPPOSITE
Jann Haworth
Donuts, Coffee and Comics, 1962–[illegible]
MIXED MEDIA

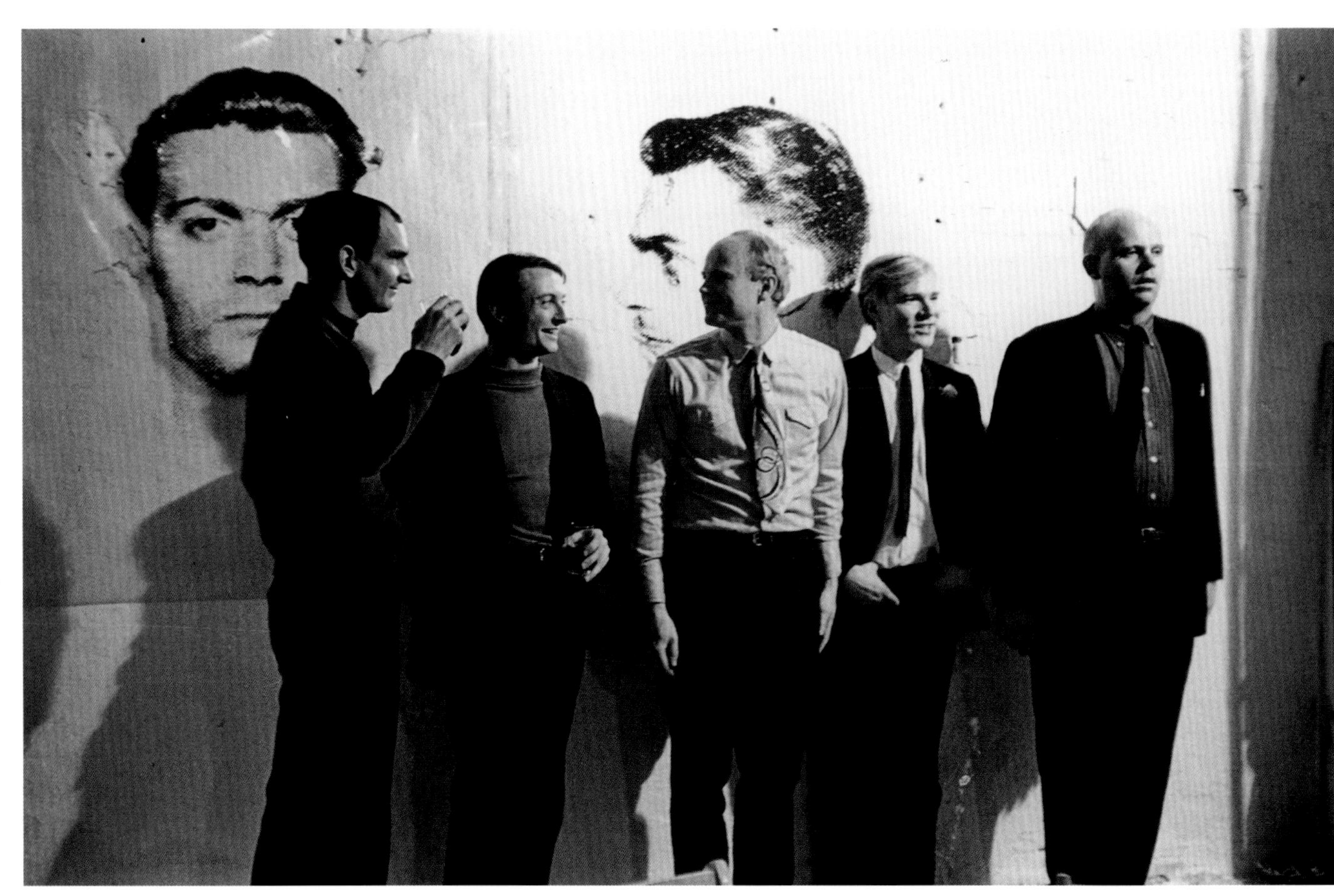

49

The 'Big Six'

1963

As curator of the exhibition *Six Painters and the Object* at the Guggenheim Museum in New York, British art critic Lawrence Alloway defined the original 'Big Six' of Pop Art. Opening in March 1963, Alloway's exhibition featured the work of Jasper Johns, Robert Rauschenberg, Andy Warhol, Roy Lichtenstein, James
43 Rosenquist and **Jim Dine**. Focusing specifically on the painted image, Alloway selected 33 contemporary examples: Johns, Rauschenberg and Lichtenstein each showed six paintings, Rosenquist, Dine and Warhol each showed five.

As Alloway made clear in the exhibition catalogue, the use of popular sources in art had been 'widespread since the 18th century, though not much charted'. *Six Painters and the Object* was, for Alloway, both a historical contribution in that sense and a playful exercise in exposing how Pop Art's collision of 'high and popular culture' typically 'embarrassed' elitist critics. In response to the exhibition, 24-year-old New York critic and art historian Barbara Rose wrote a review in *Art International* in May that year.

While conceding that Pop Art must be art (if it hung in the Guggenheim), she questioned its 'calibre'. For her, rather than being pure Pop Art, the work of Johns and Rauschenberg was actually a bridge between Abstract Expressionism and Pop. Only Dine was directly criticized: albeit fresh, his work was, she thought, 'heavy-handed' and 'the least of the artists represented'.

Travelling on from the Guggenheim
to the **Los Angeles** County 50
Museum of Art in the summer of 1963, *Six Painters and the Object* gained significant national exposure and made Pop's Big Six famous. Fifty years later, in considering Pop's principal players and their legacies – and with the significant benefit of hindsight – the art critic Arthur C. Danto would redefine the critical Big Six. While keeping Warhol, Lichtenstein and Rosenquist, he disputed Rose's assessment of Dine and retained him. However, building on her critique, he excluded Johns and Rauschenberg in favour of Claes
Oldenburg and **Tom Wesselmann**. 30

OPPOSITE
From left, Tom Wesselmann, Roy Lichtenstein, James Rosenquist, Andy Warhol and Claes Oldenburg in Warhol's loft, New York City, 1964

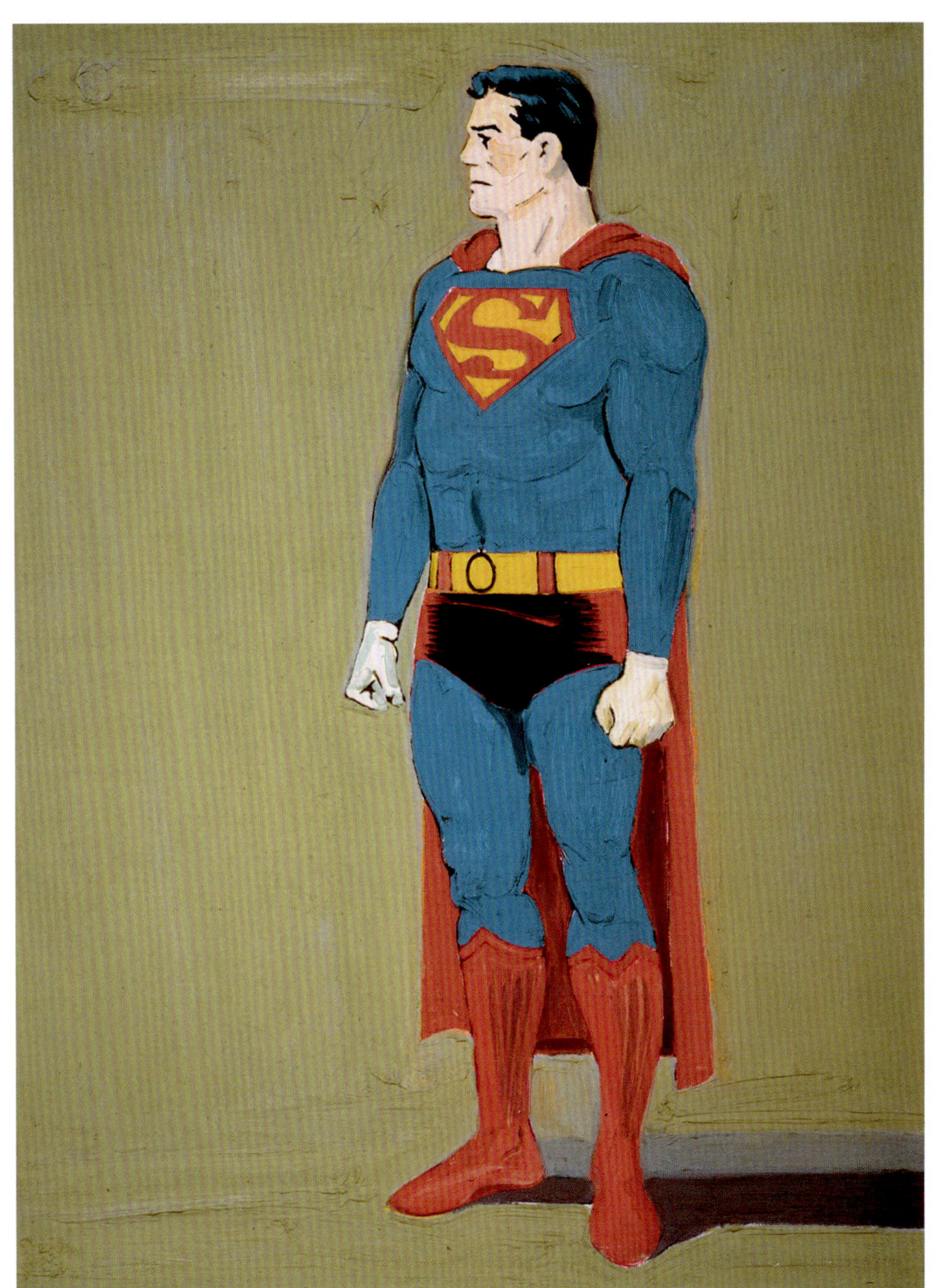

50

West Coast Pop

American Pop Art was always bicoastal. Home to the artists, dealers and patrons who came to define West Coast Pop, the 'golden state' of California inspired Pop artists from across the world. When his seminal exhibition *Six Painters and the Object* moved to the Los Angeles County Museum of Art in July 1963, British art critic Lawrence Alloway added some Californian artists, including Wayne Thiebaud,
33 **Ed Ruscha** and new Pop pin-up artist Mel Ramos, in recognition of West Coast Pop and its developments.

It was Thiebaud, progenitor of what *Time* magazine called 'The Slice of Cake School', who inaugurated West Coast Pop in February 1961 with his first solo exhibition at the forward-thinking San Francisco Museum of Modern Art. In September–October 1962, curator Walter Hopps organized the famous *New Painting of Common Objects* exhibition at the Pasadena Art Museum in Los Angeles. Placed as if in dialogue, he hung East Coasters Andy Warhol and Roy Lichtenstein alongside West Coast giants Thiebaud and Ruscha. A month after *Six Painters and the Object* closed in August 1963, Alloway's friend John Coplans, the British Pop artist and curator, organized *Pop Art USA* at the former Oakland Art Museum in San Francisco – the first large-scale exhibition originating in California, composed of works drawn from across the nation.

Critics immediately noted how displays of West Coast Pop highlighted the 'disparate' nature of the wider Pop Art movement, despite the fact that the artists involved were all sharing sources of inspiration, consistently referencing contemporary urban life and the objects that populate it. California-based artists Ruscha, Ramos and Thiebaud distinguished themselves, however, by taking common everyday objects simply as inspiration for their paintings, rather than actually imitating those objects as sculptures or installations like several of the New York Pop artists.

OPPOSITE
Mel Ramos
Superman, 1962
OIL ON CANVAS

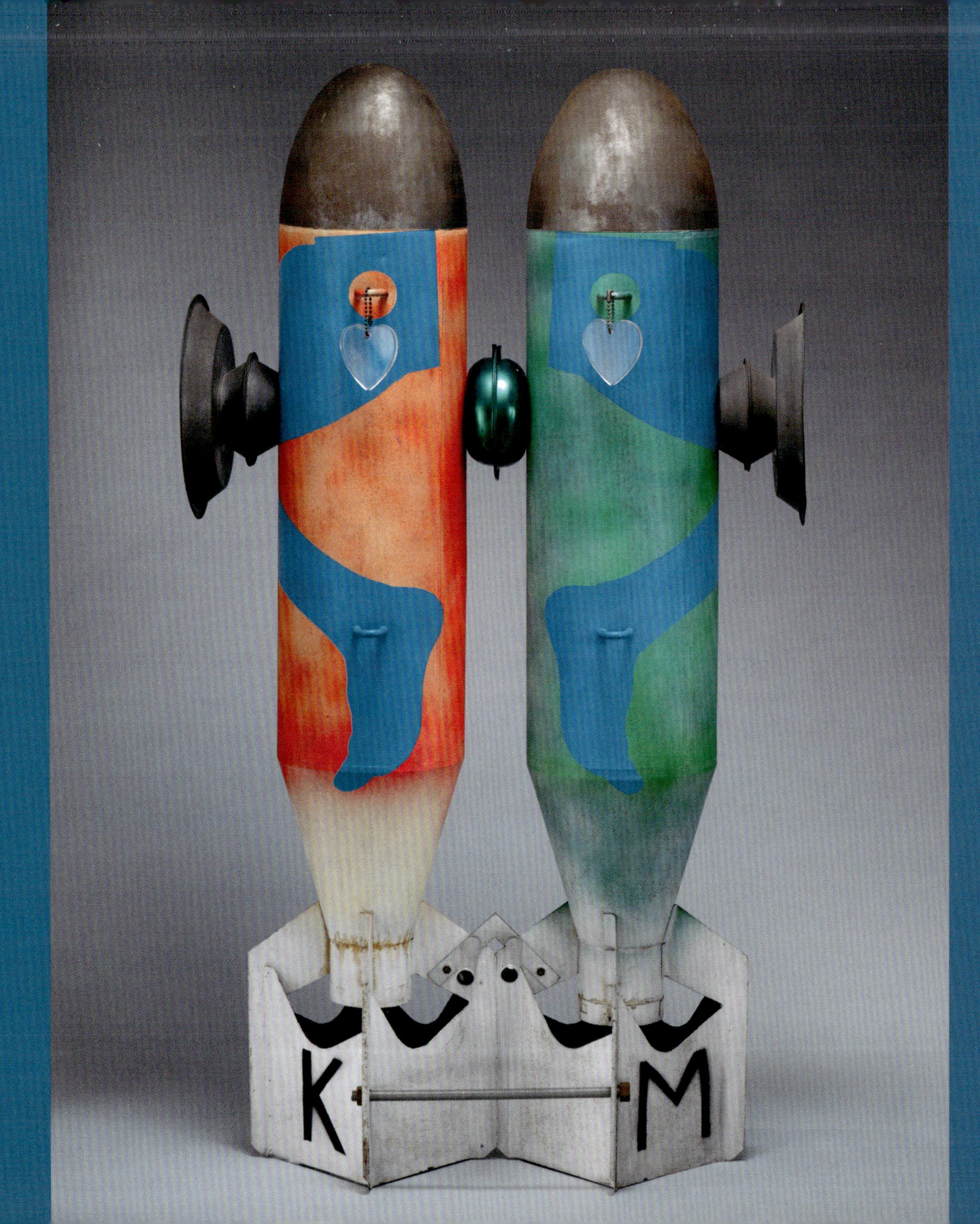
K
M

51

The Cold War

A forty-year standoff between the United States and the Soviet Union, the Cold War remained 'cold' because the existence of atomic weapons guaranteed what American strategist Donald Brennan called in 1962 'mutually assured destruction'. The stalemate had begun soon after the end of the Second World War, during the US presidency of Harry S. Truman. Pumping millions of Marshall Plan dollars into war-ravaged Western Europe was one way for Truman to guarantee US influence in the region. Truman's successor, Dwight D. Eisenhower formally pledged support for all nations 'threatened' by the expansion of Communism in both Europe and the Middle East. Over the following decades, the two superpowers engaged in more than fifty continuous 'proxy wars' across the world.

11 In consequence, bombs, **aircraft**,
57 warheads, rockets and **explosions**
were prominent in the iconography of Pop Art. Austrian Pop artist Kiki Kogelnik, for example, fascinated by the 'technical beauty of rockets', produced *Bombs in Love* (1962), a provocative and sardonic critique of a dangerously atomic age. But it was the Berlin Wall, constructed in August 1961, that became shorthand for the conflict itself. The Wall's 28-year existence almost precisely spanned the lifetime of the Pop Art movement, and its destruction symbolized the end of the Cold War and what American economist Francis Fukuyama ambitiously called the 'end of history'.

After the trauma of the Cuban Missile Crisis of 1962, when the world came close to nuclear exchange, US president John F. Kennedy and Soviet premier Nikita Khrushchev began working towards more cordial relations. In August 1963, the governments of the United Kingdom, the United States and the Soviet Union converged in Moscow to sign the historic Partial Nuclear Test Ban Treaty. Although it excluded land-based testing of nuclear weapons, the Treaty expressly banned testing 'in the Atmosphere, in Outer Space and Underwater'. Further nations would add their signatures over the coming months, so that even at the height of the Cold War the world could sleep just a little more easily.

OPPOSITE
Kiki Kogelnik
Bombs in Love, 1962
MIXED MEDIA WITH PLEXIGLAS AND ACRYLIC ON BOMB CASINGS

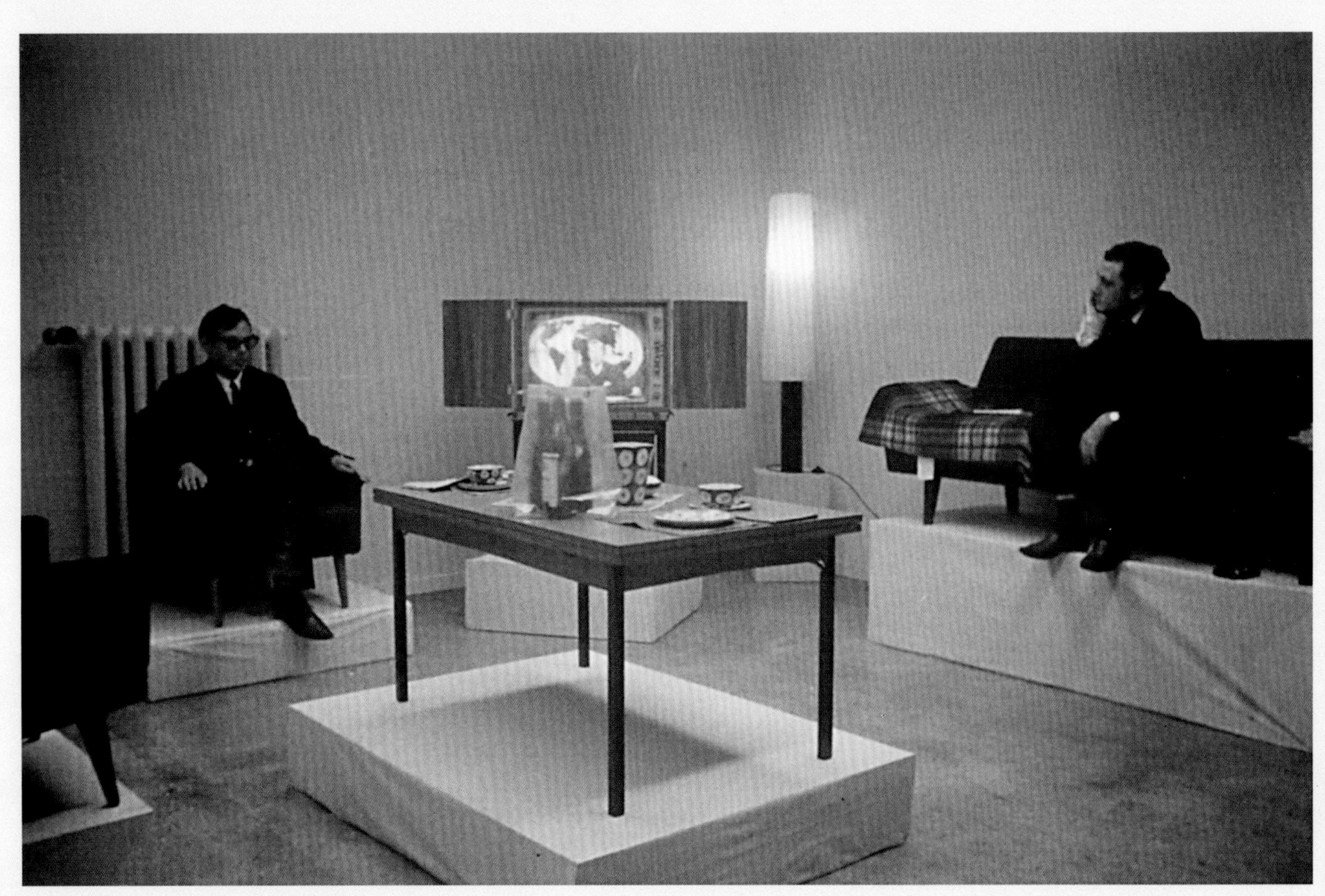

52

Capitalist Realism

German Pop Art, or Capitalist Realism (named in response to the Soviet Union's Socialist Realism), was the brainchild of a group of young artists that included Sigmar Polke, Gerhard Richter and Konrad Lueg. Inaugurated at the Berges furniture shop in Düsseldorf, West Germany, in October 1963, the 'environment' they created there announced not just Capitalist Realism but also Richter's very personal response to Pop Art.

Richter, a student at the Düsseldorf Academy of Arts at this time, had met the artist Konrad Lueg, who later became a successful dealer, two years earlier. In the summer of 1963, he and Lueg conceived of hosting an installation called *Living with Pop: A Demonstration for a Capitalist Realism* and then persuaded the shop to allow them to use the space
10 for a hyper-simulated **'happening'**. They hung their work wherever they
29 could, turned on all the **television** sets, dotted effigies of famous people about the shop – including one of
39 **John F. Kennedy, who was shot the following month** – and, as 'living sculptures', performed to spectators as anaesthetized customers in a powerful critique of rampant consumerism.

Coming of age in communist East Germany, Richter studied and initially taught at the Dresden Academy of Fine Arts. In March 1961, five months before the erection of the **Berlin Wall**, 51
he and his wife fled to West Berlin and declared themselves refugees. An artist from a communist country, Richter already understood Socialist Realism, the official communist form of art featuring heroic images created in a realistic style. Once in the West he encountered a society dominated by what philosopher Herbert Marcuse would call, in his 1964 treatise *One-Dimensional Man*, 'false needs'. For Marcuse, consumerism and the 'false needs' encouraged by it were as powerful a form of social control as more overt forms under communism. Like the Russian **Sots** 91
artists, Richter and the Capitalist Realists held up a mirror to both capitalism and communism, revealing each to be as absurdly banal as the other.

OPPOSITE
Konrad Lueg and
Gerhard Richter
Living with Pop, 1963
PHOTOGRAPH OF
PERFORMANCE

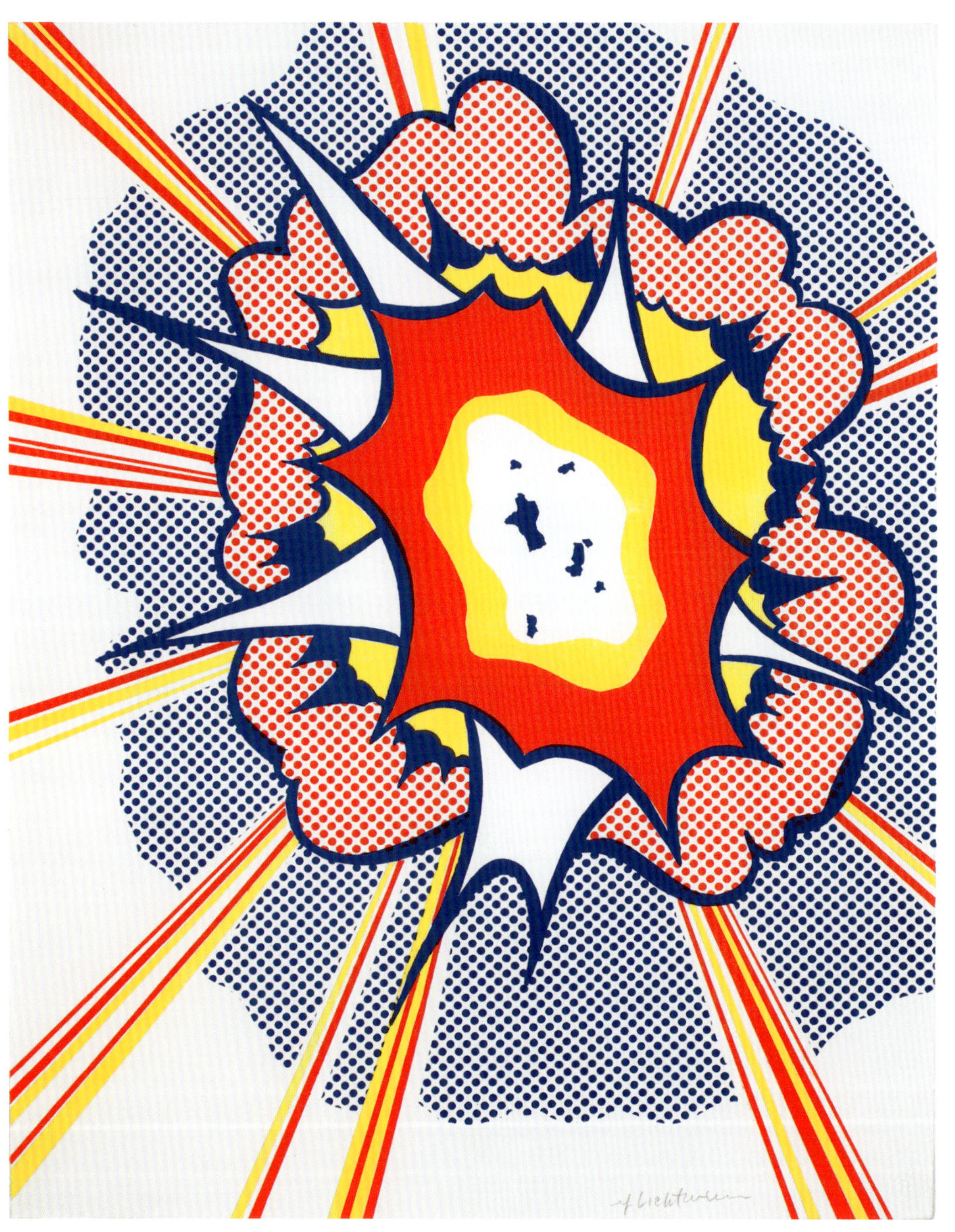

53

Ben-Day dots

First developed in the 19th century by American illustrator and printer Benjamin Day Jr, Ben-Day dots, as they came to be known, were used in the printing of comic books during the 1950s to give the effect of tonal colour shading. If Ben-Day dots are small enough, the images they constitute seem to miraculously vibrate with the perceived movement of colour and tone. Roy Lichtenstein first made use
17 55 of the technique in his **adaptations**
57 **of cartoon iconography** during the early 1960s and Ben-Day dots soon became the distinguishing formal characteristic of his work. Instantly recognizable, even today they epitomize the visual style of American Pop Art.

By 1961, Ben-Day dots were recognizably commercial: shorthand for the texture of mass-produced images. Lichtenstein loved their bright, acidic, artificial and garishly 'vulgar' colour range and he imitated them with gusto. Over the course of a thirty-year career, he explored the ways in which these dots can provide depth, perspective and 'realness' in flat, two-dimensional printed images.

Lichtenstein explained that his work is 'supposed to look like a fake'. He never actually directly copied anything he found in comic books, but by using Ben-Day dots he lent each work the look of having been printed by a machine, as one of many. In this sense his work appears to deny the presence of an authentic original and simultaneously reinforced the art-market necessity of having one. Using a template of uniform holes, Lichtenstein painstakingly painted each dot, seamlessly faking each one. His Ben-Day dots are substitutes for the 'real' manufactured ones, which themselves simulate the effects produced by handmade brushstrokes. Lichtenstein even suggested that his works are the Ben-Day dots themselves – 'data transmission', as he called it, from the ever-receding original – echoing philosopher Marshall McLuhan's 1960s phrase 'the medium is the message'.

OPPOSITE
Roy Lichtenstein
Explosion, 1965–6
LITHOGRAPH ON PAPER

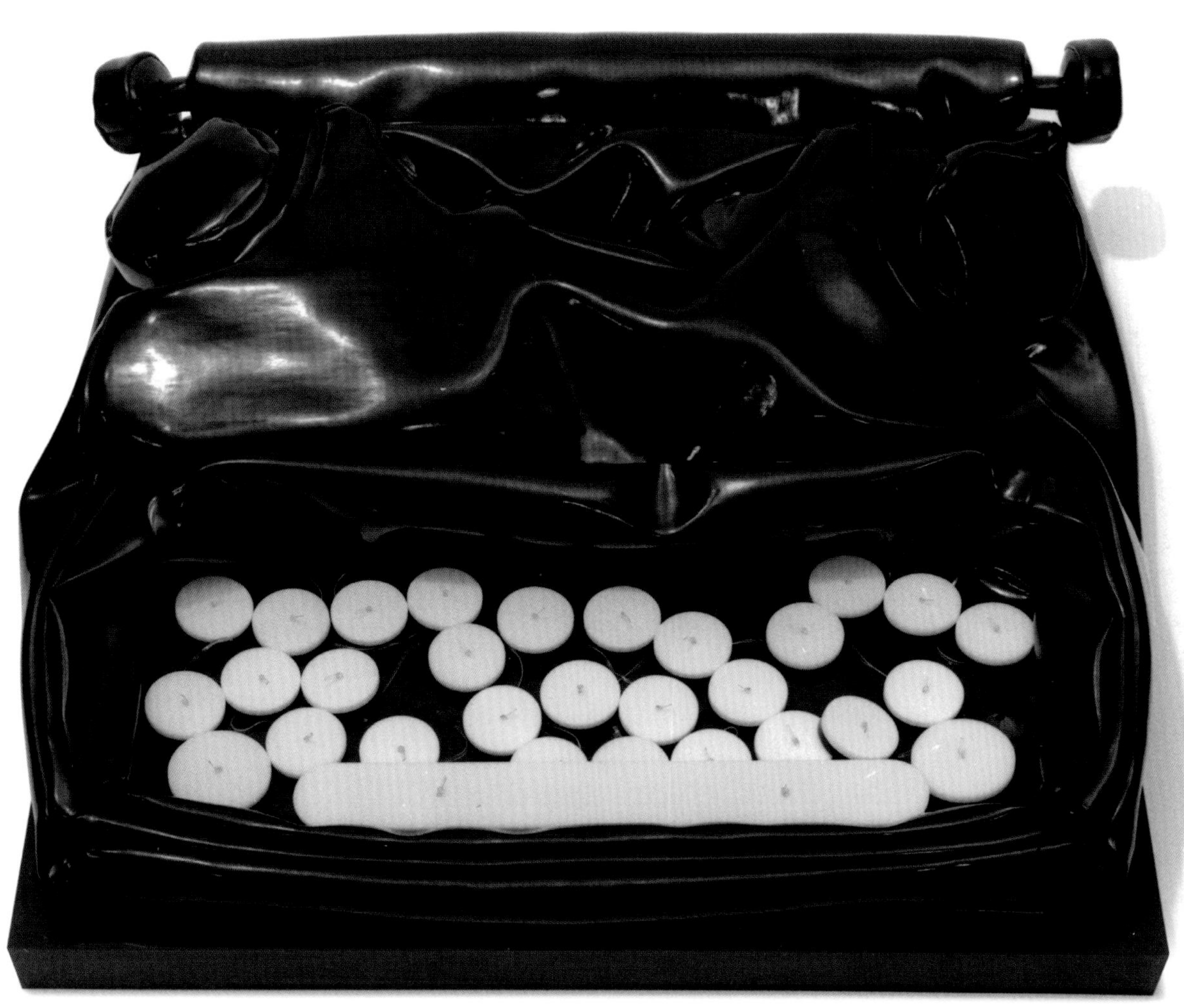

54

Soft Machines

Claes Oldenburg

1963

Fresh from a solo exhibition at the Green Gallery in New York, inclusion in the *International*
24 *Exhibition of the* ***New Realists*** at
46 the **Sidney Janis** Gallery in November
16 1962 and several **'happenings'**
that year, in 1963 Swedish-born American Pop sculptor Claes Oldenburg embarked on the creation of a radical series of soft sculptures, challenging the unquestioned convention that sculpture should be hard and taut. Oldenburg wrote that he preferred to work with 'very simple ideas' and advocated 'an art that takes its form from the lines of life itself'.

In 1963, Oldenburg shocked the New York art world by moving to
50 **Los Angeles** – in part because it was, as he said, just so 'opposite' to New York. With a reputation that preceded him, the artist was quickly offered an exhibition at the Dwan Gallery in October that year by the Los Angeles art dealer and patron Virginia Dwan. It was just before his departure for California that Oldenburg began work on his first soft sculptures – large, mutated foodstuffs such as *Floor Burger* and *Floor Cake* (both 1962), in stuffed and sewn fabric. As everyday symbols of American popular culture, Oldenburg's huge burgers, cakes and ice-cream cones are colourful and satisfying, unhealthy looking and hard to avoid. Moving from cheap everyday food to everyday objects, later in 1963 Oldenburg created his *Soft Machines* series in sewn vinyl. *Soft Pay-Telephone* and *Soft Typewriter*, emasculated, floppy and shapeless versions of the mass-produced objects they imitate, are designed according to Oldenburg as 'objects impregnated with humanity'.

Interested in the work of psychoanalyst Sigmund Freud, Oldenburg recognized through his work the power with which we imbue everyday – masculinized – machines. Literally deflating them served to expose both our heavy dependence on them and the uncomfortable truth of their and fragility. For Oldenburg, his Pop sculpture 'twists and extends and accumulates and spits and drips, and is heavy and coarse and blunt and sweet and stupid as life itself'.

OPPOSITE
Claes Oldenburg
Soft Typewriter, 1963
VINYL FILLED WITH KAPOK, PLEXIGLAS, NYLON CORD

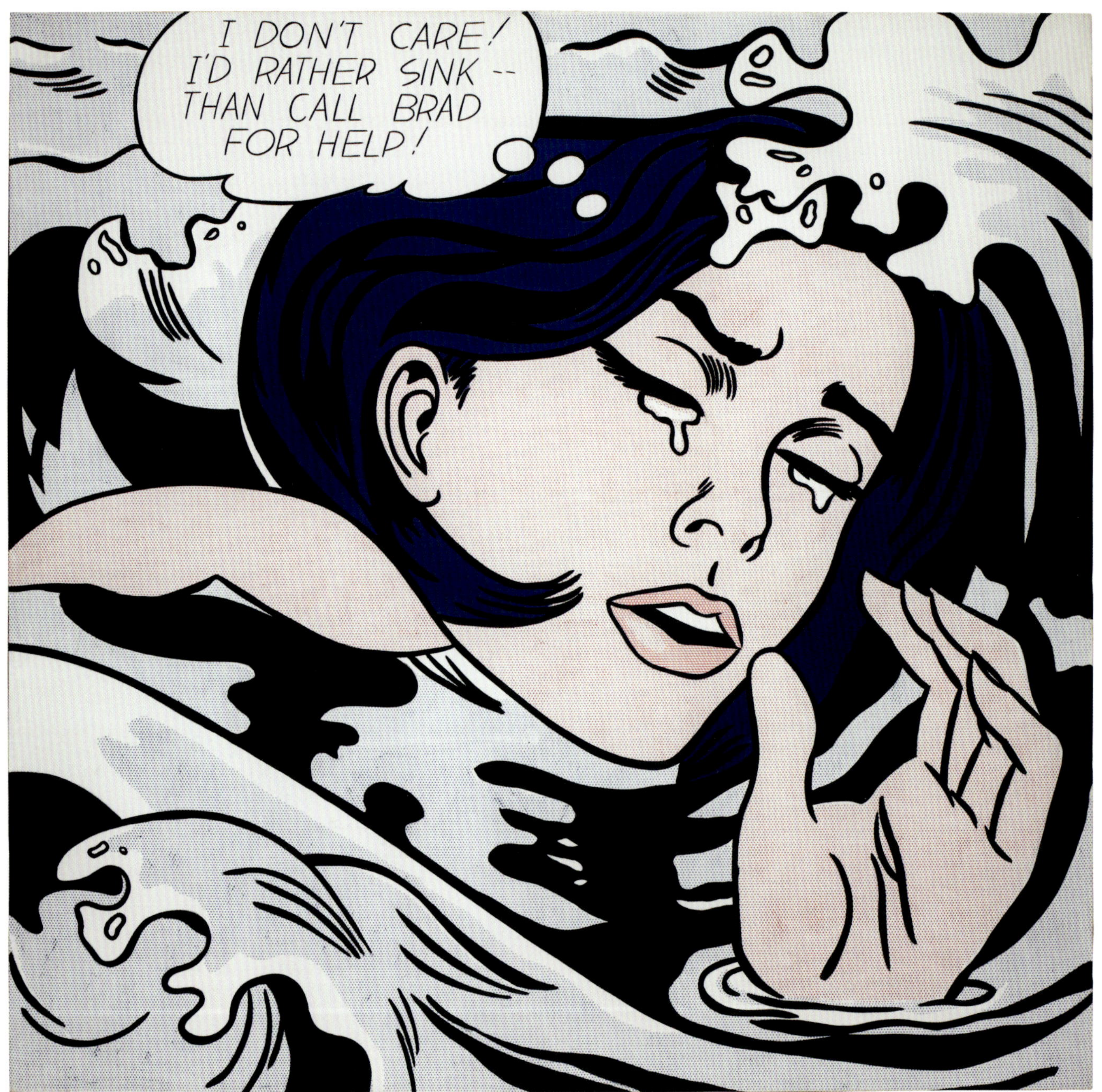
I DON'T CARE! I'D RATHER SINK -- THAN CALL BRAD FOR HELP!

55

Drowning Girl

Roy Lichtenstein

1963

Describing Roy Lichtenstein as funny, kind, modest and sexy, his ex-girlfriend Letty Eisenhauer also said that he 'wanted to see women cry'. Although 'there was no apparent meanness' about Lichtenstein, in retrospect she claimed, 'The crying girls are what he wanted women to be.' In 1963 he began work on a series of images lifted from comic strips featuring young women in distress. *Drowning Girl* is one of his earliest and best known.

Lichtenstein drew his inspiration from *Secret Hearts*, and specifically the opening page of its 'Run for Love!' story, illustrated by Tony Abruzzo and published by DC Comics in 1962. The original image included the drowning girl's boyfriend, Mal, clinging to an upturned boat and a verdant shoreline in the distance. But, with the eye of an advertising man, Lichtenstein simplified and cropped Abruzzo's image, discarding everything but the girl, her bare right shoulder and suggestively posed left hand. He then edited the girl's speech bubble, changing 'I don't care if I have a cramp!' to the more emphatic 'I don't care!' Seen in melodramatic close-up, caressed by the swirling waves, in her final moments the girl would rather drown than call her boyfriend for help. Renamed by Lichtenstein, her boyfriend, Brad, is a self-consciously heroic-sounding American archetype and a recurring off-screen character in several of his later works.

During the early 1960s, Lichtenstein became fascinated by romantic clichés. He made his name producing highly emotional content in a detached, impersonal way, denoting the commercialized and voyeuristic. 'I take a cliché and try to organize its forms to make it monumental,' he said. Lichtenstein's distressed young women were of course already clichéd but, transformed into tragic victims and stoical heroines, they became Pop Art monuments.

OPPOSITE
Roy Lichtenstein
Drowning Girl, 1963
OIL AND MAGNA ON CANVAS

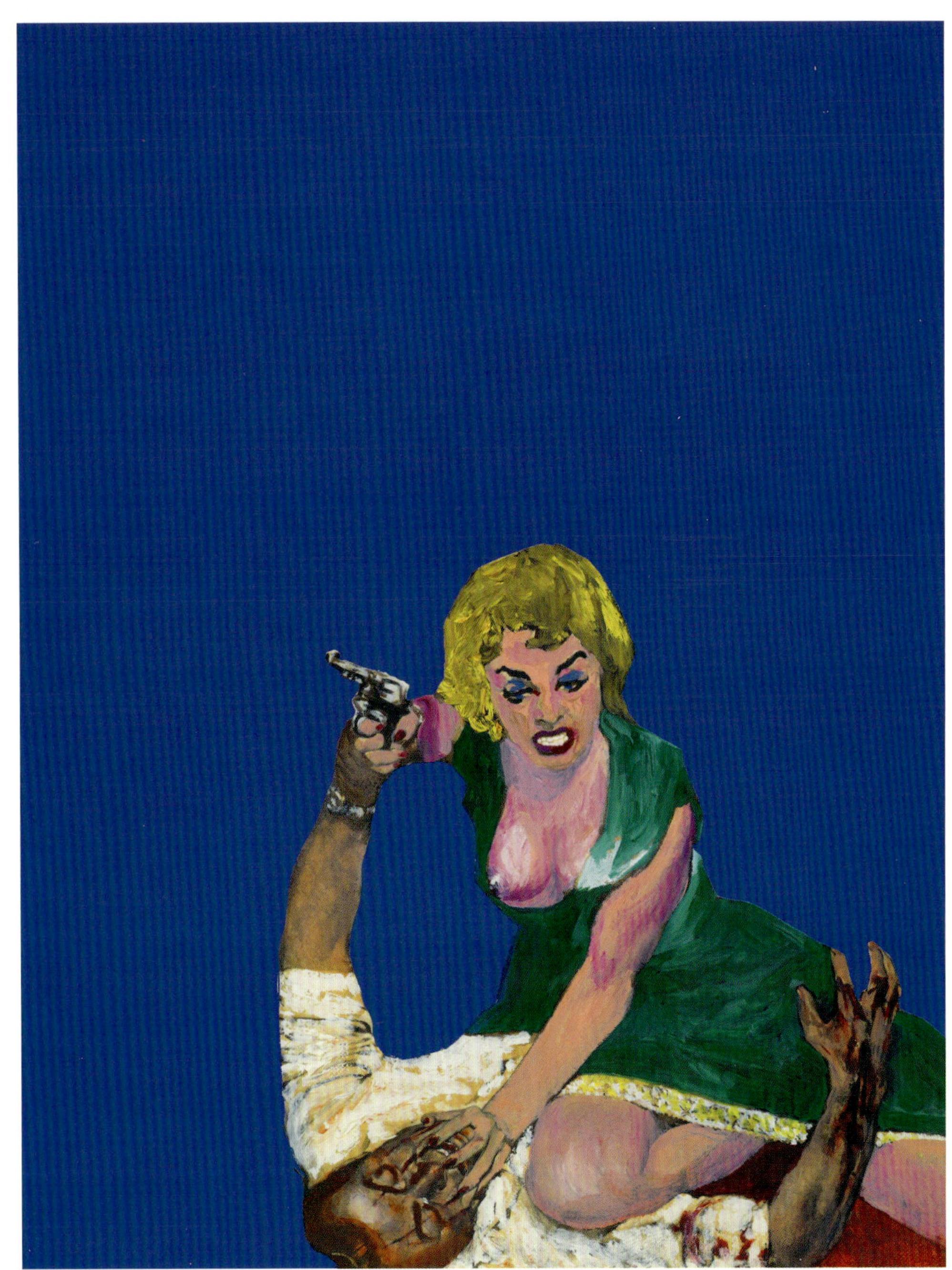

56

Self-Defense

Rosalyn Drexler

1963

The work of American Pop artist, writer and professional wrestler Rosalyn Drexler constitutes a unique commentary on the popular iconography of women. First exhibiting her work in 1960 at the short-lived Reuben Gallery in New York, Drexler made her name dramatizing the 'battle of the sexes' in arresting visual ripostes to the misogyny of the 1960s. Focusing on the exaggerated clichés of Hollywood gangster movies and cheap pulp fiction, she explored and created dynamic new visions of the divisive archetype of the femme fatale. As a wrestler, Drexler went by the name of 'Rosa Carlo' and was painted by Andy Warhol in 1963.

Cheaply produced pulp fiction – the seediest and most sensational kind, often bought 'under the counter' and characterized by the literary elite as the lowest form of literature – offered unusually spirited role models for women. Pulp fiction was so bad, so brash, so outrageous, the thinking went, it was only good for pulping – which made pulp innately Pop. And in Pop pulp fiction, women's lives took a more dynamic turn. The dangerous femme fatale might be as much a misogynist stereotype as the angelic housewife, but she often had more fun.

Drexler's *Self-Defense* of 1963 depicts a blonde woman holding a handgun, straddling and violently assaulting a man with an expression of frenzied determination. One of her breasts has fallen from her dress – not to titillate, but as an ironic nod to the kinds of publications that did. Never mind the handgun, it's her breast that takes vengeful aim, like a warhead bursting from its casing. The depiction of a violent woman was rare during the early 1960s; still rarer was it to depict a man's forced submission. Produced the same year as *Put It This Way*, in which Drexler depicted a man violently assaulting a blonde woman against the same uniform blue backdrop, *Self-Defense* is her Pop revenge.

OPPOSITE
Rosalyn Drexler
Self-Defense, 1963
ACRYLIC AND PAPER COLLAGE ON CANVAS BOARD

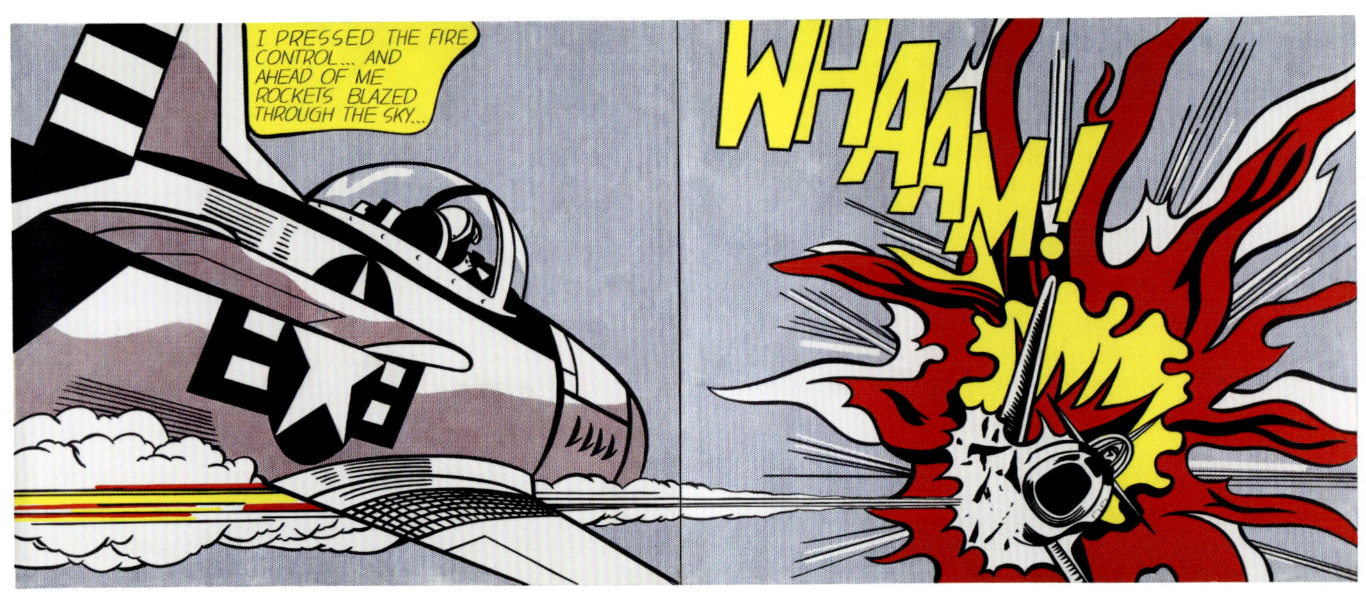
I PRESSED THE FIRE CONTROL... AND AHEAD OF ME ROCKETS BLAZED THROUGH THE SKY...
WHAAM!

57

Whaam!

Roy Lichtenstein

1963

Roy Lichtenstein's 1963 diptych *Whaam!* received generally positive reviews on its debut at the Leo Castelli Gallery in New York. Produced the year that US president Lyndon B. Johnson accelerated American bombing of Vietnam and parodying what critic Max Kozloff called the 'phallic dream of national glory', Lichtenstein conceived of *Whaam!* as being firmly within the European tradition of history painting. Yet when it was purchased three years later by the Tate Gallery in London, the critic Herbert Read described *Whaam!* as 'just nonsense'.

Inspired by an image from an *All-American Men of War* comic book drawn by Irv Novick and published by DC Comics in 1962, Lichtenstein's painting is a 'detached' caricature of
51 modern **warfare**. With its cinematic impact – 'WHAAM!' screams dramatically across the right-hand panel of Lichtenstein's diptych –
53 commercial **Ben-Day-dot** technique and comic-book idiom, *Whaam!* depicts, in sanitized form, the clichés of war.

As with his earlier **comic-book adaptations**, Lichtenstein edited, cropped and enlarged his source material and reordered the colour palette. The two halves of the diptych are connected by a blast line that slices across the lower sections of the canvases from one aircraft towards the gaping hole in the other. Lichtenstein thought of the pilots in his images as 'fascist types' he just couldn't 'take seriously'. Despite the pilot's dreamily ecstatic speech bubble and his partially glimpsed helmet, embedded in the aircraft, in common with the original, the pilot feels curiously absent from this image. His absence isolates him and us – from the violence depicted. Ironically, we also have no sense of the victim, without whom there would be no satisfying 'WHAAM!' It's not really bombs and aircraft colliding here, but the childish fantasy of war and a Pop ironic approach to the subject and its depiction in popular culture.

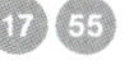
17 55

OPPOSITE
Roy Lichtenstein
Whaam! 1963
OIL AND MAGNA ON CANVAS

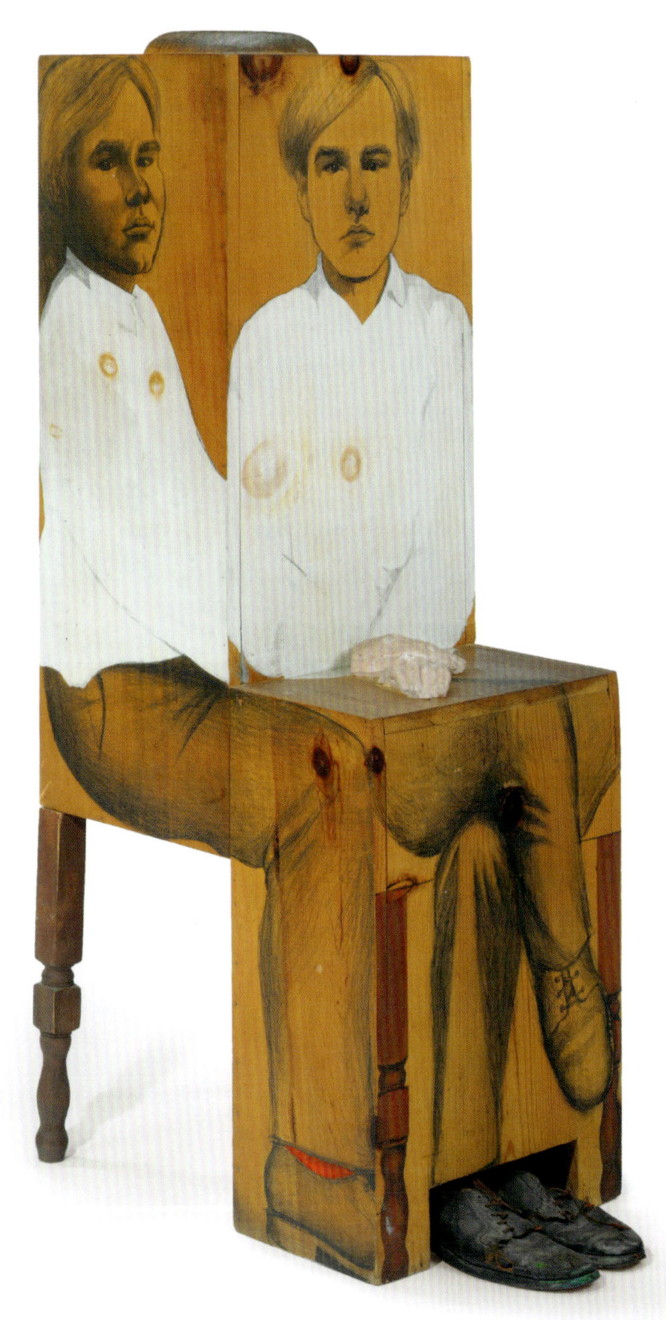

58

Marisol sculpts Andy Warhol

1963

A year before Andy Warhol cast her in his films *Kiss* and *The Thirteen Most Beautiful Women*, in 1963 **Marisol** made him the subject of her sculpture *Andy*. Glamorous and freethinking, by 1963 these unique Pop artists were famous – as artists, friends and mutual muses. Both were performers who loved **dragging up**, he in make-up and wigs and she in men's suits that landed her on best-dressed lists. Both were happy to publicize their work, he as the ultimate Pop celebrity and she as a *Vogue* model. Both were, in fact, quiet and introverted Catholics with solitary and ultimately rootless natures. In the masculine, heterosexual atmosphere of the 1960s art world, both felt snubbed and somewhat alienated. When it came to sexuality, outside their small avant-garde circles, both were outsiders. She was a self-described 'promiscuous' woman at a time of suffocating gender conformity and he was a gay man during a period of intense persecution. Pop's celebration [illegible] behind which each of them felt safe.

Marisol's pencil portrait of a cross-legged Warhol presents him from three different perspectives and is superimposed onto a broken, upturned triangular prism sculpted in plaster and wood. Marisol also drew on swirl marks that mimic and overemphasize the natural grain of the wood. As well as incorporating a turned supporting chair leg behind, she even included a pair of Warhol's own shoes, which deliberately jar with the image itself. In *Andy*, Warhol appears awkward and lonely, almost adolescent, encased and imprisoned inside the wood.

Marisol looked upon her own work with wary confidence. While some might think her Pop sculptures wildly amusing, she certainly didn't. 'No, they're not funny,' she said. 'I remember one night…I got so scared by my work, it looked so alive I had to leave the studio. They looked like real people. Good art is very peculiar. It's a mystery.' For Marisol, Pop sculptures were powerful charms.

OPPOSITE
Marisol
Andy, 1963
GRAPHITE, OIL AND
[illegible]
ANDY WARHOL'S SHOES

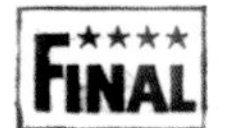

DAILY NEWS
NEW YORK'S PICTURE NEWSPAPER ®

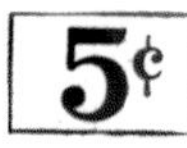

Vol. 45. No. 130 Copr. 1963 News Syndicate Co. Inc. New York, N.Y. 10017, Saturday, November 23, 1963* WEATHER: Cloudy, showers, windy, mild

KENNEDY ASSASSINATED

Johnson Sworn as President; Left-Wing Suspect Seized

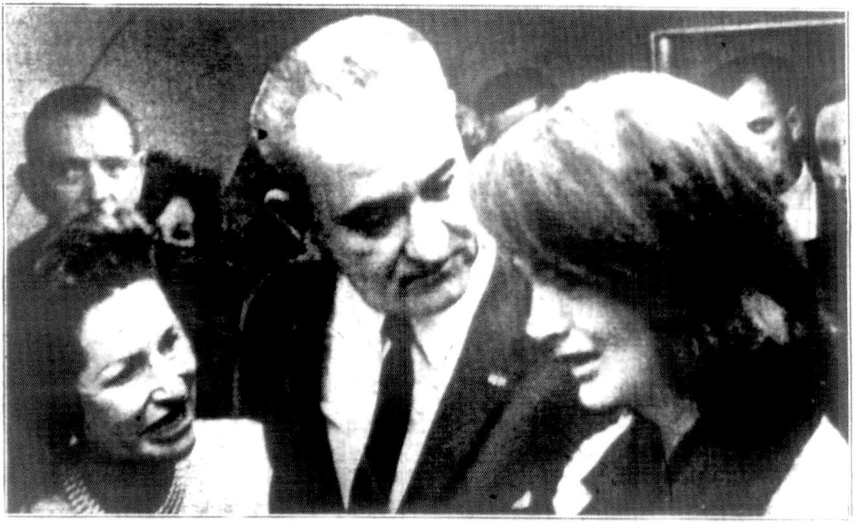

(Associated Press Wirefoto)

Just sworn in as the nation's President, Lyndon Johnson turns to console John F. Kennedy's widow as Mrs. Johnson looks on.

6 MORE PAGES OF PICTURES – PAGES 18, A, B, C, D AND BACK PAGE. STORIES START ON PAGE 2

59

22 November 1963

On both sides of the Atlantic, popular culture of the early 1960s was saturated with images of US president John F. Kennedy and his wife, Jackie. Young, good-looking and fashionable, the Kennedys became ubiquitous Pop Art motifs, synonymous with modern America itself.

One of the youngest presidents, Kennedy and his stylish, French-speaking First Lady were distinguished by their Hollywood glamour and their progressive politics. A Democratic senator for the state of Massachusetts, Kennedy was elected the 35th president in January 1961 and is best remembered for supporting civil rights in the racially segregated American South. The Kennedy future was to be bright and youthful for America. But on Friday 22 November 1963, while on a campaign tour in Dallas, driving through late-morning crowds in an open-topped Lincoln limousine, President Kennedy was assassinated – a moment that was horrifyingly caught forever on film. Pronounced dead at a nearby hospital about half an hour later, his body was returned to Washington, DC, on Air Force One that afternoon, as his escort and deputy Lyndon B. Johnson was sworn in as the next president. Two days later, while being transferred from police custody to the county jail, Kennedy's apparent assassin, former US Marine Lee Harvey Oswald, was himself shot by Dallas nightclub owner Jack Ruby and again the moment was caught on film. The images of both events would haunt a stunned nation for decades.

Pop artists including Andy Warhol and Gerhard Richter responded to press photographs and TV images of Jackie Kennedy's mourning by casting her as an icon of collective grief. National trauma, endlessly recycled, had an ambivalent significance for them, however. As Warhol said, 'It didn't bother me that much that he was dead. What bothered me was the way the **television** and radio were programming everybody to feel so bad.' (25)

OPPOSITE
Daily Mirror front page,
23 November 1963

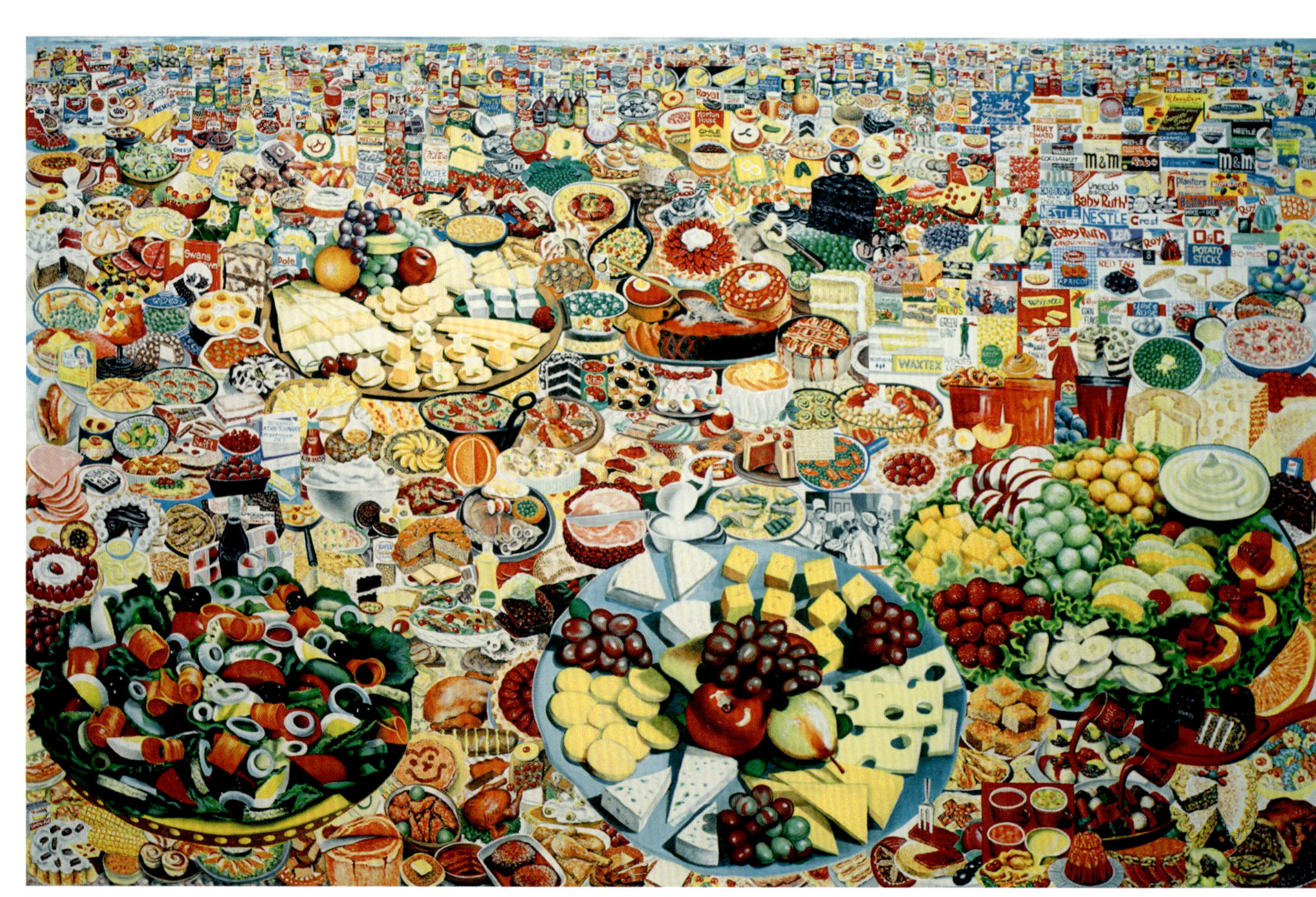
Royal
Swans Down
Dole
m&m
m&m
Uneeda
Baby Ruth
NESTLE
NESTLE
Crest
Planters
Baby Ruth
O&C
POTATO STICKS
RED TAG
WAXTEX

60

Erró meets James Rosenquist

1963

Icelandic Pop artist Erró visited New York for the first time in 1963 and met James Rosenquist, recently hailed by Guggenheim curator Lawrence Alloway as one
49 of Pop's **'Big Six'**. Sharing several motifs and a love of epic, large-scale canvases, the two began a lifelong transatlantic friendship.

Guðmundur Guðmundsson – later known professionally as Erró – was brought up in isolated rural Iceland. Having studied first in the capital Reykjavík, then in Oslo in Norway and in Florence in Italy, he went on to gain critical success after solo exhibitions in Europe and the Middle East in the late 1950s. He paid several visits to New York in 1963, during which he met Rosenquist and other members of the Big Six, including Roy Lichtenstein,
43 Robert Rauschenberg and **Jim Dine**, finding fresh inspiration in that most urban of modern cities.

Despite his prolific output and wide acclaim in Europe, Erró's 1964 solo exhibition at the Gertrude Stein Gallery was his first and last in New York. While unmistakably Pop, his eccentric and fantastical paintings didn't just reference the excesses of popular culture, comic books and consumerism. His works were subversive – almost Surrealist – satires on contemporary politics that were deeply rooted in the traditions of Renaissance art. Though welcoming at first, New Yorkers, with the exception of Rosenquist, resisted the broader cultural allusions of Erró's idiosyncratic work.

Although he has achieved international success, Erró – one of the youngest of the Pop generation – has lamented
Pop Art's courting of money: 'Money 74
is dominating the world. Everyone thinks about it and everyone wants to be rich. It's a pain in the arse really... I thought it would stay in America, but now it dominates the world.'

OPPOSITE
Erró
Foodscape, 1964
OIL ON CANVAS

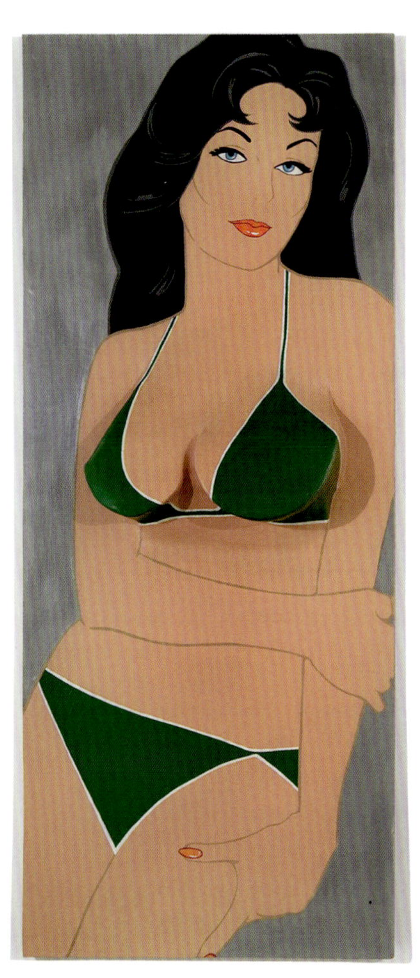
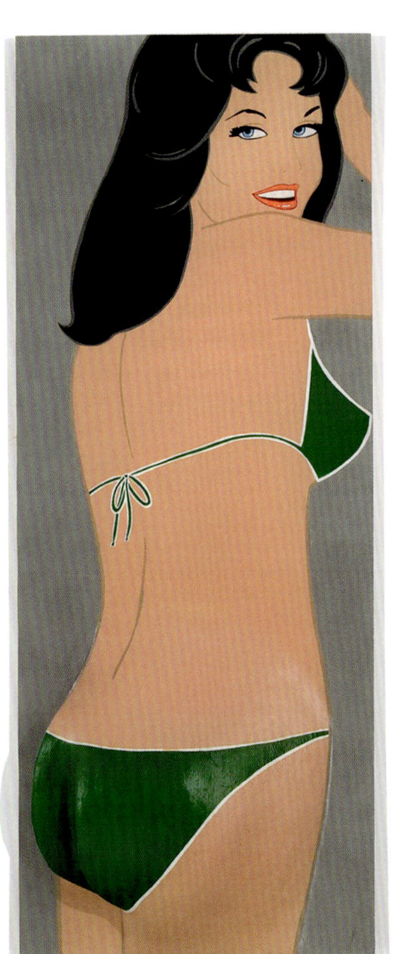
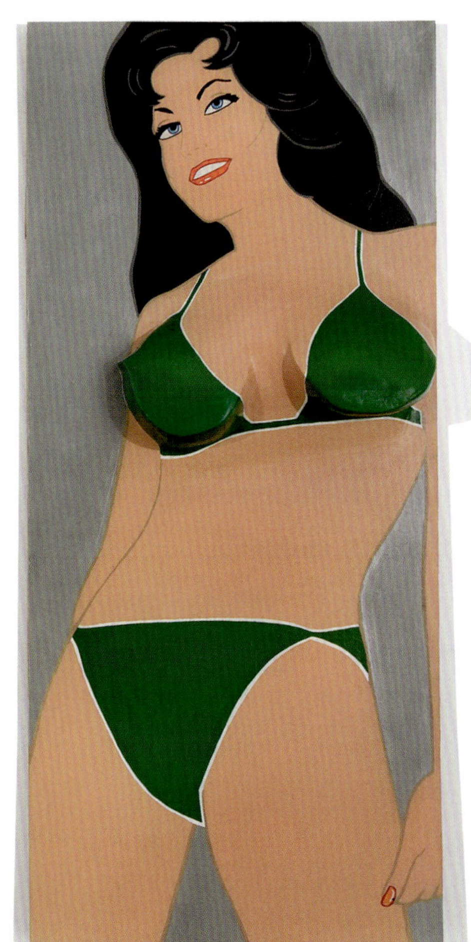

61

First International Girlie Show exhibition

1964

At the beginning of January 1964, 25-year-old art dealer Arne Glimcher opened the *First International Girlie Show* group exhibition at his Pace Gallery in midtown New York. Featuring stirring work by ten contemporary Pop artists, including
30 Roy Lichtenstein, Andy Warhol, **Tom Wesselmann** and Mel Ramos, its theme was the girlie pin-up. Despite, or perhaps because of, the subject matter, Glimcher's exhibition included the work of only two female Pop artists: Rosalyn Drexler and Marjorie Strider, whose career the exhibition launched.

For her Pace Gallery debut, Oklahoma-born Strider produced several large-scale relief paintings based on images of alluring, scantily clad men's magazine pin-ups – what she called her 'Bikini Nudes'. Represented at near full-length, seemingly available young women seductively meet the viewer's gaze, their breasts protruding from the surface of the paintings. These 'build-outs', as Strider called them, were sculpted in pine and laminated to Masonite panels. Soon she would begin producing build-outs from lighter, epoxy-coated Styrofoam. Painted in acrylics in uniform colours and with a manufactured sheen effect, her reliefs were striking. With their protruding breasts, these simulated life-size pin-ups, like hyper-real sex dolls, look oddly, uncannily alive.

Satirizing the iconography of popular men's magazines, Strider's build-outs highlighted the strange disparity between women as seen in print and the women of everyday life. Specialist media had created, she felt, a new species of women who didn't really exist. Her work used irony to expose the ways in which Pop media had distended the heterosexual male's expectation of both women and sexuality.

OPPOSITE
Marjorie Strider
Green Triptych, 1963
ACRYLIC PAINT, LAMINATED PINE ON MASONITE PANELS

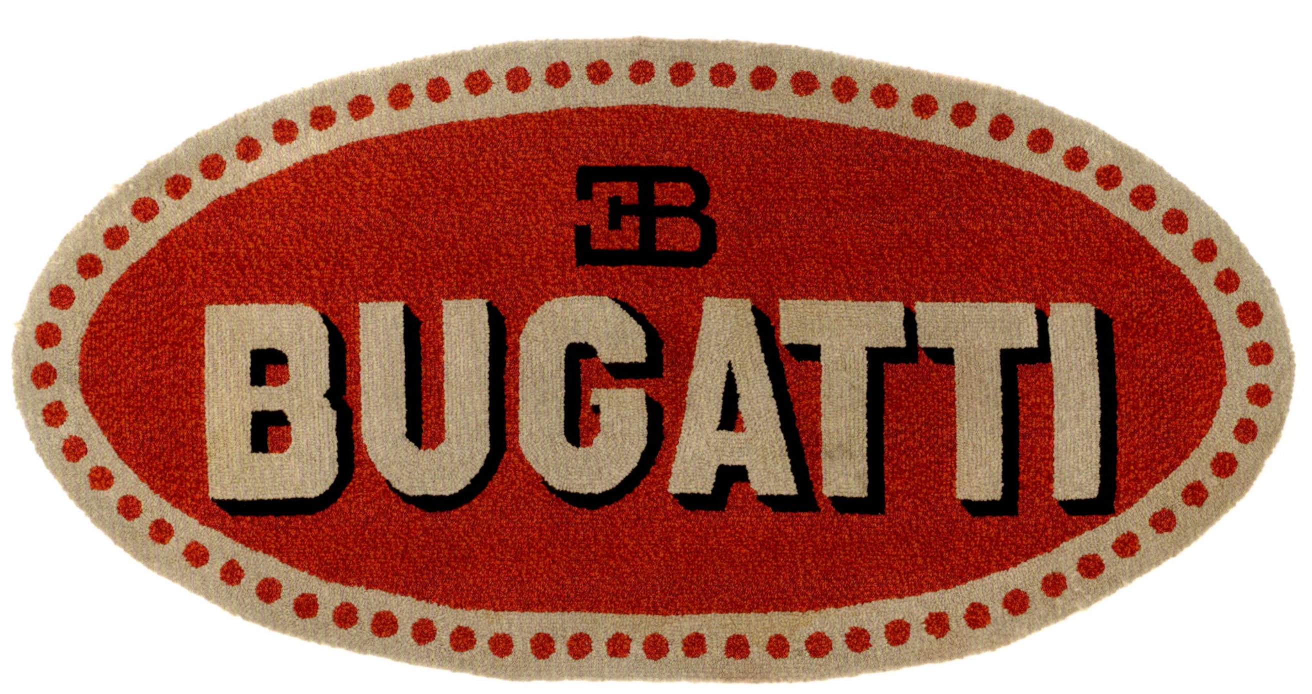
EB
BUGATTI

62

Dorothy Grebenak

With its focus on objects of everyday life, it's no surprise that Pop Art encompassed an interior design craze. During the 1960s, little-known American Pop designer Dorothy Grebenak, a former high school teacher based in Brooklyn, New York, created handcrafted rugs decorated with popular everyday icons of modernity. Despite claiming, 'I don't think what I do is Pop Art,' in 1964 she enjoyed a solo exhibition entitled *Odd Man In* at the Upper East Side gallery of Pop Art dealer and collector Allan Stone.

Grebenak's hand-hooked designer rugs represent a bridge between vernacular folk techniques and contemporary Pop Art, between the traditionally 'minor' decorative arts and the new fine art that Pop was fast becoming. The Allan Stone Gallery displayed rugs inspired by $5 bills, comic-book scenes, advertisements for cleaning products, wartime propaganda, manhole covers from Brooklyn streets, NYPD police badges, US stamps and the logo of the French car manufacturers Bugatti; there was even one rug that simply screamed, 'OBSCENE'. As Grebenak said, enlarged and placed on a gallery wall, these things 'make me laugh'. If Pop artists were populating their canvases with 'vulgar' everyday objects, why not do the same with rugs, themselves everyday objects? 'I think transposing something from one medium to another is droll,' she told the *New York Times* the following year.

Although several high-profile collectors bought her rugs and actually used them (so well in fact that few originals have survived), Grebenak didn't make them to be placed on the floor. Instead, she saw them as modern-day tapestries to be hung on the wall and admired, just as they were in *Odd Man In*. Challenging conventional expectations, Grebenak's rugs weren't merely stylish additions to the avant-garde home but works of Pop Art in their own right.

OPPOSITE
Dorothy Grebenak
Bugatti Rug, 1964
WOOL

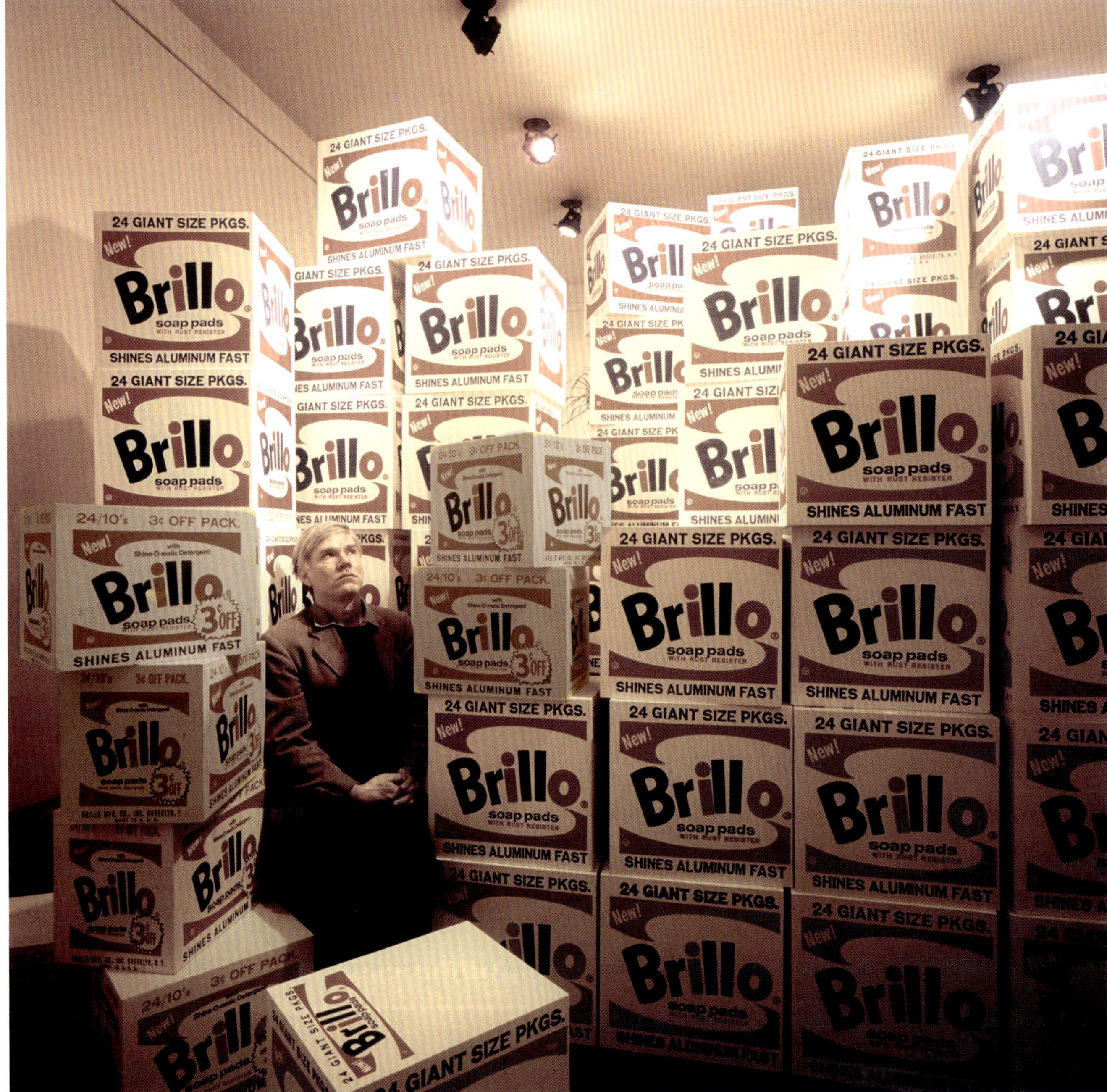
24 GIANT SIZE PKGS.
New!
Brillo
soap pads
WITH RUST RESISTER
SHINES ALUMINUM FAST
24/10's
3¢ OFF PACK.
with Shine-O-matic Detergent!
3¢ OFF

03

Brillo Box (Soap Pads)

Andy Warhol

1964

After the early success of his ***Campbell's Soup Cans***, Andy 38 Warhol briefly mused on painting still-life arrangements of soup cans alongside or on top of large Brillo soap-pad boxes. He came to the conclusion, however, that the combination of soap and soup 'looked funny because it didn't look real'. So, in 1964, he began concentrating on the boxes themselves. *Brillo Box (Soap Pads)* represents Warhol's taking refuge in the banal, his 'delight in the trivial'.

When challenged by *Art News* in November 1963, Warhol emphasized that the reason he painted the way he did was 'because I want to be a machine'. The creator of the original Brillo boxes was Abstract Expressionist artist and part-time commercial designer James Harvey. Reproducing perfect versions of Harvey's Brillo boxes, and going on to reproduce Del Monte fruit boxes, Heinz tomato ketchup boxes and Campbell's tomato juice boxes, Warhol achieved something of that commercialized 'machine' status. As he said, 'I like boring things.' But Warhol's 'boring' iterations were a form of therapy, designed to rid the modern consumer of the anxiety and lack of fulfilment created by the capitalist environment. After all, as Warhol said, 'The more you look at the exact same thing, the more the meaning goes away, and the better and emptier you feel.' Might Pop Art, conceived of as a repetitive, numbing, even alienating portrait of our immersive, commercialized surroundings, be good for the nerves?

With his 1961 ***Captain Webb*** 27 ***Matchbox***, it was British Pop artist Peter Blake who was the first to reproduce a well-known everyday product. But Blake enlarged his matchbox and obscured much of the branding. Warhol's simulation is, however, an almost direct copy, the same size and with its branding fully intact. But while the original Brillo box was manufactured in corrugated cardboard, *Brillo Box (Soap Pads)* was made by **silkscreening** a more 36 durable plywood. Made of wood, Warhol's weighty Brillo boxes remain at odds with the lightweight throwaway products that inspired them, yet retain their promise of domestic Pop hygiene.

OPPOSITE
Andy Warhol surrounded by stacks of Brillo boxes, 1964

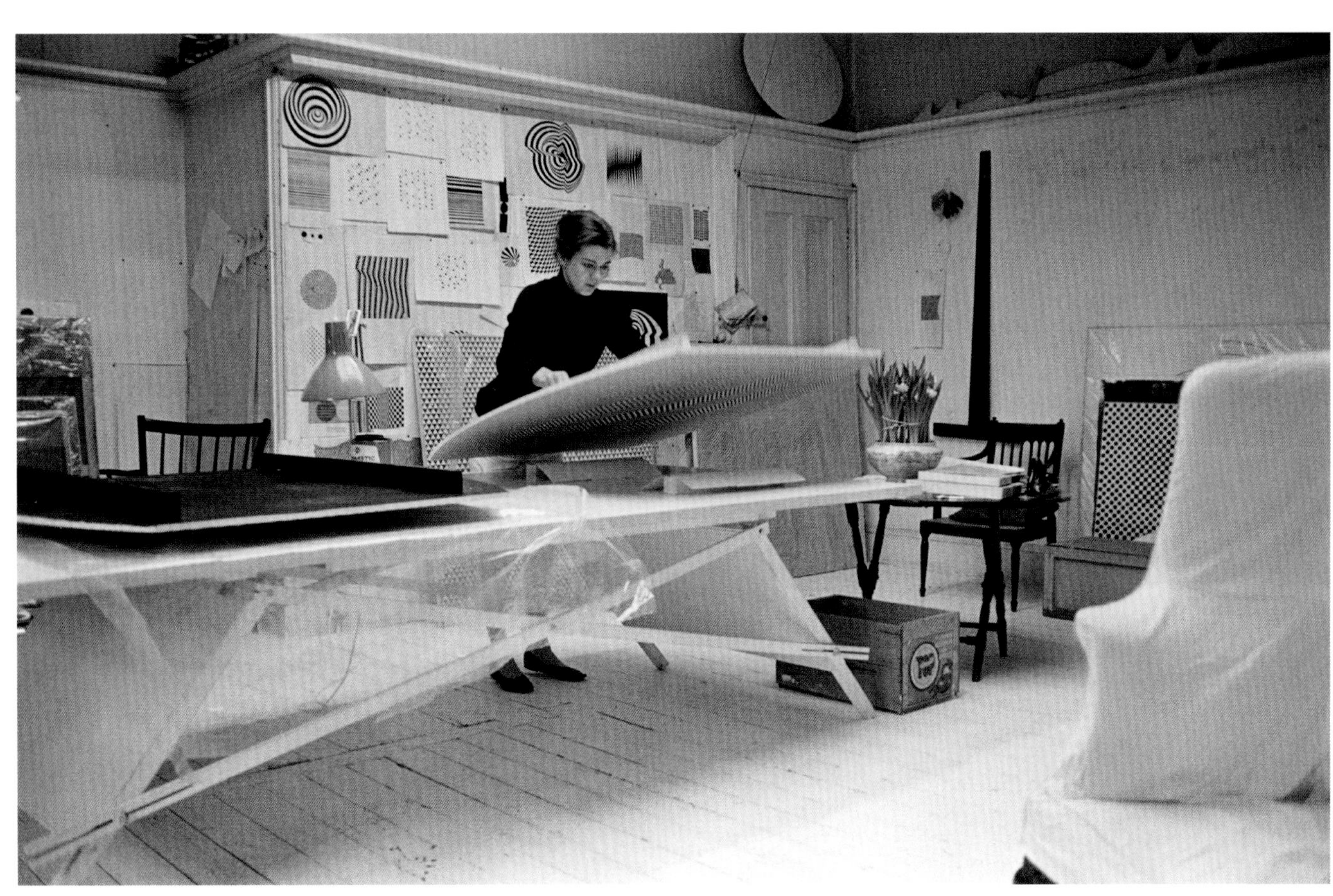

01

Op Art

In response to American artist Julian Stanczak's solo exhibition *Optical Paintings* at the Martha Jackson Gallery in New York, the term 'Optical Art', or Op Art, as it quickly became known, was first coined by *Time* magazine in September 1964. Visually arresting, this movement was to emerge as an important bridge between the new Pop Art and its old adversary, Abstract Expressionism.

Op artists such as Bridget Riley had a mathematical interest in abstract shape and colour and, in particular, their psychological effects upon the viewer. In their concern with the formal qualities of painting, they shared something with the proponents of Abstract Expressionism. However, like Pop Art, Op Art was heavily influenced by the techniques of commercial graphic design and the 'surface' of the mass-produced object. And just like Pop Art, Op Art designs would soon be co-opted by the advertising industry.

Indebted to early 20th-century modernist movements, including Dadaism, some of the earliest Op Art works were, in fact, produced by British Pop artist John McHale
for the exhibition ***This is Tomorrow*** 12
at London's Whitechapel Gallery in 1956. It was London art dealer and collector Victor Musgrave, an early
champion of **New Realist** artist 24
Yves Klein and founder of Gallery One in Soho, who in the spring of 1962 gave British Op artist Riley her first solo exhibition. Before becoming Op Art's best-known practitioner, during the 1950s Riley studied alongside Pop artist Peter Blake at the Royal College of Art and had worked as both an art teacher and a commercial illustrator. Her early black-and-white, and sometimes grey, geometric optical paintings would be shown in February 1965 at *The Responsive Eye* exhibition at the Museum of Modern Art in New York. Developing as a parallel movement to Pop Art in both London and New York, Op Art was a close relation.

OPPOSITE
Bridget Riley at work, April 1964

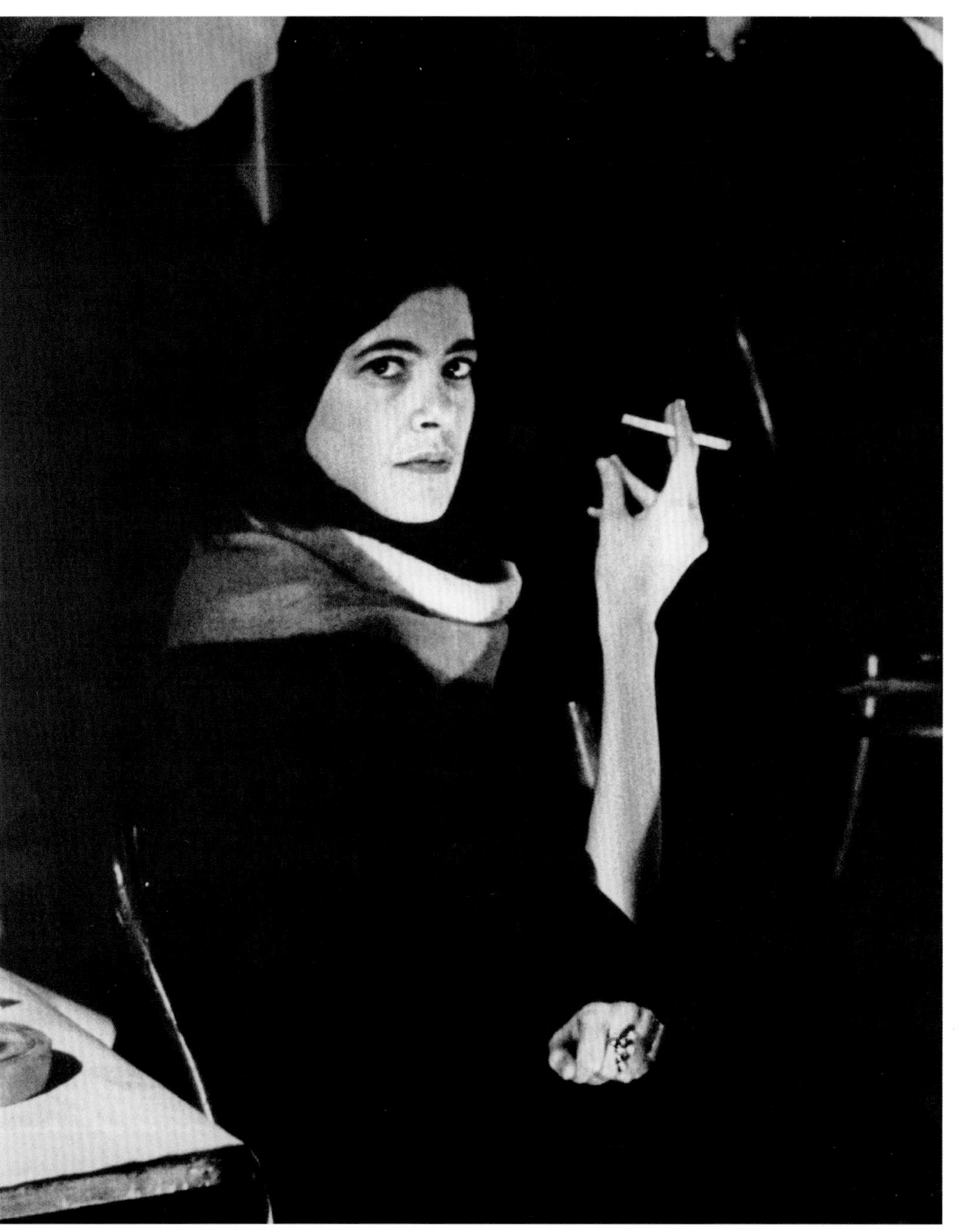

[illegible]

Susan Sontag and 'Notes on Camp'

1964

Writing in the New Jersey-based journal *Partisan Review* in the autumn of 1964, critic Susan Sontag outlined her ground-breaking 'Notes on Camp'. Developing critic Walter Benjamin's ideas on 'kitsch', outlined thirty years before, Sontag's essay famously defined what 'camp' actually meant and indirectly suggested its similarity to Pop Art. Her essay voyaged into new cultural terrain by naming what had 'not been named' and describing what had 'never been described'.

Locating its origins in the aphorisms of Oscar Wilde and designs of the Art Nouveau movement – even discerning elements in 16th-century Mannerism and 18th-century Rococo – Sontag defines camp as being, like Pop Art, not a movement as such but an attitude. Her definition has much in common with British
15 Pop artist **Richard Hamilton's classic 1957 description of Pop Art** as youthful, throwaway and fun.

Camp is similarly ironic, irreverent, coolly detached, disruptively innocent, banal and fantastic. Like Pop Art, the modern camp sensibility values pure artifice above all else. Both life and art are theatre and identity merely 'Playing-a-Role'. Pop and camp redefine taste by declaring 'the equivalence of all objects'; what is good is 'good *because* it's awful'. Crucially, for Sontag, for Andy Warhol and for many others, camp solves the problem of 'how to be a dandy in the age of mass culture'.

While Hamilton privately described this new attitude, Sontag publicly analysed it. One attraction of camp – just as Warhol said of Pop – is that once you get it you join a new and subversive cultural elite. Sontag gave Pop Art camp credentials and Warhol's film *Camp*, released the following year, made camp itself mainstream.

OPPOSITE
Susan Sontag, New York, 1962

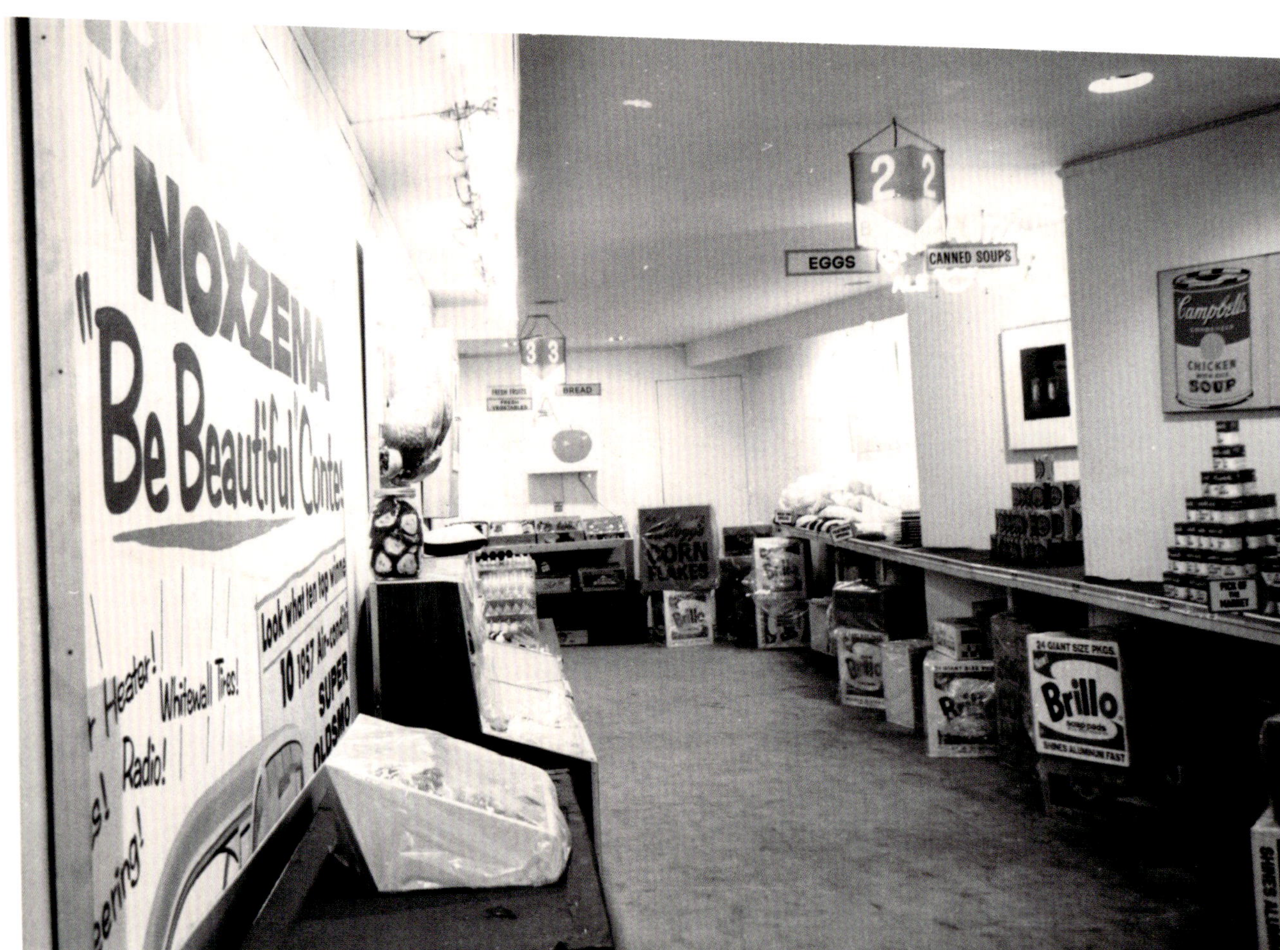

NOXZEMA
"Be Beautiful"
Whitewall Tires!
Radio!
SUPER
EGGS
CANNED SOUPS
BREAD
CORN FLAKES
Campbell's
CHICKEN
SOUP
24 GIANT SIZE PKGS.
Brillo
SHINES ALUMINUM FAST

60

The American Supermarket

1964

In October 1964 at his Upper East Side Gallery, the New York art dealer Paul Bianchini opened *The American Supermarket*, a curated installation of Pop art and sculpture celebrating American consumerism. Developing
32 Claes Oldenburg's ***The Store*** from three years earlier, Bianchini's
16 **'happening'** sought to further blur the line between the grocery store and the art gallery, even between the commercial gallery and the historical museum. Ever alive to the relativity of context, objects and spaces, Andy Warhol famously said, 'Lock up a department store today, open the door after a hundred years and you will have a museum of art.'

49 Joining some of the **'Big Six'** – Warhol, Oldenburg, Roy Lichtenstein, Jasper
[illegible] Johns and **Tom Wesselmann** – was American Pop sculptor Robert Watts (fresh from an exhibition at the nearby Leo Castelli Gallery), who cast eggs and fresh fruit in an unlikely combination of chrome and felt, pricing them at $12 each. Pop sculptor Billy Apple, a New Zealander recently arrived in New York from London, where he'd studied at the Royal College of Art with David Hockney and **Pauline** 72
Boty, displayed a $500 painted bronze watermelon. The only woman artist featured in the show was little-known Pop sculptor Mary Inman. She made her living for forty years as a commercial display artist and for *The American Supermarket* produced painted wax beef steaks, roast chickens, lobsters, pastrami and cheeses.

Passers-by and guests alike were genuinely fooled into believing the fantasy. Real Ballantine Ale bottles were displayed alongside the bronze versions by Johns (see pages 80–1). Guests thought Warhol's wooden soup cans were real, even while he signed and sold real **Campbell's soup cans** 38
at three for $18 or $6.50 each. The most popular item for sale, however, was a Warhol-designed $12 paper bag featuring a Campbell's soup printed on its side. Deeply indebted to Dada, the exhibition's strange combinations and novelty works of Pop Art **turned a profit**. After all, 74
as Warhol said, 'Buying is more American than thinking.'

OPPOSITE
The American Supermarket, 1964

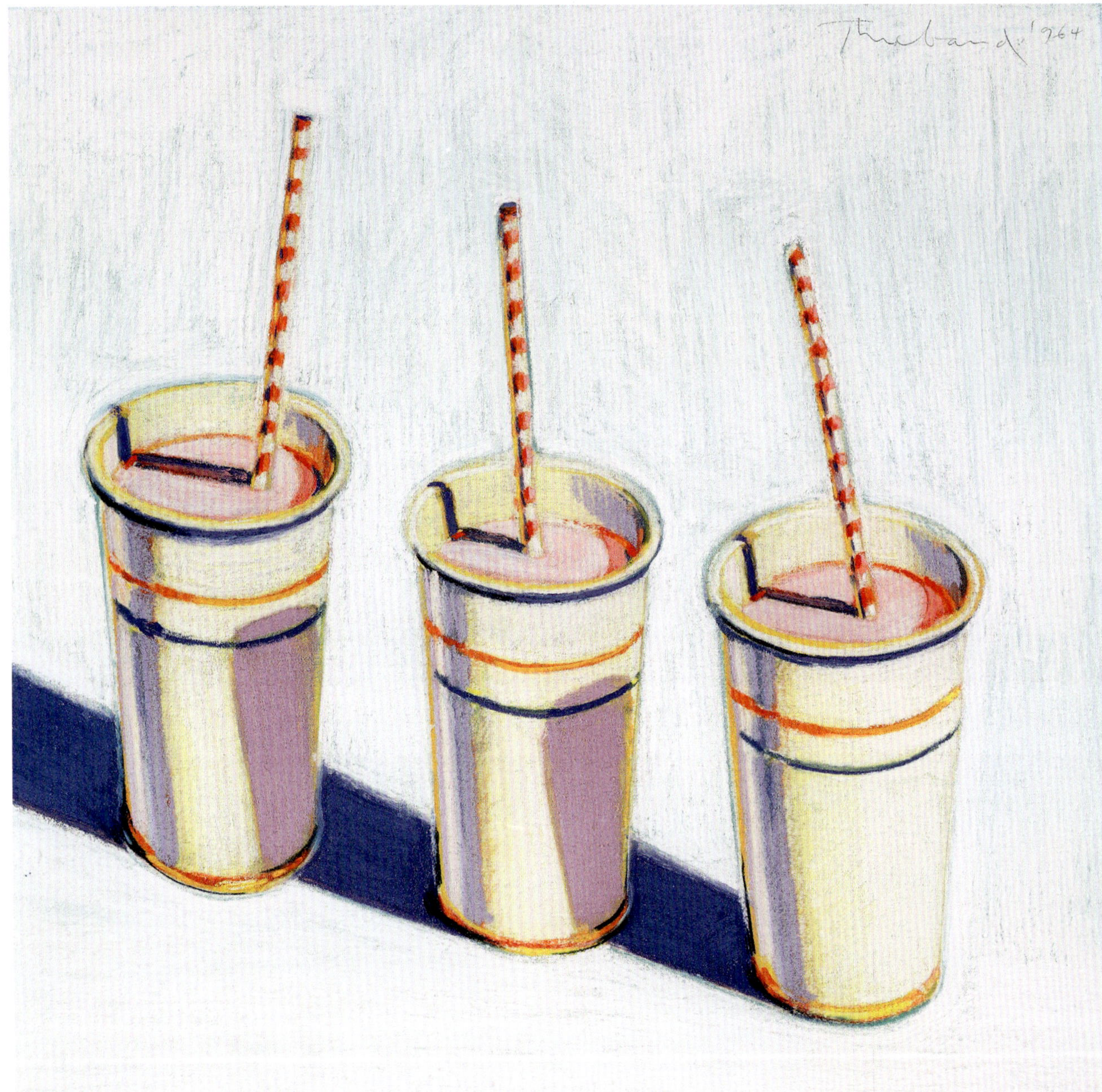
Thiebaud '964

67

Three Malts

Wayne Thiebaud

1964

50 The work of **Californian** Pop artist Wayne Thiebaud defined what *Life* magazine called 'The Slice of Cake School'. Having exhibited widely and to great acclaim in both California and New York, by 1964 Thiebaud was known for his quintessentially American paintings of cakes, sandwiches, malts and milkshakes, which suggested the emergent Pop lifestyle of those who, twenty years before, *Life* magazine had first called 'teen-agers'. His sunny 1964 painting *Three Malts*, for example, represents a satisfyingly all-American adolescent snack. Thiebaud's Pop diner aesthetic reflected the language of American post-war prosperity and had, even by the early 1960s, become emblematically nostalgic for the previous decade.

Arizona-born Thiebaud was brought up in Los Angeles and later studied at Sacramento State College in Northern California. He began his career as an apprentice illustrator at the Walt Disney Studios in the 1930s and during the Second World War worked in propagandist film production for the US Air Force. According to Andy Warhol, 'In late 1950s and early 1960s California everything looked Pop.' California was 'the future', but there were 'people walking around in it without knowing it'.

Thiebaud was not one of them. He instinctively felt a native home-grown affection, not only for Warhol's Californian 'future', but for California's present and its recent past. His summertime Pop aesthetic of the fairground, the bakery and the diner celebrated the powerful simplicity of idealized fantasies of the **American Dream**. As British Pop novelist **J. G. Ballard** wrote, 'Desperate for the new, but disappointed with anything but the familiar, we recolonize past and future.'

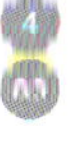

OPPOSITE
Wayne Thiebaud
Three Malts, 1964
CHALK AND OIL ON BOARD

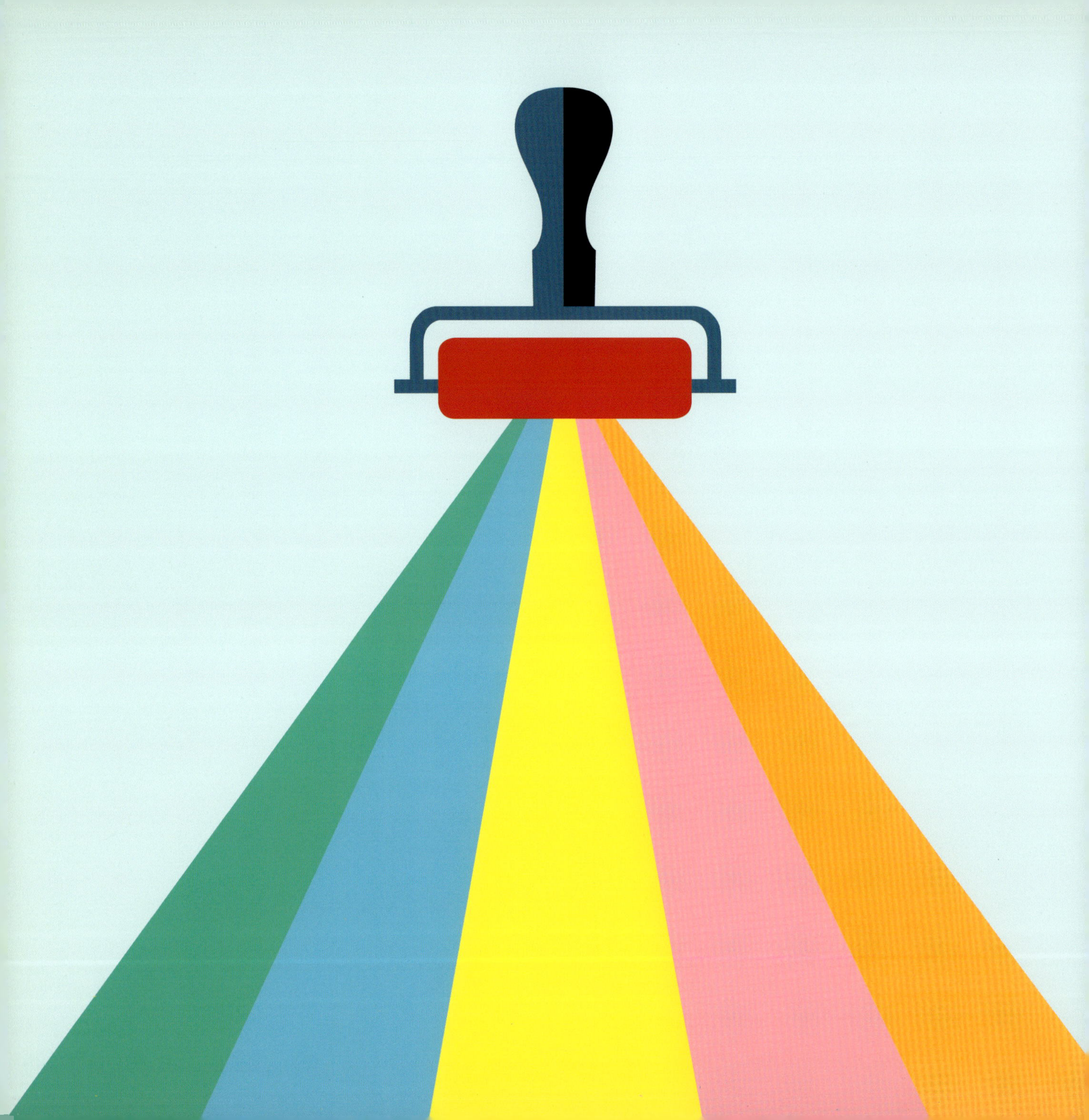

UU

Lithography

That several Pop artists, including Jasper Johns, Robert Rauschenberg, Andy Warhol and Roy Lichtenstein, enjoyed using lithography, a printmaking technique invented in the 18th century, seems at first surprising, incompatible as it sounds with the cool, slick image of Pop Art. In fact, lithography couldn't be more Pop. Invented as a cheap and relatively easy way to reproduce artworks for the mass market, its potential was recognized and exploited by Pop artists.

Modern lithography, developed in the 19th century, allowed for the printing of graphics onto mass-produced packaging. Taking its name from the ancient Greek words *lithos* ('stone') and *graphein* ('to write'), the process involves applying a reversed design in fat, oil or wax to – originally – a very smooth-surfaced limestone tablet. During the 20th century, limestone was often replaced by a smooth metal plate or versatile rubber sheet.

A solution of acid and natural tree gum would be applied, delicately etching the applied design into the porous surface and allowing the rest of the greased surface to repel liquid. At this point an oil-based ink could be rolled across the plate, attaching only to the design surface, which was then transferred to paper. Although the surface could not be recycled for new designs, it would, in its modern iteration, forever reproduce the same recurring image.

Trained at art schools and often teaching in art schools themselves, Pop artists were well aware of a diversity of artistic practices and how each might be used to produce varied effects. For his 1964 print of *Crying Girl*, for example, Lichtenstein used lithography to produce a smooth, flawless surface that serves to emphasize the artificial, mechanical quality of his famous **Ben-Day dots**.

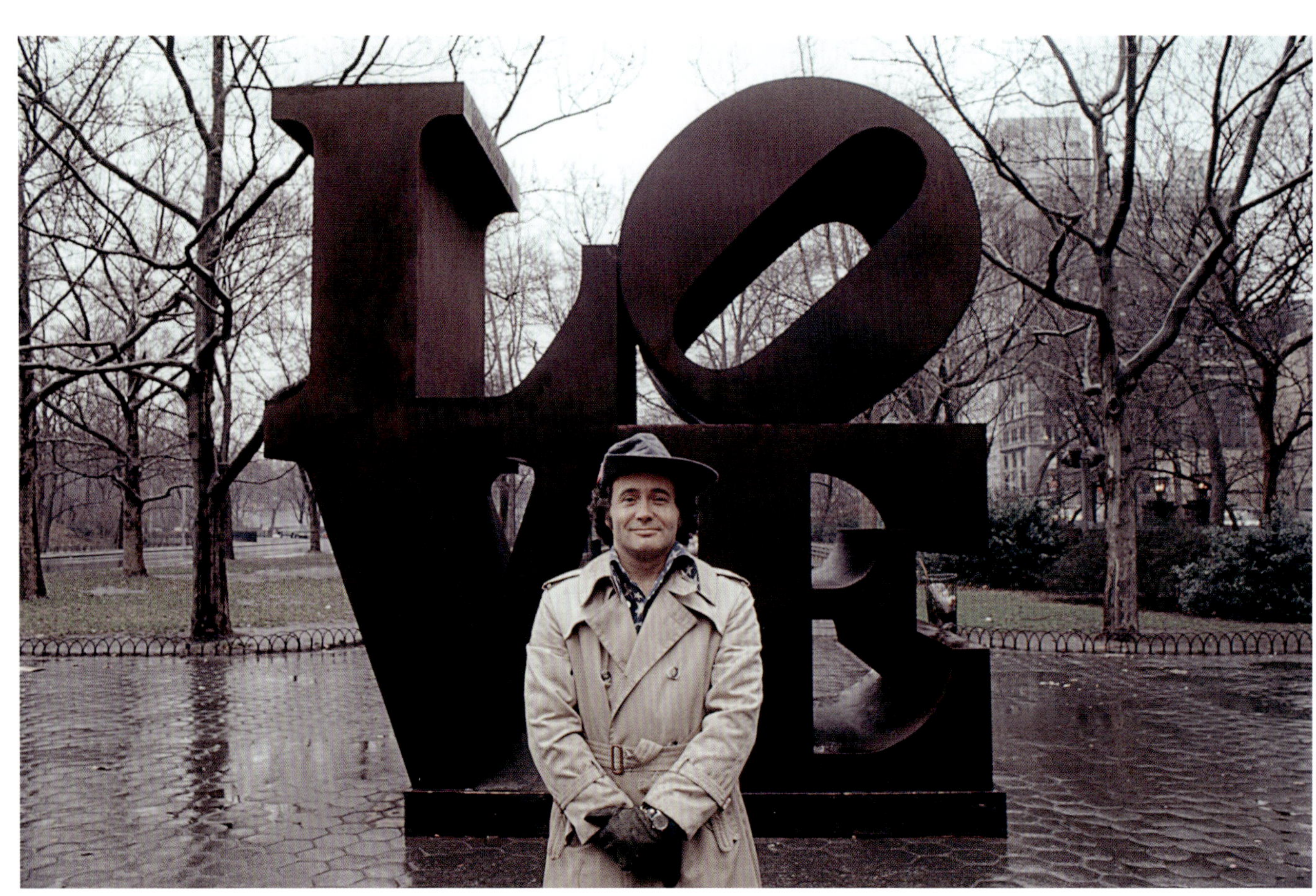
LOVE

69

Robert Indiana

Best known for his iconic 1964 word sculpture *LOVE* (and his 1966 painted version), politicized Pop artist Robert Indiana produced work that became emblematic of the 1960s Free Love Generation. Direct and accessible, his Pop motifs included simple words, numbers, signs, geometric shapes and even a roulette wheel.

Born Robert Clark, he served in the US Air Force before training at the Art Institute of Chicago and in Scotland at Edinburgh College of Art. After moving to downtown New York in 1954, he playfully rebranded himself at the age of thirty, changing his surname to Indiana after the Midwestern state of his birth. Boyfriend of American abstract artist Ellsworth Kelly, Indiana understood the nature of risk during a period of intense persecution of gay Americans. No doubt in response, and as a critique of the myth of the **American Dream**, he introduced the motif of the gambler's roulette wheel in a series of paintings that meditate on jeopardy. The first of these, *The American Dream I* – bought by the Museum of Modern Art, New York, in 1961 suggests that to be American and gay at the time involved a dangerous degree of uncertainty.

Indiana's work gained impressive exposure in New York during the early 1960s, featuring in the *New Forms, New Media* exhibition at the Martha Jackson Gallery in 1960, *The Art of Assemblage* at MoMA in 1961 and the *International Exhibition of the* **New Realists** at  24
the **Sidney Janis** Gallery. In 1962,  46
Indiana had his first solo exhibition, at **Eleanor Ward's** Stable Gallery.  44
The following year he created his Pop word sculpture *Eat* and, as a promotional feature, starred in Andy Warhol's film of the same name, in which the camera watches him endlessly eating a mushroom. In 1964, Indiana recycled his *Eat* motif as a huge flashing sign for the New York State Pavilion at the New York World's Fair, but it ended up having to be removed because too many hungry visitors thought – understandably – that it literally indicated the whereabouts of a restaurant.

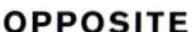
OPPOSITE
Robert Indiana with his *LOVE* sculpture in Central Park, New York City, 1971

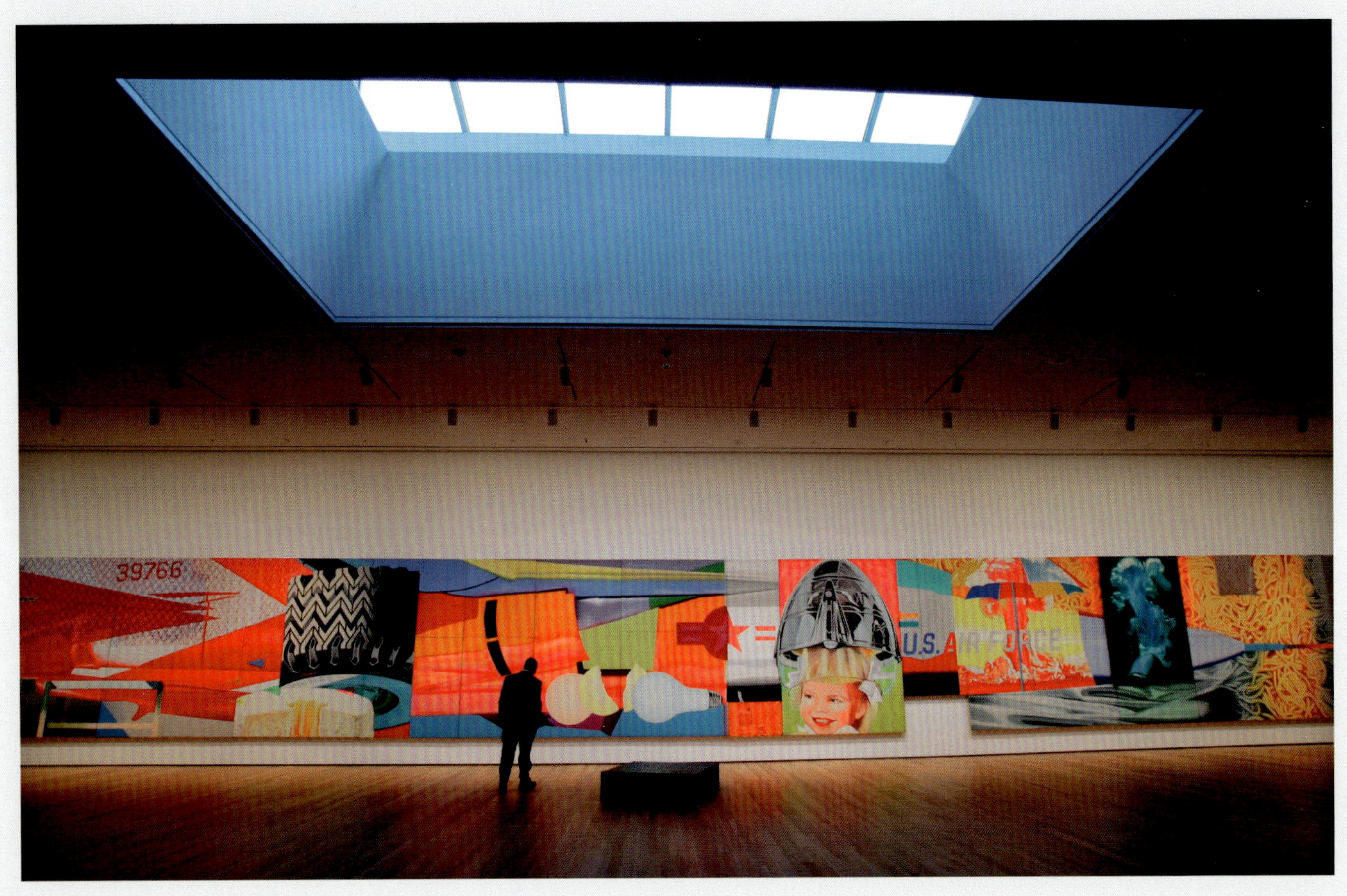
39766
U.S. AIR FORCE

70

F-111

James Rosenquist

1964–5

Drawing heavily on what he called
9 the 'power and gusto' of **billboard painting**, Pop artist James Rosenquist's monumental *F-111* was designed in 1964–5 for installation at the Leo Castelli Gallery in New York's Upper East Side. Composed of 23 panels, arranged in an 86-foot-long panoramic sequence across the gallery's four walls, this was called the largest and the 'grandest' work of
23 Pop Art by **Henry Geldzahler**, who became a curator at the Metropolitan Museum of Art and championed the movement.

Fascinated by peripheral vision – the way we perceive without precisely seeing – Rosenquist designed *F-111* as a 360-degree wraparound vision of contemporary America. The large-scale work bombarded viewers with a visual cacophony of juxtaposed elements: close-ups of tinned spaghetti, a young girl underneath a blow-dryer that morphs into the nose of an F-111 attack aircraft, flashing light bulbs, a diver gasping for breath and a nuclear explosion beneath a child's umbrella (an image playing on the idea of the 'nuclear umbrella', by which atomic states pledge to protect those that don't possess such weapons).

Painted in a photographic style at the height of the Vietnam War, Rosenquist's work was inspired by the US military's newest bomber, first flown a few days before Christmas in 1964 yet soon found to be redundant. His painted *F-111* is, however, 4 metres (13 feet) longer than the aircraft it actually depicts. Imagining the technicians contracted to build the F-111 – their salaries paid by the military-industrial complex,
enabling the buying of new **cars** 7
and suburban houses and the births of new babies – Rosenquist highlights how what he called the 'economy
of surplus' was driven by **war**. In 51
representing the modern economy this way, he forces the viewer to confront some of the most disturbing aspects of contemporary America.

OPPOSITE
James Rosenquist
F-111, 1964–5, shown in the MoMA, 2004

OIL ON CANVAS WITH ALUMINIUM, 23 SECTIONS

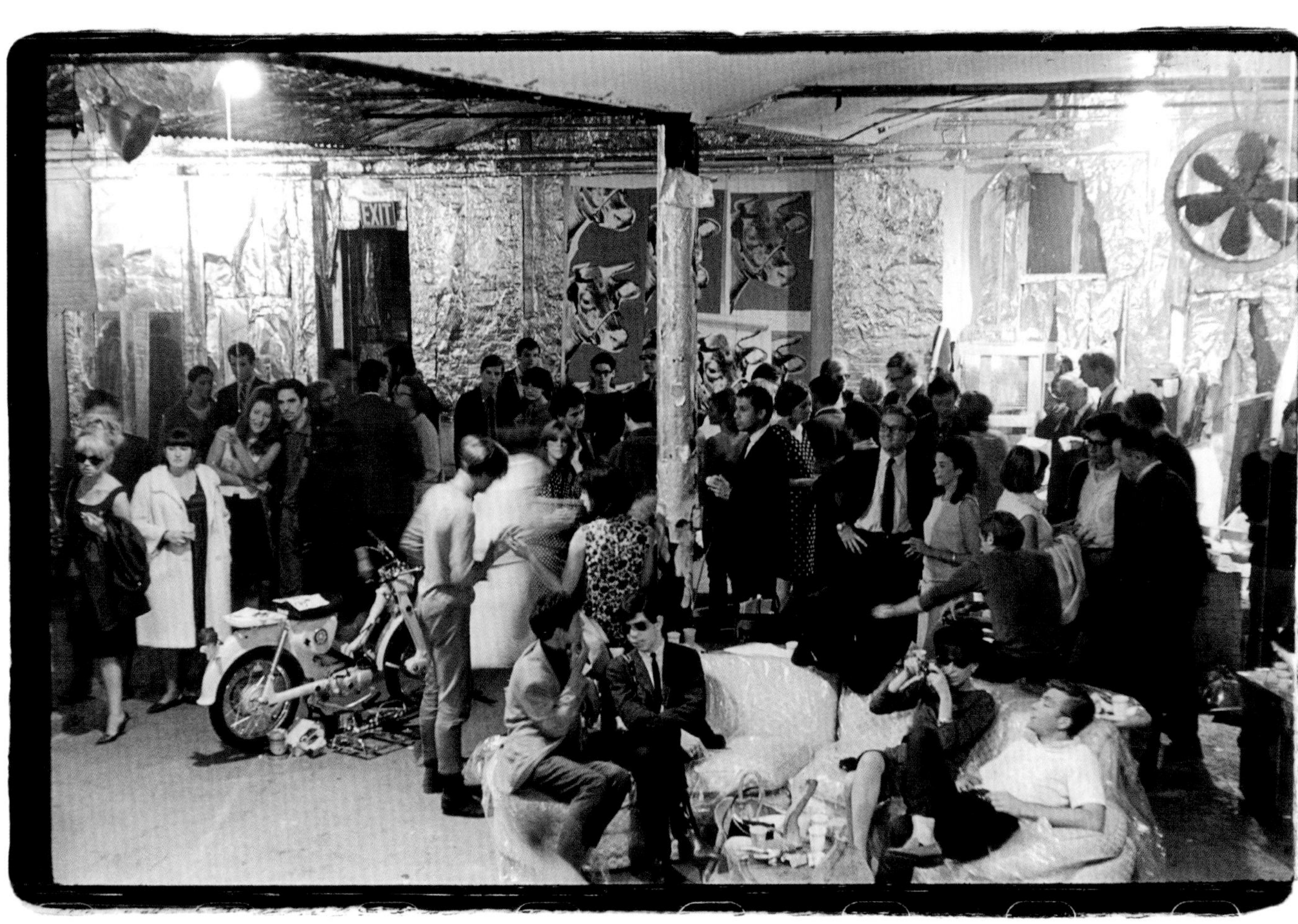
EXIT

71

The Factory

Andy Warhol's New York studio, known as the Factory, produced an
16 extensive list of radical **'happenings'** and controversial films in addition to
36 the sculptures and **silkscreens** for which it is most famous. In January 1966, Warhol inaugurated the first of these happenings, known as the *Exploding Plastic Inevitable*. To a backdrop of projections of his films and music by the Velvet Underground, Factory celebrities including Edie Sedgwick, Joe Dallesandro, Candy Darling and Paul America cavorted in a vortex of deliberately poetic performances that became as famous as they were confusing.

Filmed in the summer of 1966 and released that September, the most commercially successful of Warhol's Factory films was *Chelsea Girls*. Presented in split screen – colour on the left, black and white on the right – the film's cast featured superstars such as the singer Nico, artist Brigid Berlin, actor Ondine, model International
90 Velvet, and **drag** performer Mario Montez. For the film's London release, graphic designer Alan Aldridge's Surrealist poster famously featured the naked body of 16-year-old artist Clare Shenstone, with shuttered windows looking out from her torso.

Based at three different locations in downtown Manhattan between 1962 and 1984, the Factory served as both a hang-out for Warhol's friends and muses and a prolific headquarters for Andy Warhol Enterprises. The original Factory, in which the *Exploding Plastic Inevitable* took place, was also known as the Silver Factory, after its distinctive décor. Set designer Billy Name was responsible for this design, which Warhol commissioned, having been taken by **mail artist** 22
Ray Johnson to one of Name's outrageous early 1960s 'haircutting parties' and seeing the walls covered in silver tin foil and the furniture painted in silver acrylic. Name would soon become Warhol's lover and the stills photographer for all Factory films. In many ways, and for a time at least, he was Warhol's indispensable right-hand man.

OPPOSITE
A party at the Factory, New York City, 1965

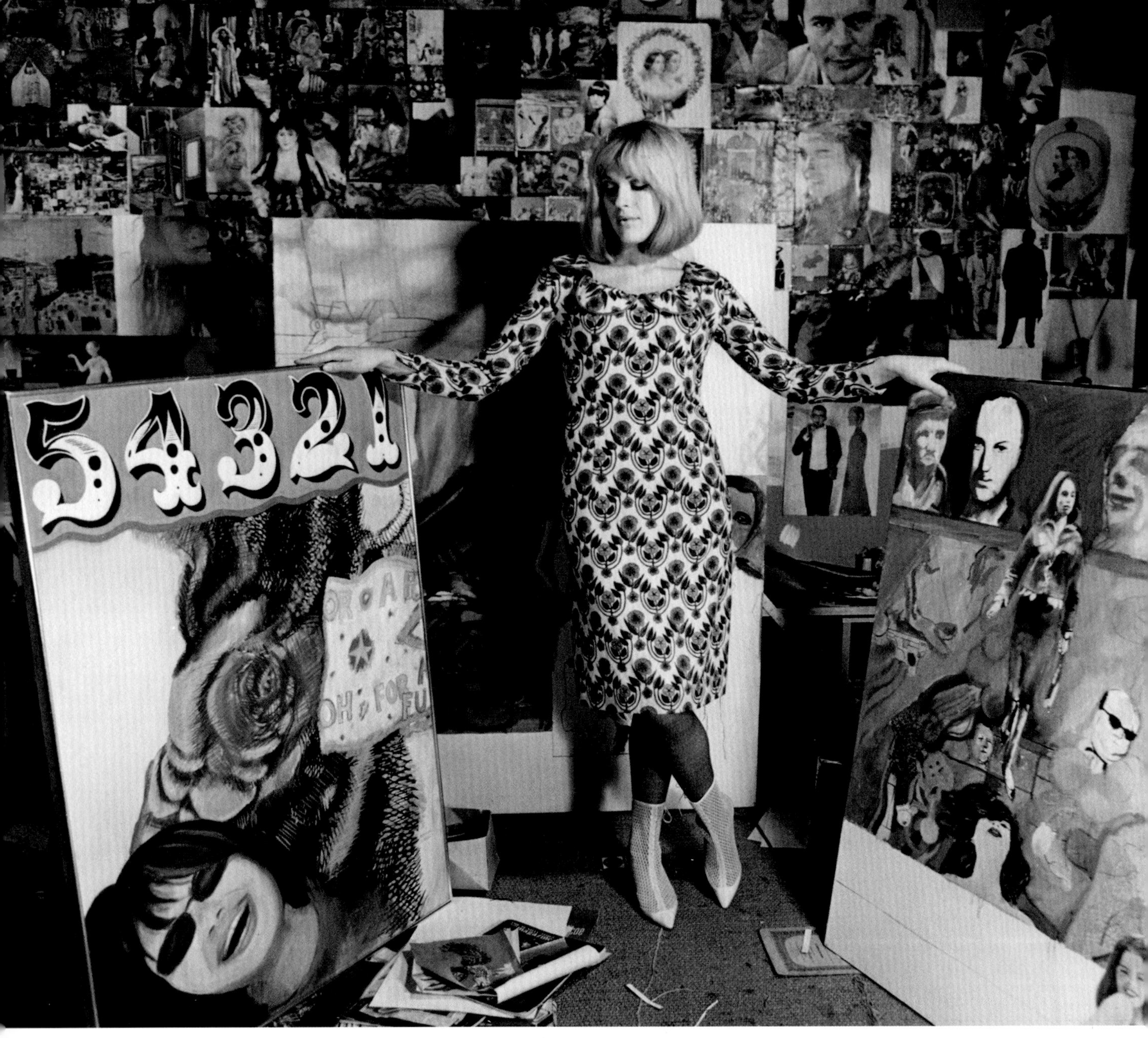
54321

72

Pauline Boty

After a decade-long career as a pioneering British Pop artist, Pauline Boty died of leukaemia in July 1966 at the age of just 28. As a student at London's Royal College of Art in the late 1950s and early 1960s she had become friends with David Hockney, Peter Blake and Derek Boshier and was the only British woman involved in the Pop Art movement. She produced exuberant paintings and unusual collages that were, until recently, neglected by critics.

Having trained initially at Wimbledon School of Art in London, Boty continued her studies at the prestigious RCA during an era when fine art – oil painting on canvas – was considered the most prestigious, and therefore masculine, of artistic practices. As a result, she was encouraged to enrol as a designer of stained glass. Soon, however, she began painting and collaging in her spare time and, in November 1961, exhibited twenty of her works alongside those of Blake at the Artists' International Association Gallery near Leicester Square. Yet exactly a year later, *Scene* magazine wrote in patronizing terms: 'Actresses often have tiny brains. Painters often have large beards. Imagine a brainy actress who is also a painter and also a blonde, and you have Pauline Boty.'

Boty understood the powerful magnetism of Hollywood. Clarifying Pop's role in contemporary culture, she said, 'Film stars are the 20th-century gods and goddesses. People need them, and the myths that surround them, because their own lives are enriched by them. Pop Art colours those myths.' Boty's work can be seen, at least in one interpretation, as a critical exploration of the ways in which Hollywood developed and maintained unhealthy female stereotypes. Boty's reputation as the 'Wimbledon Bardot' unfairly diminished the critical reception of her work, both during her life and after her untimely death.

OPPOSITE
Pauline Boty in her studio, 1963

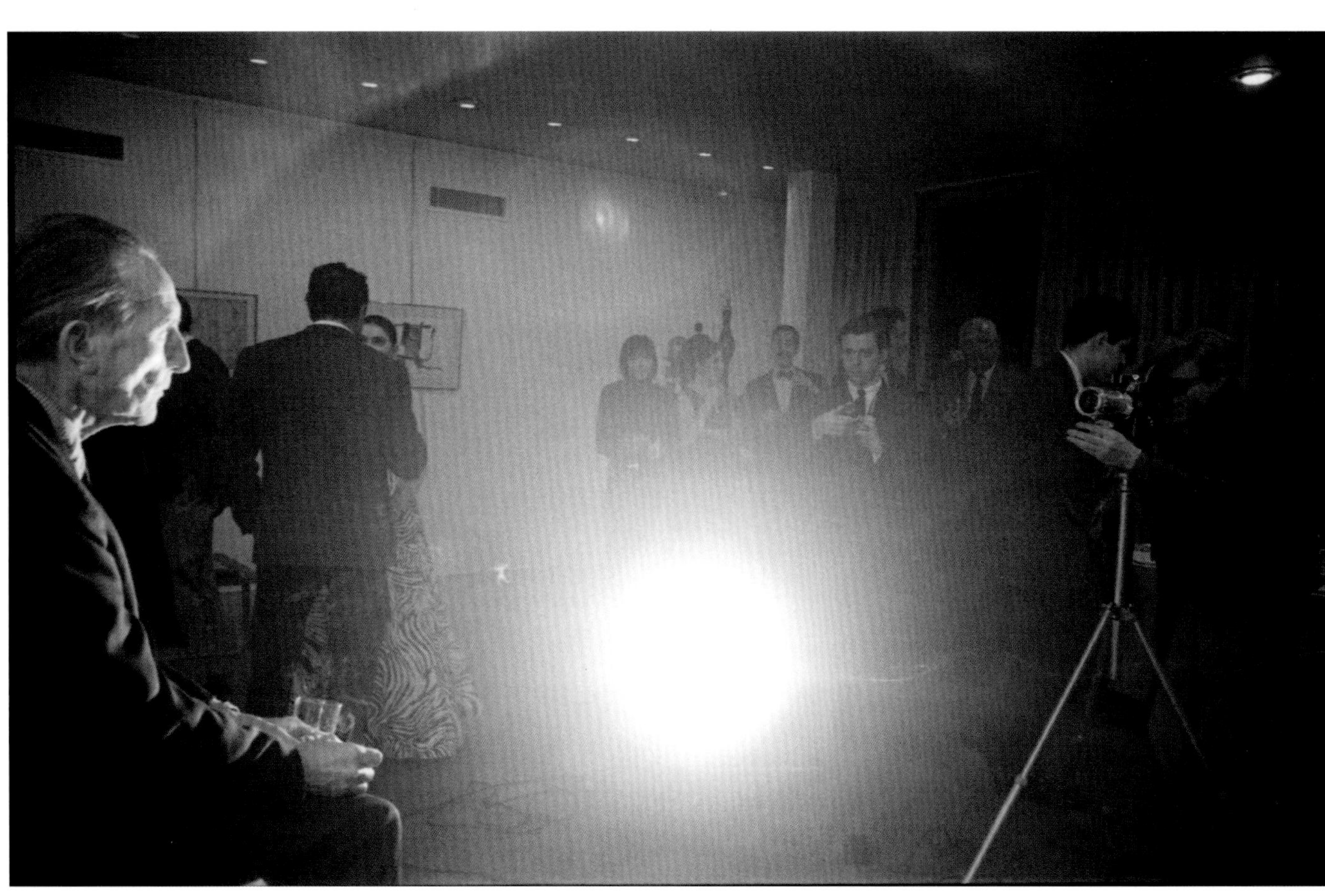

73

Andy Warhol meets Marcel Duchamp

1966

It's hard to overemphasize the
1 profound influence that **Marcel Duchamp** had on Andy Warhol. By the time Warhol actually met his artistic hero, he'd already been collecting his work for several years; when Warhol died, in 1987, he had more than thirty pieces. Both artists had attended the
47 1962 **MoMA Pop Art symposium** and had met – very briefly – the following year at Duchamp's 1963 retrospective at the Pasadena Art
50 Museum in **Los Angeles**. Both would survive assassination attempts – Duchamp in Paris in 1965 and
82 **Warhol in 1968** – and both were, perhaps surprisingly, camera-shy.

The first well-documented meeting between Duchamp and Warhol occurred in February 1966 on the opening night of an exhibition at the Cordier & Ekstrom Gallery on New York's Madison Avenue. Later, and with typical disingenuousness, Warhol claimed, 'I didn't know he was famous.' And yet that night he engineered a meeting with Duchamp that's been described by photographer Nat Finkelstein, who was present at the time, as a 'guerrilla attack'. Warhol turned up uninvited with his camera, ready to capture Duchamp on three separate films – each lasting nearly three minutes – for his silent series *Screen Tests*. They kept their distance for most of the evening, but when they finally met, 37-year-old Warhol and 78-year-old Duchamp were distinctly awkward, even frosty, around one another, neither speaking a word until Warhol eventually offered, 'Well, Mr Duchamp, it's been nice meeting you,' before Duchamp resumed puffing his cigar and returned to his newspaper. Nevertheless, Warhol had captured his hero on film.

That same year, Duchamp completed his last major work, *Étant donnés*. Undertaken in complete secrecy over a twenty-year period, like Warhol's *Screen Tests* it concerns the voyeurist-exhibitionist impulse, anticipating contemporary
pornography and the digital age. [illegible]

OPPOSITE
Marcel Duchamp (left) and Andy Warhol (right), during filming for Andy Warhol's *Screen Test 79*, 1966

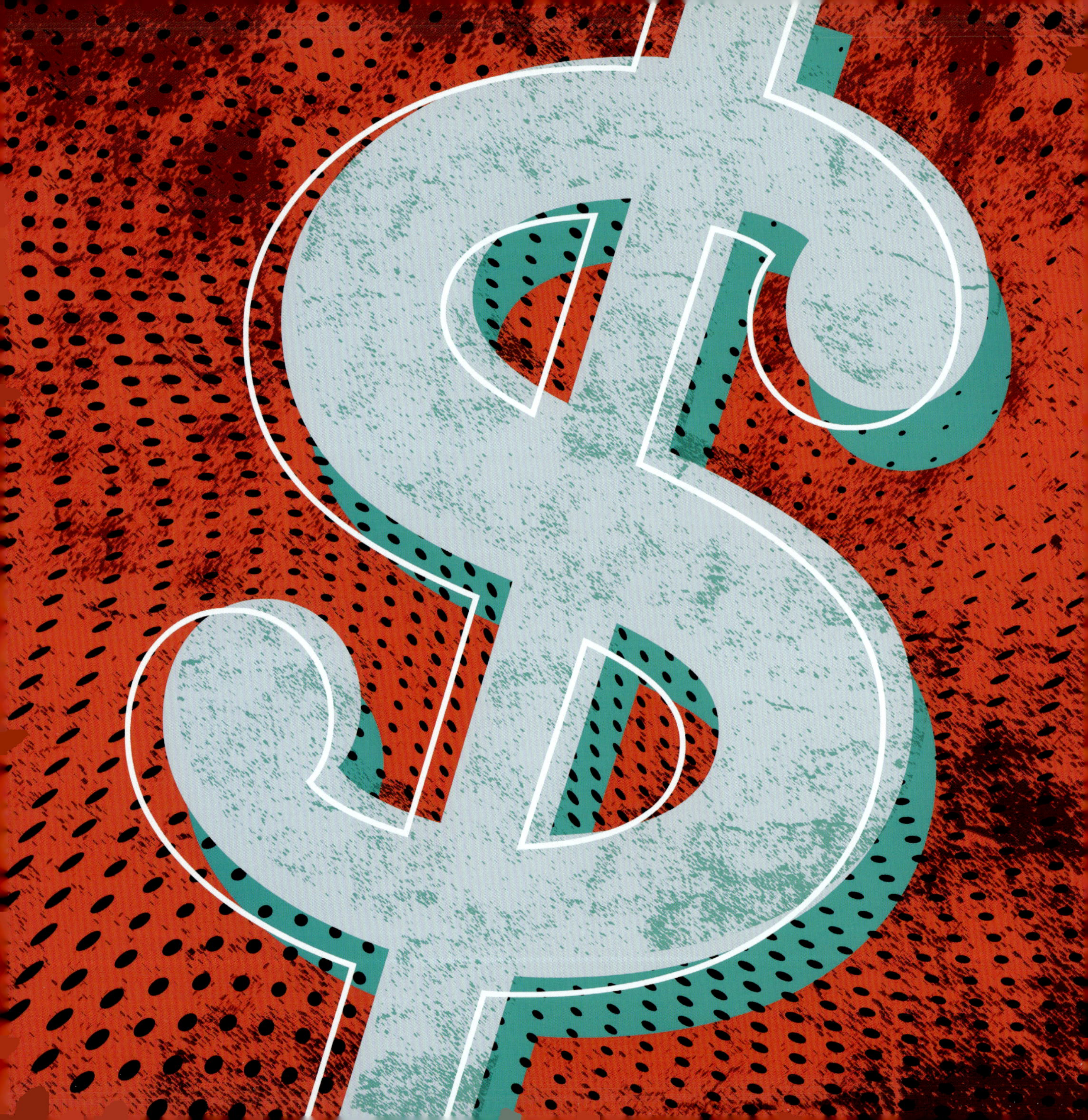

74

Art as business

Wealth and conspicuous consumption were not merely Pop motifs. Pop artists were often very happy to play the commercial game, court big money, exploit the art market and earn themselves extraordinary fortunes. While some left-wing artists have always struggled to resolve the tension between success and wealth, for many Pop artists these were happily synonymous.

Breaking saleroom records, Pop artists quickly rose to fame and notoriety in the 1960s, with Pop Art works becoming some of the most expensive in the world. In 1962, art critic Irving Sandler commented that Andy Warhol appeared not to 'satirize vulgarity and idiocy but to accept its values complacently'. And he was right. A decade later Warhol would claim:

Business art is the step that comes after art. I started as a commercial artist, and I want to finish as a business artist... Being good in business is the most fascinating kind of art. During the hippie era people put down the idea of business – they'd say, 'Money is bad,' and 'Working is bad,' but making money is art and working is art and good business is the best art.

—

Pop Art started out depicting the aspirational products of consumer culture, but within a decade it had itself become an aspirational commodity. James Rosenquist's ***F-111*** was sold to an American collector the year it was exhibited for the then-extraordinary sum of $45,000 (over $300,000 today). In 1966, many British commentators were shocked when the Tate Gallery in London bought Roy Lichtenstein's ***Whaam!*** for the relatively modest price of nearly £4,000 (over £30,000 today). Nearly fifty years later, in 2015, Lichtenstein's painting *Nurse* sold for over $95 million. But Warhol would be thrilled to know that the highest-selling work of Pop Art to date remains his *Silver Car Crash (Double Disaster)*, sold for the phenomenal sum of $105 million in 2013.

70

57

SEX WAR SEX CARS SEX

CLEANLINESS IS NEXT TO GODLINESS

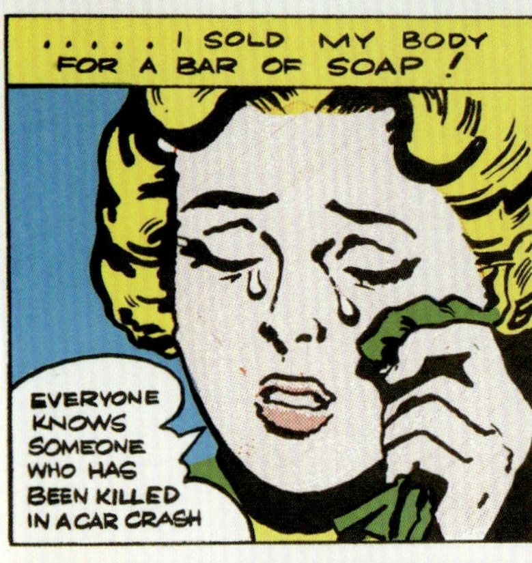

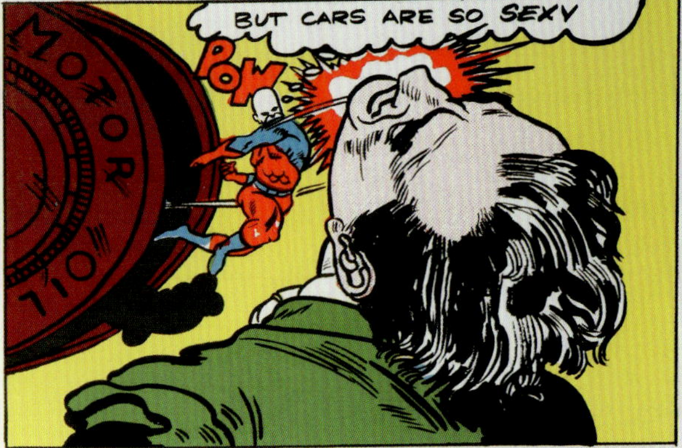

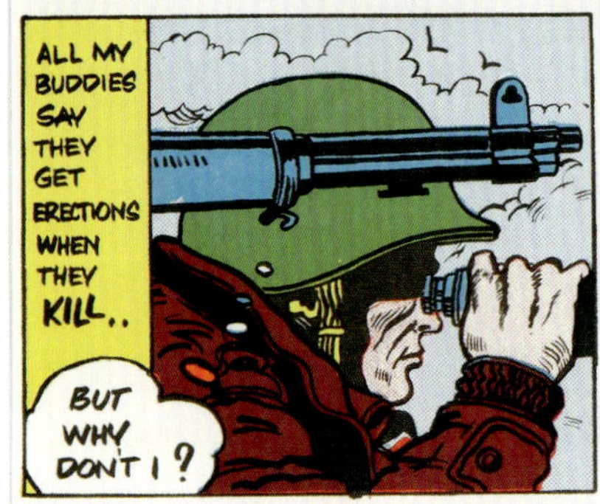

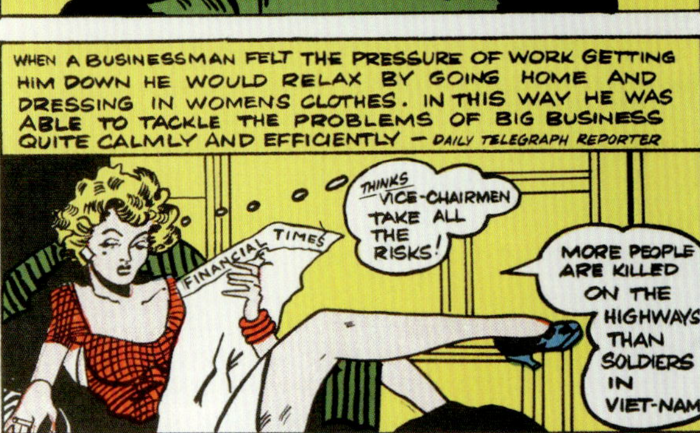

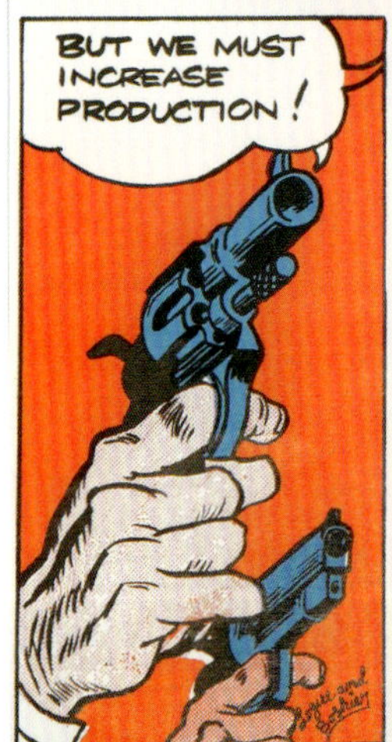

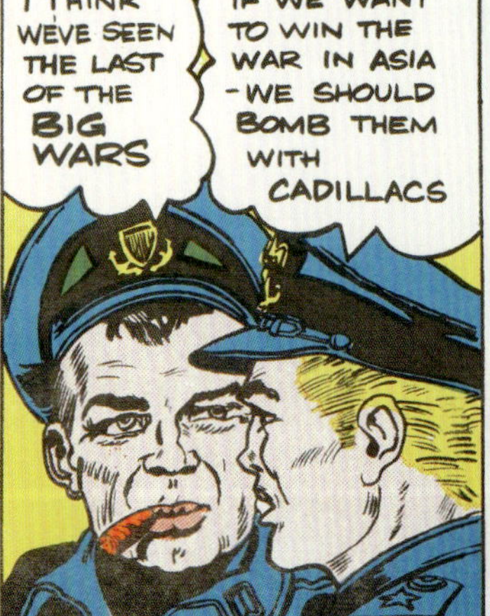

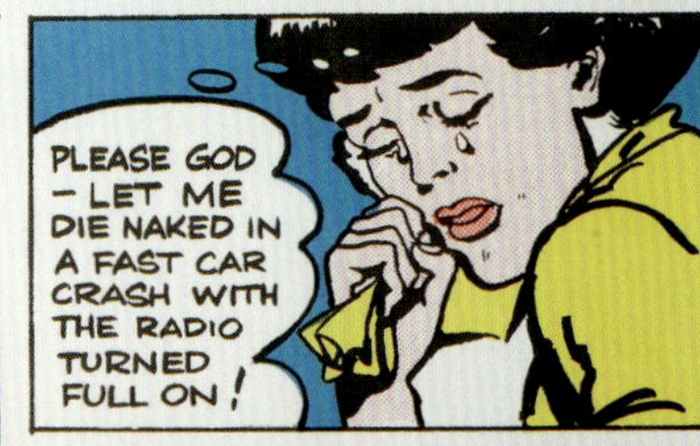

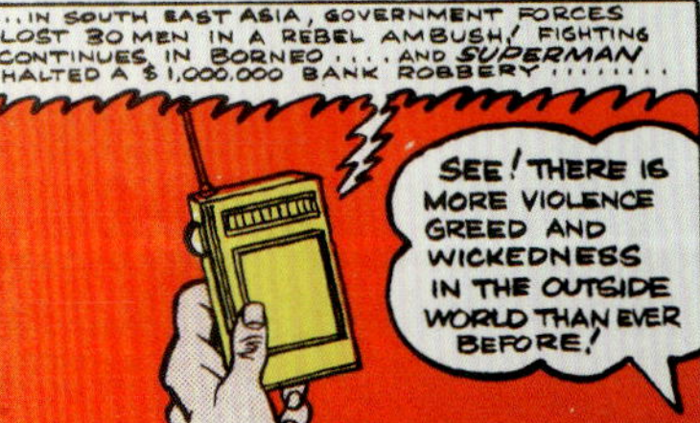

75

Sex War Sex Cars Sex

Derek Boshier and Christopher Logue

1966

In 1966, in collaboration with his friend the British poet Christopher Logue, British Pop artist Derek Boshier produced the comic-strip
68 **lithograph** *Sex War Sex Cars Sex.* Registering discomfort at Britain's support of America's war in Vietnam, it is a radical Pop satire on modern life in which eight brightly coloured cartoon panels display weeping and aggressive figures racked with
61 **Cold War** fear and sexual anxiety.

In 1961, while studying at the Royal College of Art in London, Boshier had exhibited at the *Young Contemporaries* exhibition at the Royal Society of British Artists. In 1963, he represented Britain at the Paris Biennale, and he participated in the *New Generation* exhibition, which opened the following March at the Whitechapel Gallery in London. By the mid-1960s, Logue had begun writing his bloody interpretation of Homer's Iliad, the ancient Greek epic about the decade-long Trojan War.

In *Sex War Sex Cars Sex*, Logue's powerful words evoke the panic and brutality of wartime culture. A speech bubble screams, 'See! There is more violence greed and wickedness in the outside world than ever before!' Our attention is deliberately focused on devalued bodies and physicalized responses to violence and disaster. A woman, we are told, sold her body 'for a bar of soap', soldiers claim to gain erections when they kill (one worrying that he doesn't) and, in response to stress, a businessman takes to
drag in order to relax and tackle 'big 90
business' both 'calmly and efficiently'.
Cars appear, meanwhile, as more of 7
a threat even than guns. 'Everybody knows someone who has been killed in a car crash,' says one weeping women. Another, reflecting the modern desire for extreme sensations, says, 'Please God – let me die naked in a fast car crash with the radio turned full on!' In asserting the provocative connection between technology, violence and arousal, Boshier and Logue here anticipated **J. G. Ballard's** sensational novel *Crash* by seven years.

OPPOSITE
Derek Boshier and Christopher Logue
Sex War Sex Cars Sex, 1966
SCREENPRINT

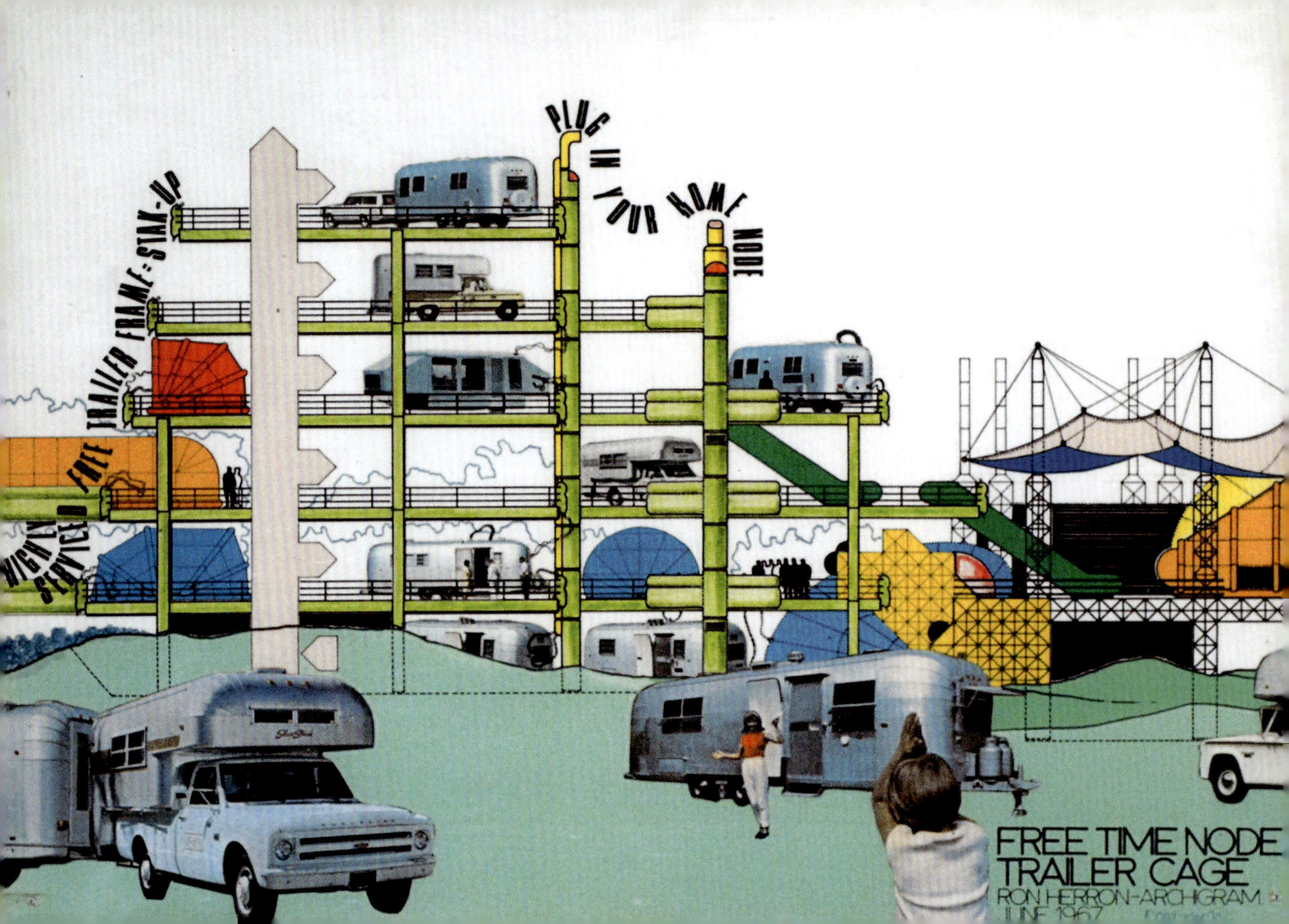
SERVICED
FREE
TRAILER FRAME: STAK-UP
PLUG IN YOUR HOME NODE
FREE TIME NODE
TRAILER CAGE
RON HERRON-ARCHIGRAM
JUNE 1967

76

Archigram

Launching their challenge to modernist architectural practice, in 1961 an informal group of young British architecture graduates calling themselves Archigram, colliding the words 'architecture' and 'telegram', produced the first (two-page) edition of their eponymous London-based manifesto. *Archigram*, which ran to ten issues, detailed the ideas of one of the most innovative, Pop-inspired architectural collectives in Europe.

Archigram's key members were Peter Cook, Warren Chalk, Dennis Crompton, David Greene, Ron Herron and Michael Webb. Their work was guided by what Greene has described as an 'altered reading of the familiar' and by what architectural historian Simon Sadler has identified as 'space-age technology, computing, serial production, consumerism and the demands of a newly expanded leisure class'. Across their publications, Archigram employed the Pop aesthetic of brightly coloured, kaleidoscopic collage design to encourage a younger and more diverse audience to engage with contemporary architecture. Their first exhibition, *Living City*, was staged in 1963 at London's Institute of Contemporary Arts and the collective famously exhibited at the 1968 Milan Triennale, designing the accompanying 'Milanogram' poster.

Some of Archigram's most outlandish Pop designs include the 1964 *Walking City*: an alien reptile-like structure; the 1966 *Living Pod*: an organically shaped travelling capsule-home; and *Instant City*: a nomadic airship archive of urban cultural resources completed in 1970. While most of their projects remained unrealized, Archigram's conceptual contribution in developing architecture from modernist idealism to postmodernist pragmatism was considerable. Their collective Pop-inspired influence can be seen, perhaps most notably, in postmodern works like Renzo Piano and Richard Rogers's 1977 Centre Pompidou in Paris.

OPPOSITE
Ron Herron
Free Time Node Trailer Cage, 1967
COLLAGE

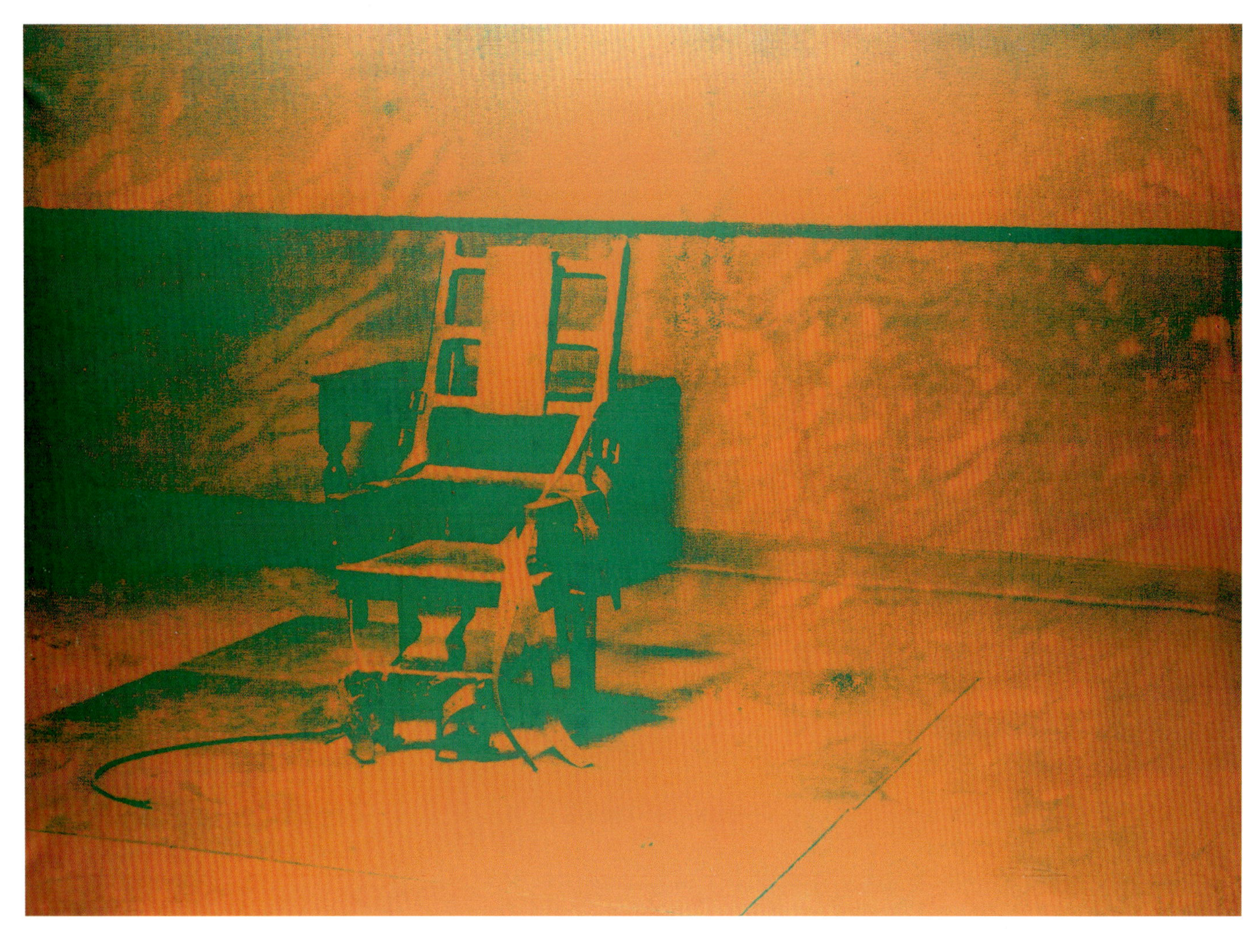

77

Big Electric Chair

Andy Warhol

1967

42 Part of the ***Death and Disaster* series**, the creation of which had been prompted five years earlier by
23 **Henry Geldzahler**, now curator at the Metropolitan Museum of Art, Andy
36 Warhol's **silkscreen** *Big Electric Chair* became one of a number of mature responses to his first 1964 *Electric Chair* silkscreen. By returning again and again to the same images, drawn this time from the darker recesses of contemporary culture, and creating several near-identical and compulsively repetitive works, Warhol reflects back to us a dispassionate and clinical attitude to death. Based on a 1923 black-and-white photo of the New York state execution chamber and its electric chair, Warhol's macabre *Big Electric Chair*, with its acidic greens and oranges, has a coolly distancing effect.

Later *Electric Chair* images focus on 'Old Sparky', New York state's electric chair. For seventy years it was situated in the centre of an empty chamber at Sing Sing prison, north of Manhattan, on the banks of the Hudson River in the suburban town of Ossining (home to *Mad Men*'s fictional Don and Betty Draper). Since 1891, over six hundred people had been executed 'in the hot seat' and, in August 1963, murderer Eddie Lee Mays was the last. By 1967, all executions in New York – except, in theory, for the murder of police officers – had been outlawed by progressive state governor Nelson Rockefeller.

Warhol approached 'Old Sparky' as the subject of both a still-life study and an exercise in portraiture. Designed to be occupied, the chair is expected to house a body but instead there remains a haunting absence. We cannot resist voyeuristically imagining the horrors of an electric execution – exactly what would it look like? And feel like? – so that the chair begins, before our eyes, to contain the shape of a ghostly presence. Warhol's hot seat is a grotesque Pop throne, whose occupants, both real and imagined, take on outsized psychological and social significance as contemporary Pop symbols of **fame** and notoriety. 

OPPOSITE
Andy Warhol
Big Electric Chair, 1967
INK AND ACRYLIC ON CANVAS

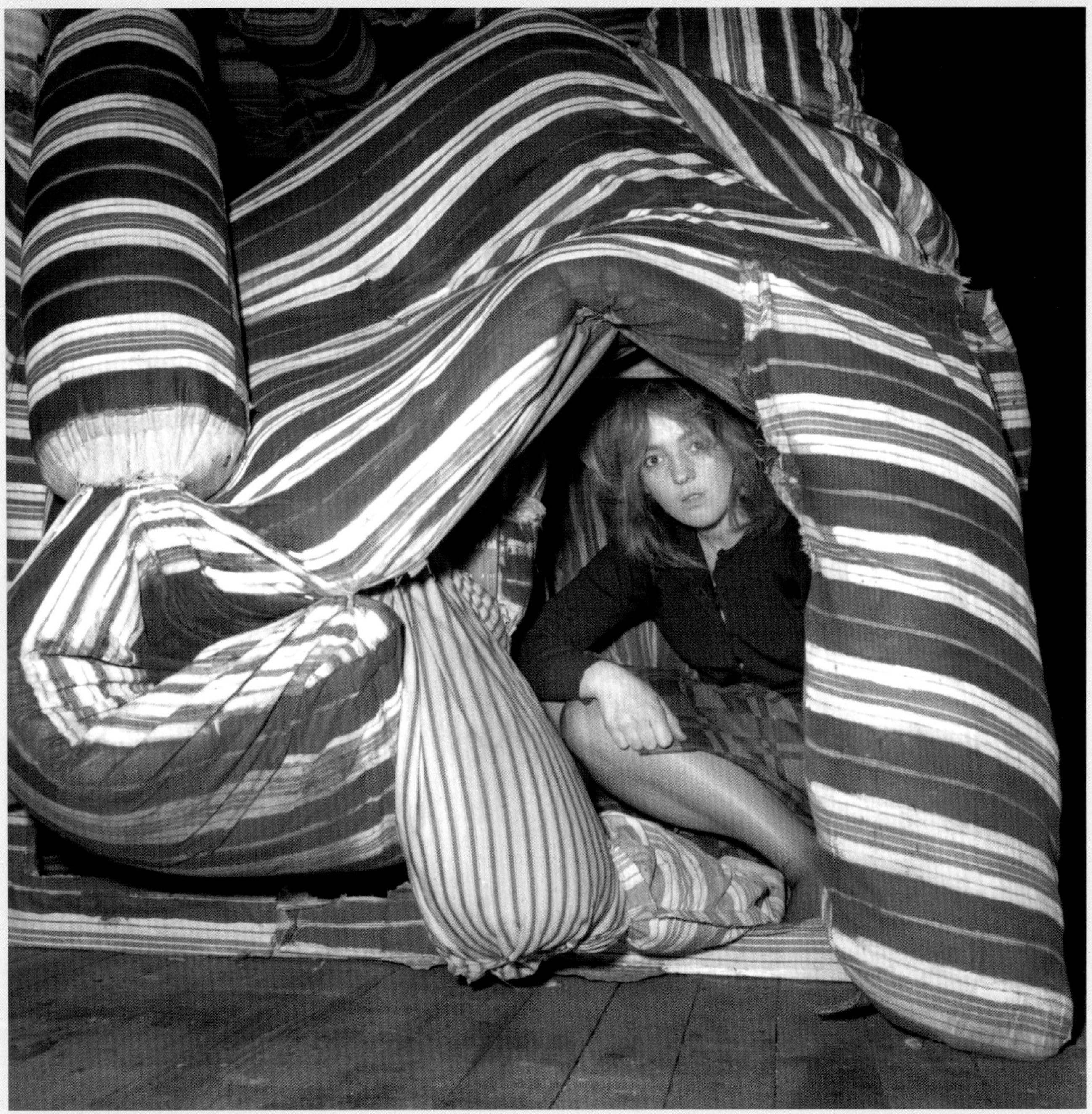

78

Marta Minujín

Argentinian Pop artist Marta Minujín – 'the Latin answer to Pop' and one of the movement's most influential practitioners – was a pioneer of
16 the 1960s artistic **'happening'**.
Influenced by American Pop artist Allan Kaprow, Minujín's work embodied what her friend the French artist Jean-Jacques Lebel called an 'intensification of feeling, the play of instinct, a sense of festivity, social agitation'.

Born in Buenos Aires, the exuberant Minujín studied at the National University Institute of Art during the late 1950s before winning a travelling scholarship, allowing her to settle in Paris for a year. Loosely associated
24 with the **New Realist** movement,
Minujín produced early work that represented what critic Pierre Restany called the 'direct appropriation of reality'. In early 1960s Paris, French Pop was, in her words, 'the only new and really different' art form.

Interested in the decaying qualities of everyday 'found objects', in 1961 Minujín orchestrated a happening called *The Destruction*. Gathering several old mattresses, she installed them on an empty piece of wasteland in Paris's southern Necker district and encouraged her artist friends to deface them, eventually setting them alight while she freed five hundred caged birds and a hundred caged
rabbits. Like **Niki de Saint Phalle**, 37
Minujín wanted to 'create while destroying' in what she called an 'indisputably orgiastic' Pop event.

Minujín later returned to Buenos Aires, where she orchestrated several large-scale interactive Pop happenings before moving to New York in 1966. She created the radically prescient, high-tech installation performance *Minuphone* the following year. Here, the viewer-participant was placed at the centre of the work in what appeared to be a telephone booth, where the dialling of a particular number would fill the booth with bright colours and sounds. The floor would then be
transformed into a **television** screen 25
reflecting the viewer-participant back at themselves, watching themselves being watched. 'For me,' Minujín said, 'art was a way of intensifying life, of impacting the viewer, shaking up, removing…inertia.'

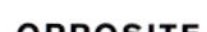

OPPOSITE
Marta Minujín at a happening in Paris, 8 June 1963

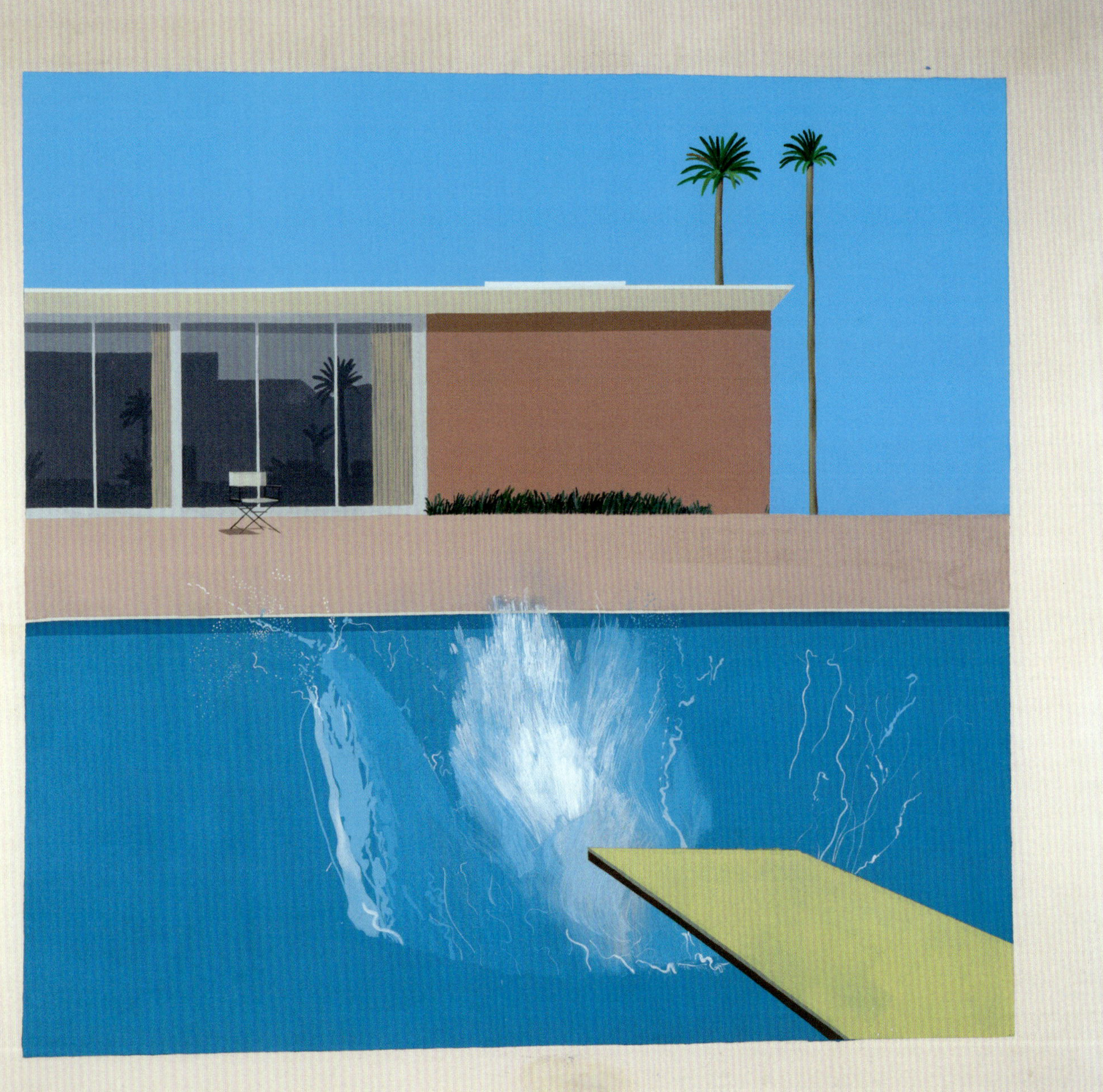

79

A Bigger Splash

David Hockney

1967

British Pop artist David Hockney briefly visited America as a student in 1961, dyeing his hair blond for the first time, and returned again just before Christmas in 1963. The following year, 50 he settled full time in **Los Angeles**. Painted in the spring of 1967, *A Bigger Splash* is the last of three 'splash' paintings depicting swimming pools that distil the popular British dream of California and epitomize Hockney's 1960s Pop style. The painting's title would – seven years later – give its name to a partly fictionalized biopic about Hockney directed by Jack Hazan. Contemporary critics considered the film – as some did the painting and Pop Art itself – both 'elegant' and 'vapid'.

Southern California and what one contemporary critic called the 'idyllic bizarreness of Los Angeles' had a profound effect on Bradford-born Hockney. *A Bigger Splash* – with its uniform light, deep blue sky, palm trees, modernist villa and swimming pool – has captured an intimate fantasy of LA. To frame it, Hockney flattened the painting's perspective and gave the image a border so that it looks like a **Polaroid** photograph. 19 Witnessing the scene at one remove – from afar, as it were – the viewer is a trespasser. Our interest is piqued by the splash of the title, rising from the surface of the pool and suspended in midair. The 'absence' of the diver lends the image a curious immediacy, so that each time we view it the painting feels new and fresh.

In 1966, while teaching at University of California, Los Angeles, Hockney met his Californian muse and partner of five years, the artist and photographer Peter Schlesinger. Until their move to London in 1968, Hockney was a Californian pioneer, joyously discovering with innocent British eyes the Pop iconography of Hollywood.

OPPOSITE
David Hockney
A Bigger Splash, 1967
ACRYLIC ON CANVAS

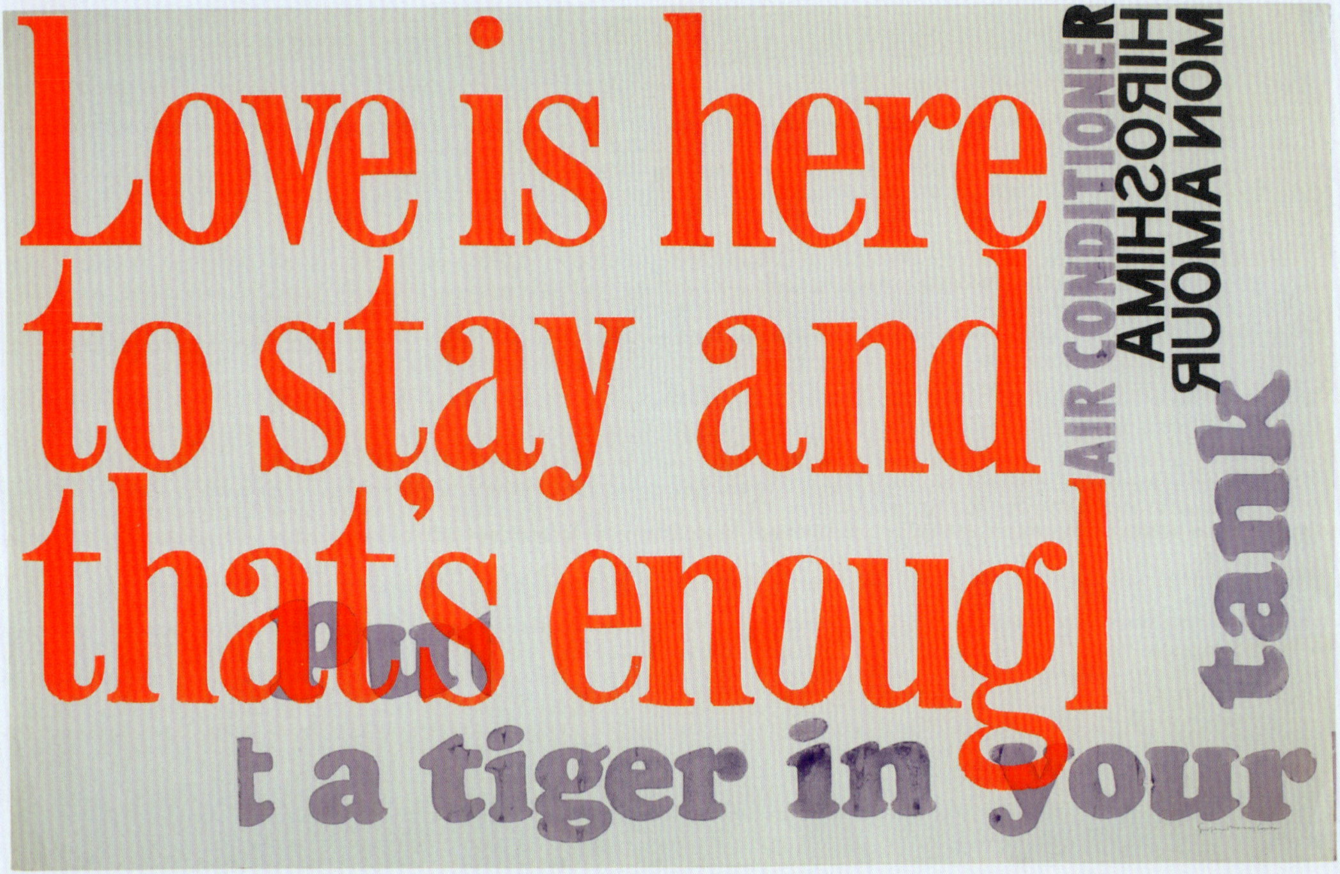

Love is here
to stay and
that's enougl
t a tiger in your
tank

AIR CONDITIONER
HIROSHIMA
MON AMOUR

80

Corita Kent

An artist and professor of fine art at Immaculate Heart College in 50 **Los Angeles**, Sister Mary Corita was named Woman of the Year in 1966 by the *Los Angeles Times*. The following year she was profiled by *Newsweek* magazine and featured on the front cover of the magazine's Christmas edition. Her popular approach was encapsulated when she wrote, 'Art does not come from thinking, but from responding.' Kent advocated what she called 'plork'. Combining the words 'play' and 'work', plorking was for Kent a 'responsible act necessary for human advancement'.

Sister Mary Corita was perhaps the most unlikely of Pop artists. The little-known high priestess of 'protest Pop', she was a progressive social activist – christened 'the joyous revolutionary' by Social Realist artist Ben Shahn – who personified a radical collision of Pop Art and Catholicism. One of several female Pop artists to do so during the late 1960s, she explicitly politicized the Pop Art movement.

Seeing fellow Catholic Andy Warhol's work in a 1962 Los Angeles exhibition, Kent found they shared a common approach to the images and objects of everyday contemporary life. Using a 35mm slide holder – or 'finder' as she called it – to identify subjects, Kent saw the popular and mass-produced with a playful enthusiasm. Lifting inspirational quotes from the Bible, The Beatles and Martin Luther King Jr, Kent created striking **silkscreen** 36 prints with powerful slogans. Her unique style combined the techniques and iconography of graphic design, brand advertising and commercial sloganeering to spread a spiritual and political message that promoted peace and love.

In response to the Catholic hierarchy's condemnation of her Pop Art as blasphemous, Kent left the Church in 1968 for life in the secular world. Her unique Pop Art legacy was described by the equally radical 1960s priest and poet Father Daniel Berrigan as gifting 'joy, joy, joy!' to popular Catholicism.

OPPOSITE
Corita Kent
Tiger, 1965

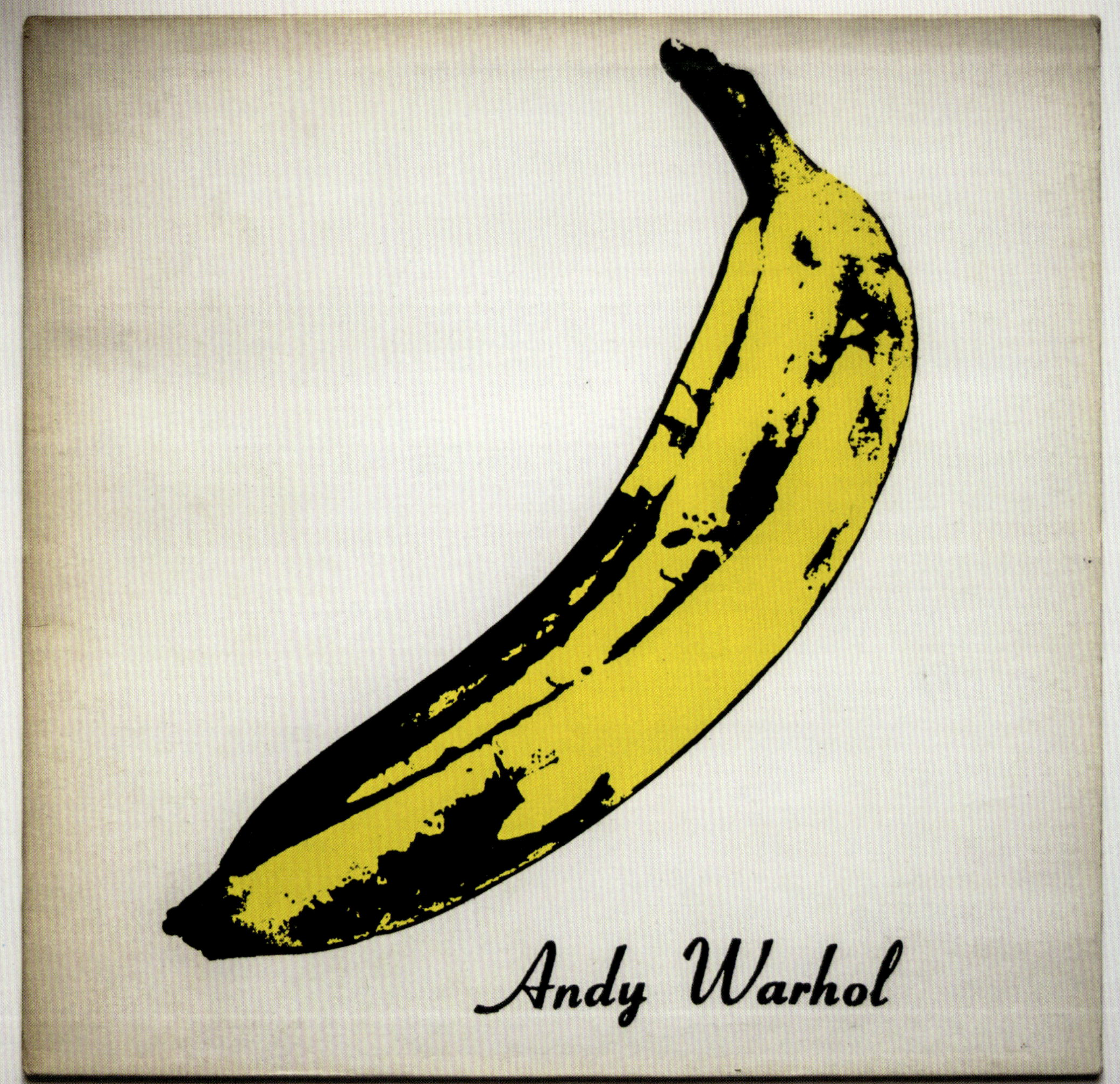
Andy Warhol

81

Pop Art pop

Pop artists defined the visual iconography of some of the best-known albums of the 1960s and 1970s. In 1968, Anglo-American Pop Art husband-and-wife team
48 Peter Blake and **Jann Haworth** designed what was then the most expensive album cover of all time for one of the biggest-selling pop bands of all time – The Beatles. Created for an, at the time, incredible £3,000, Blake and Haworth's colourful and
2 now-iconic **photomontage** for *Sgt. Pepper's Lonely Hearts Club Band* featured images of over fifty celebrities (nine of which were actually waxworks) and won them the 1968 Grammy Award for Best Album Cover.

As in so many areas, it was Andy Warhol – as Andrew Warhola, an
[illegible] unknown **commercial designer** during the 1950s – who pioneered Pop Art's relationship with popular, or at least mass-produced, music albums. He drew and painted several cover designs for classical musicians, his first, at the age of 21, for an album of Mexican music. After his rise to artistic fame and at the height of the **Factory** years, Warhol famously 71
created a provocatively phallic banana for the cover *The Velvet Underground & Nico*, the band's 1967 debut album. Perhaps best known, however, is the 1971 *Sticky Fingers* album cover for the Rolling Stones, featuring the denim outline of a penis beside an inviting zip.

During the last two decades of his life, Warhol produced an extensive body of cover and sleeve portraits for the albums of several best-selling pop musicians. In 1976, he collaborated with the singer Paul Anka on the cover of his album *The Painter*. In the following years he depicted Liza Minnelli on the cover of *Live at Carnegie Hall* (1981), Diana Ross on *Silk Electric* (1982), Aretha Franklin on *Aretha* and Debbie Harry on *Rockbird* (both 1986).

OPPOSITE
Andy Warhol
The Velvet Underground & Nico, Verve Records, 1967
ALBUM COVER DESIGN

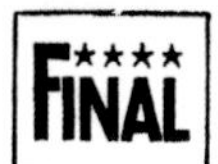

DAILY NEWS

NEW YORK'S PICTURE NEWSPAPER ®

8¢

10¢ OUTSIDE L.I. AND SUBURBS

Vol. 49. No. 296 Copr. 1968 News Syndicate Co. Inc. New York, N.Y. 10017, Tuesday, June 4, 1968★ WEATHER: Sunny and warm.

ACTRESS SHOOTS ANDY WARHOL

Cries 'He Controlled My Life'

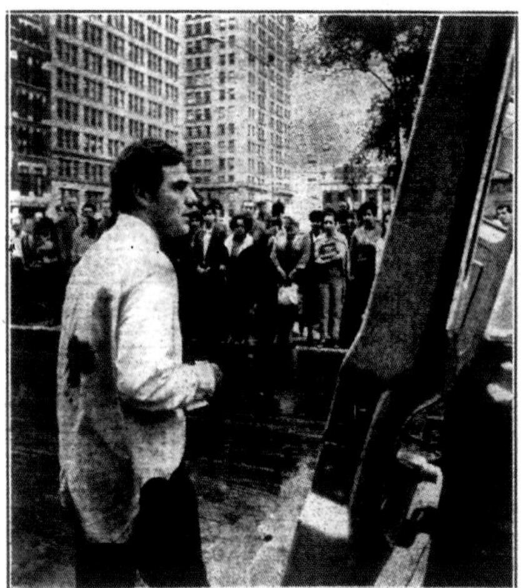

NEWS photo by Jack Smith

Guest From London Shot With Pop Art Movie Man

Shot in attack on underground movie producer Andy Warhol, London art gallery owner Mario Amaya, about 30, walks to ambulance. Warhol was shot and critically wounded by one of his female stars, Valerie Solanas, 28, the "girl on the staircase" in one of his recent films. She walked into Andy's sixth-floor office at 33 Union Square West late yesterday afternoon and got off at least five shots. Valerie later surrendered. See → *—Stories on page 3*

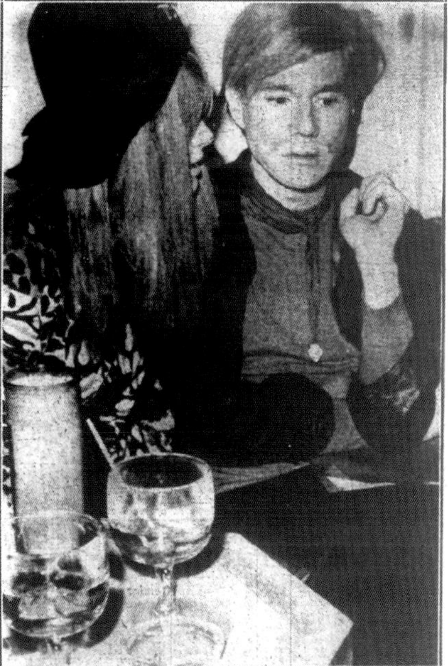

NEWS photo by Tom Monaster

Warhol (r.) was doing his thing with friend in Village spot recently.

02

Shooting Andy Warhol

1968

In the late afternoon of 3 June 1968, two months before his 40th birthday, Andy Warhol was shot by 32-year-old American activist Valerie Solanas, who had briefly featured the previous year in his film *I, a Man*. Her bullet tore through both of Warhol's lungs, his intestines, spleen, liver and oesophagus, and he was pronounced dead for one and a half minutes before open-heart massage revived him. As a result of his injuries, Warhol was forced to wear a surgical support every day for the rest of his life. In the autumn of 1968 he told the *New York Times*, 'Since I was shot, everything is such a dream to me. I don't know what anything is about…Like I don't even know whether or not I'm really alive or – whether I died. It's sad.'

Moving to New York in the mid-1960s, New Jersey-born psychology graduate Solanas lived at the famously bohemian Chelsea Hotel and supported herself financially as a freelance writer and sex worker. In 1965, she wrote a 'provocative' feminist play called *Up Your Ass* and, on meeting Warhol two years later on the street outside the **Factory**, 71 offered him her manuscript as a potential film project. Although he read it, he rejected it and apparently lost the manuscript. Demanding payment for the loss, Solanas was instead offered – and apparently enjoyed taking – roles in his 1967 films *Bikeboy* and *I, a Man*. In her extremist manifesto *SCUM* (Society for Cutting Up Men), Solanas advocated that women should 'overthrow the government, eliminate the money system, institute complete automation and eliminate the male sex'. Three days after the shooting she told local press, 'Read my manifesto and it will tell you what I am.'

Later diagnosed as a paranoid schizophrenic, Solanas claimed Warhol had 'too much control' over her life. After the shooting she gave herself up, was declared 'insane' and went to prison until 1971. For Warhol, **Pop fame** clearly had its risks. After her 
release, Solanas briefly stalked him and harassed him over the phone, causing Warhol to remain fearful of further attacks until his death in 1987.

OPPOSITE
Daily News front page, 4 June 1968

Neo-Pop, late 1960s–present

While initially an unashamed celebration of popular culture, towards the end of the 1960s and beyond, Pop Art became particularly critical of it. With the capacity of mainstream Pop to shock now diminishing and with new social and political movements emerging, 'Neo-Pop' came to represent the dissident 'outsider' attitudes of 1970s radical feminists, **drag queens** 90 and graffiti artists. Their angry and visceral approach to art, politics and the body – a kind of messy **Punk** 94 Pop – defined an era of extremes and stood in opposition to the parallel, coolly clinical Minimalist Art movement. Surviving an **assassination attempt** 82, and as if aware that Pop had finally peaked, at this time Andy Warhol began to consider his legacy. During the 1970s he 'wrote' his memoirs as well as his ***Philosophy*** 93 and created for posterity hundreds of cardboard time capsules filled with the everyday objects of his life.

In common with British novelist **J. G. Ballard** 89, the bard of postmodernism, American Pop collagist Martha Rosler and British Pop sculptor **Allen Jones** 85 each sought to highlight in their own ways the new violent and **pornographic** 87 convergence of domestic and public life. Around the same time emerged **Sots Art** 91 – a subversive Soviet Russian Pop – which clarified the ideological link between the iconographies of Western and Soviet cultures. By the end of the 1970s the New York City-based **Pictures Generation** 95, which included the photographer Cindy Sherman, was beginning to explore the construction of 'reality' and question its very nature.

With the unleashing of the free market during the 1980s, Neo-Pop artists **Jean-Michel Basquiat** 96 (the first black Pop artist), **Keith Haring** 97 and **Jeff Koons** 98 evolved radical and unique ways to make a lot of money. Soon embracing the new Digital Age, and building on Warhol's 1985 inauguration of digital art, in the late-1990s British Neo-Pop artist **Julian Opie** 99 created computer-generated portraits now synonymous with 'Cool Britannia'. Seeking to reject the influence of the art market, over the last few decades the most influential inheritor of the Punk Pop analogue tradition is perhaps British graffiti artist **Banksy** 100 – who has infused Pop's afterlife with humour, compassion and a social conscience.

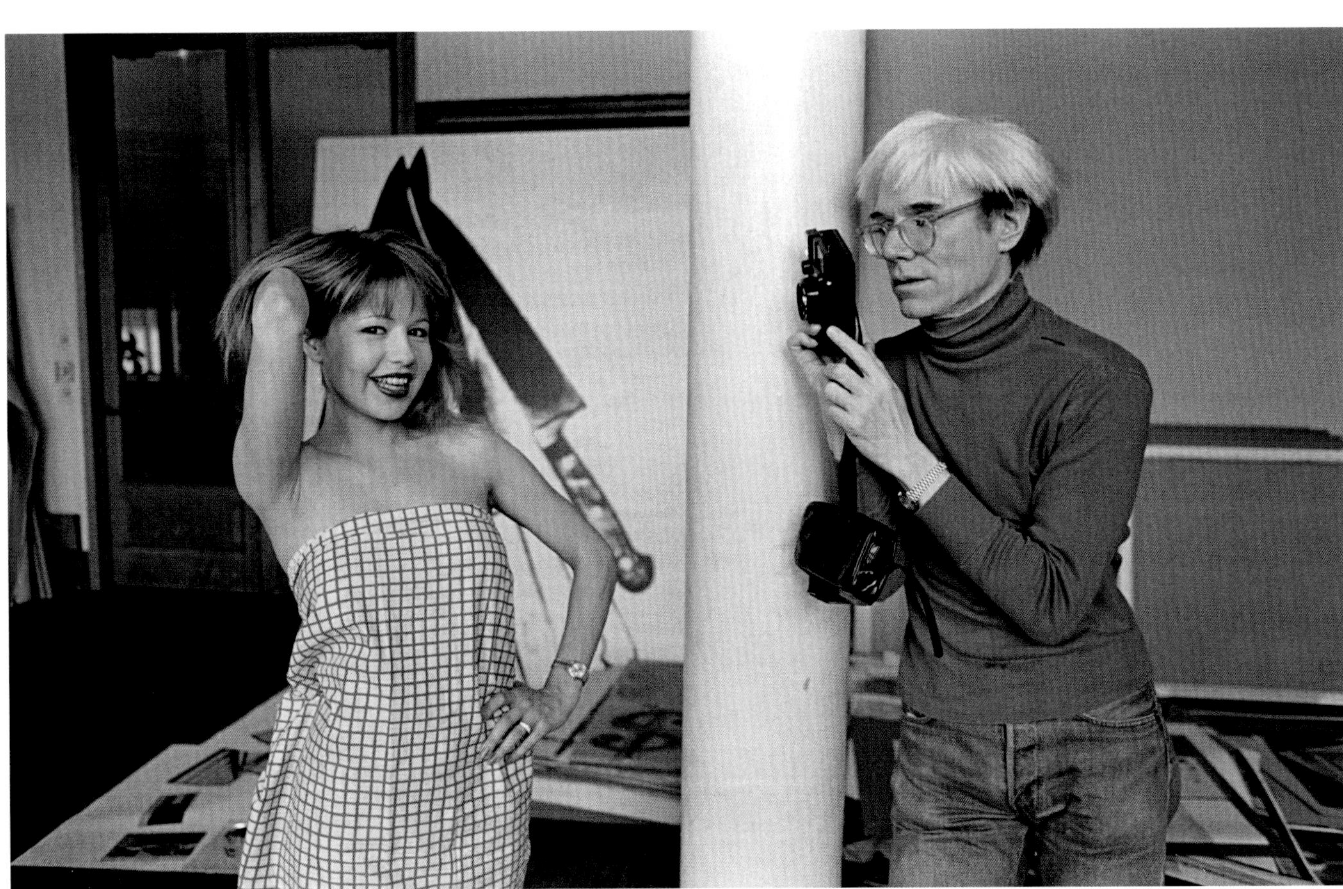

83

‘In the future, everyone will be world-famous for 15 minutes’

As Hollywood yielded to the influence
25 of popular **television** and the
conventional camera began to look
dowdy alongside the fashionably
19 disposable **Polaroid**, Andy Warhol
predicted the democratic spread of glamour, fame and notoriety. For him, the postmodern future wasn’t just bright, it was starlit – full of celebrities, as everyone and everything began to assimilate and standardize under the influence of widening mass media and spreading consumer affluence. ‘New categories of people are now being put up there as stars’, even ‘crooks’, he claimed. In the future we would all both watch and be watched. Iconic status – if enjoyed for only 15 minutes – would be the new Pop normal.

Warhol’s most famous quote can be traced to Swedish curator Pontus Hulten’s book, written to accompany the February opening of Warhol’s 1968 solo exhibition in Stockholm. In response to claims that Warhol never said it, Hulten plausibly countered ‘If he didn’t say it, he could very well have said it.’ By 1968, Pop plausibility had replaced incontrovertible fact. Warhol’s public persona was by then so well established that his attitude, style and speech pattern were familiar enough to allow for the possibility of mimicry and satire.

Revelling in what art critic Arthur C. Danto described as ‘his own fantasy of being a celebrity in a world of celebrities’, Warhol not only reflected the culture of popular stardom but also embodied it. A prolific self-portraitist, during the 1980s he embraced new digital technology and hosted the MTV series *Andy Warhol’s 15 Minutes*, defining and anticipating selfie culture, sensationalized reality TV and the cult of hyper-celebrity. Television was, he declared, ‘the new everything’, although, with some humorous irony, he wanted one of his early TV shows to be called ‘Nothing Special’. Fame, Warhol suggests – both glamorous and, as he discovered, life-threatening – is everything and nothing all at once.

OPPOSITE
Andy Warhol photographing actress and singer Pia Zadora
1983

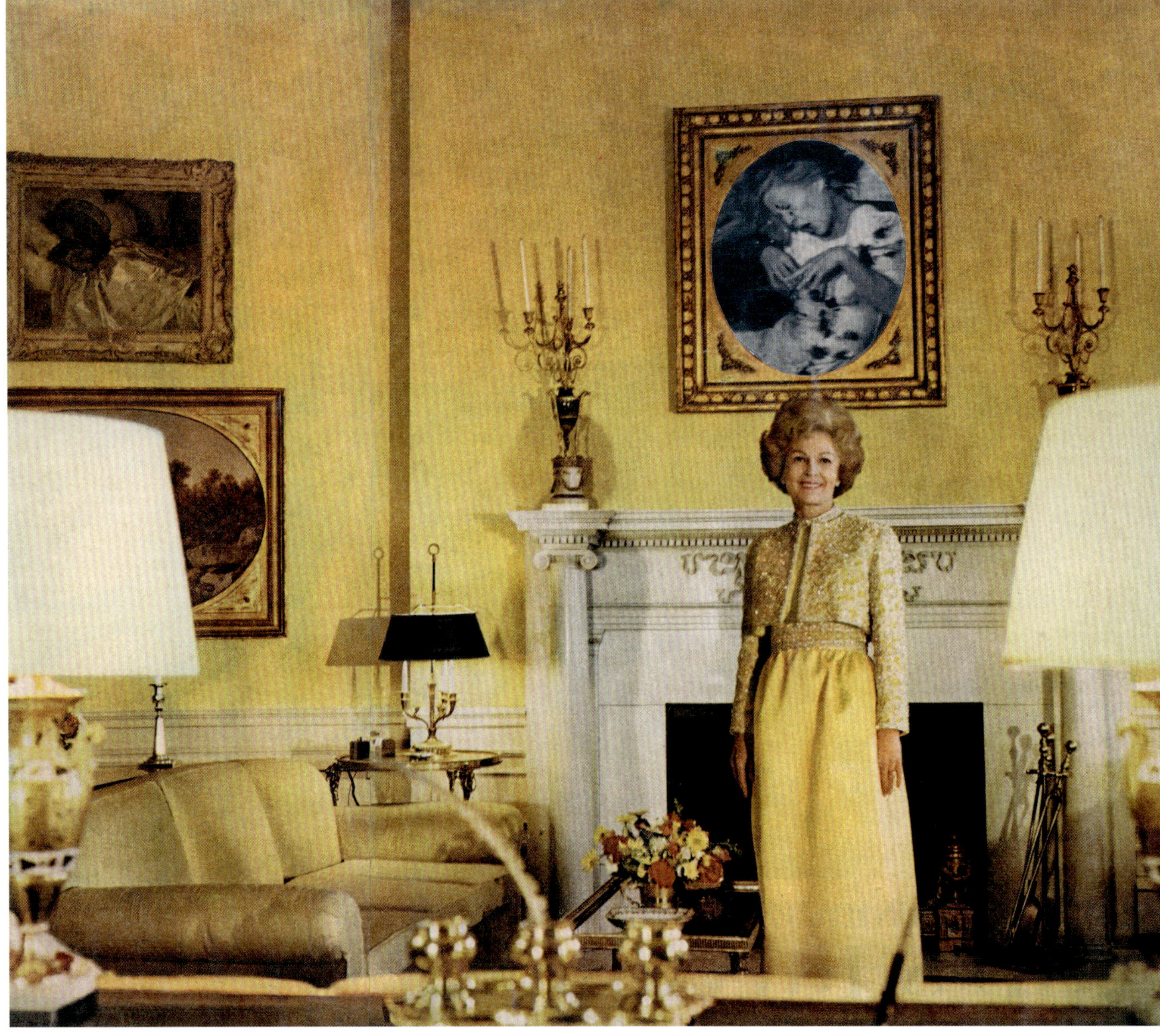

84

First Lady (Pat Nixon)

Martha Rosler

1967–72

Borrowing images from *Life* magazine, American Pop artist Martha Rosler
2 produced the disturbing **photomontage** *First Lady (Pat Nixon)*, showing the wife of the newly inaugurated President in an official photograph. Here we see Mrs Nixon standing gracefully in a gold-themed White House drawing room, with what is apparently a photograph of a dying woman hanging above the mantelpiece. The image in fact is that of the actress Faye Dunaway in the gangster film *Bonnie and Clyde* (1967), which was highly influential for young people, as it represented the federal government relentlessly pursuing and killing those who rebelled against it. For Rosler, the image represented the texture of life in late 1960s America, described by critic Seymour Krim as a 'bad pot-dream, paranoid and cruelly absurd', in which modern art reflected 'our squawking American nightmare'. A clear indictment of the Vietnam War, this work remains one of the most arresting examples of Pop Art.

Part of Rosler's satirical series *House Beautiful: Bringing the War Home* – produced from approximately 1967, when American public support for the Vietnam War was flagging, through 1972, when Nixon signed the Paris Peace Accords that signalled the end of American involvement – *First Lady* was the culmination of an extensive investigation into the possibilities of collage and photomontage. Inspired by the transgressive work of Max Ernst, the San Francisco artist Jess, and John Heartfield, and produced in the form of flyers to advertise political marches, Rosler's Pop collages focused critical
attention on American **wars** and the 51
lives of American women. By 1967, American women were organizing and protesting vocally against the oppressions they faced. International wars were, for Rosler, inextricably intertwined with everyday domestic conflicts of power and subjugation. Visual shock tactics, she felt, would draw attention to the blindnesses of modern society. By cutting and pasting mass-media images of organized violence alongside those of aspirational lifestyles, Rosler sought to bring out the disparity between the idealized lives depicted by the media and the brutal conflict in faraway Vietnam those portrayals simply ignored. Her work brought the horrors of war into the American home, revolutionizing Pop Art in the process.

OPPOSITE
Martha Rosler
First Lady (Pat Nixon),
1967–72
COLLAGE

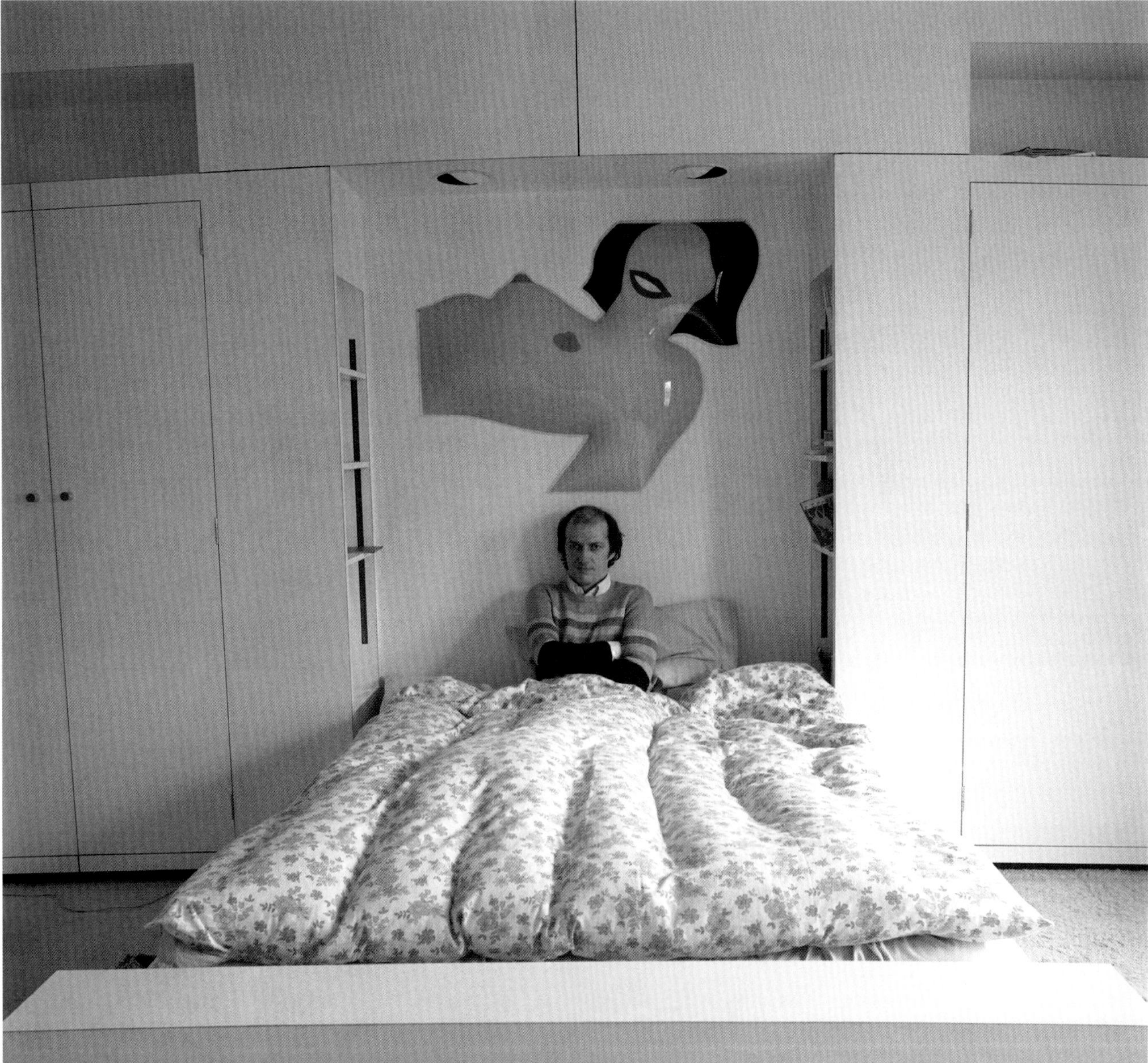

05

Allen Jones

In 1969, British Pop artist Allen Jones, a contemporary of David Hockney and Derek Boshier at the Royal College of Art in London – at least in his first year, before he was expelled – produced, at a cost of nearly £5,000, three provocative pieces of 'adult comic strip' sculpture. *Hatstand*, *Table* and *Chair* were each moulded in fibreglass by the shop mannequin firm Gems Wax Models Ltd and partially clad in black leather. Now infamous, these 'forniphilic' sculptures inspired director Stanley Kubrick's 'women tables' in his 1971 dystopian film, *A Clockwork Orange*.

Jones's work was, in part, motivated by what he described as the new 'sexual charge' of post-Pill Swinging London. Jones sought, as he says, 'to try to represent the figure free of fine art associations so that the viewer would have to confront figurative sculpture on their own terms.' The popular modern-day nude led him, perhaps inevitably, to
87 commercial **pornography**. Reflecting the misogyny of mainstream porn, his work depicts in a very direct way the sexualized slavery of women. Emerging, Jones says, 'from the same social milieu that produced the militant voice of feminism', the feminist critic Laura Mulvey nevertheless felt that Jones's sculptures expressed 'a strange male underworld of fear and desire'. These uncomfortable 'psychological constructions' underscore the fact that sex can be a form of power, sexualization a mode and technique of suppression. Jones's partially clad sculptures of exploited women are only one step away from the
American nudes of **Tom Wesselmann** 30
and Mel Ramos, who advertise the female body as another consumable Pop product. Jones, however, takes this notion to its extreme and highlights how that fetishization of the female form obscures the dignity – and reality – of women.

Surprisingly well received when it was exhibited in 1970 at London's Arthur Tooth & Sons Gallery in Mayfair, it took sixteen years for *Chair* to become the focus of serious controversy. Whilst on display at London's Tate Gallery in 1986, on International Women's Day that year *Chair* was attacked with paint stripper by angry protesters. Jones's work retains its power to polarize opinion and provides an example of the confusions often inherent in Pop irony.

OPPOSITE
Allen Jones, 1969. Above him hangs Tom Wesselmann's *Great American Nude #74*, 1965 (painted, moulded plastic)

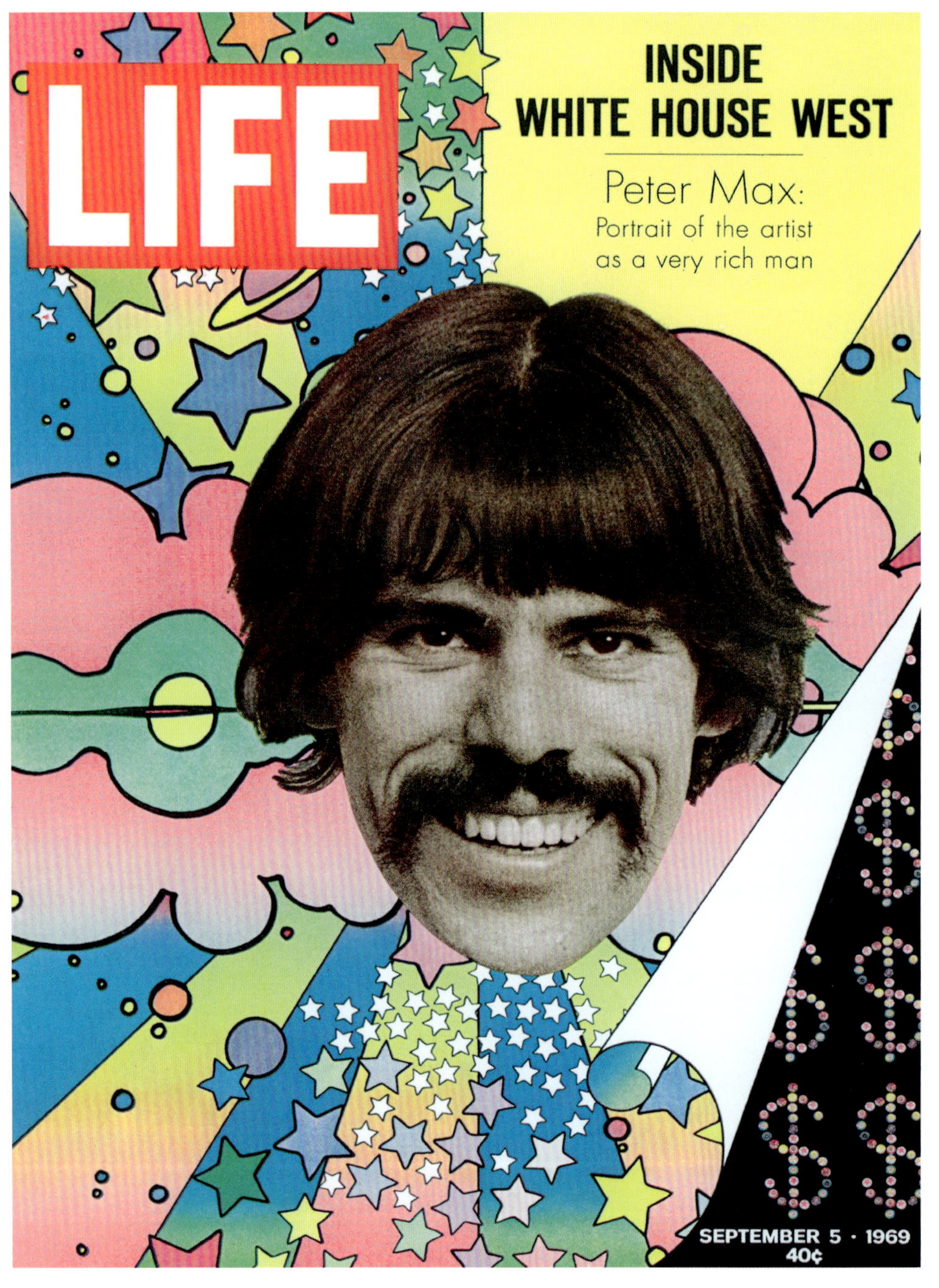
LIFE
INSIDE
WHITE HOUSE WEST
Peter Max:
Portrait of the artist
as a very rich man
SEPTEMBER 5 · 1969
40¢

86

Peter Max

High priest of Psychedelic Pop, artist Peter Max – with his pudding-bowl haircut and handlebar moustache – graced the front cover of the September 1969 edition of *Life* magazine with the James Joyce-inspired tagline 'Portrait of the artist as a very rich man'. Promoting his highly colourful and fantastical Pop posters to the younger hippy generation and inspired by Andy
74 Warhol's **'art as business'** mantra, Max had recently taken the decision to brand and license his own work. Although at the time licensing work was unusual – particularly for a young artist – it certainly paid off: Max made an extraordinary $2 million in 1970 alone.

Defining the iconography of the 1960s counterculture, Max's 'cosmic Pop' posters captured what he called the 'visual mood' of the decade. Inevitably inspired by commercial graphics, his new approach towards Pop design was also influenced by Art Nouveau and even, unexpectedly, astronomy. The *Life* cover bursts with colourful clouds and smoke, rays of sunshine and multiple stars (on a lifting page corner that revealed his bejewelled dollar sign designs beneath).

Born in Berlin in 1937 to Jewish parents who subsequently fled the country, Max spent the first decade of his life in Shanghai, China. He later studied in New York, where **Marilyn** 45
Monroe once recognized him on the street and complimented him on his work. Acidic colours and dreamy, psychedelic shapes suddenly became hip among young people, and, as he said, 'I gave them what they wanted.' His most famous series of images, inspired by the Statue of Liberty, was loved and collected by US president Ronald Reagan. Comfortable with big business, Max went on to produce a diverse set of Pop commissions – not
just for presidents, but for **car** and 7
aircraft manufacturing companies too – and would appear on the front covers of *Newsweek* and *Time*.

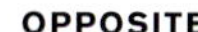

OPPOSITE
Peter Max
Life magazine cover, 5 September 1969

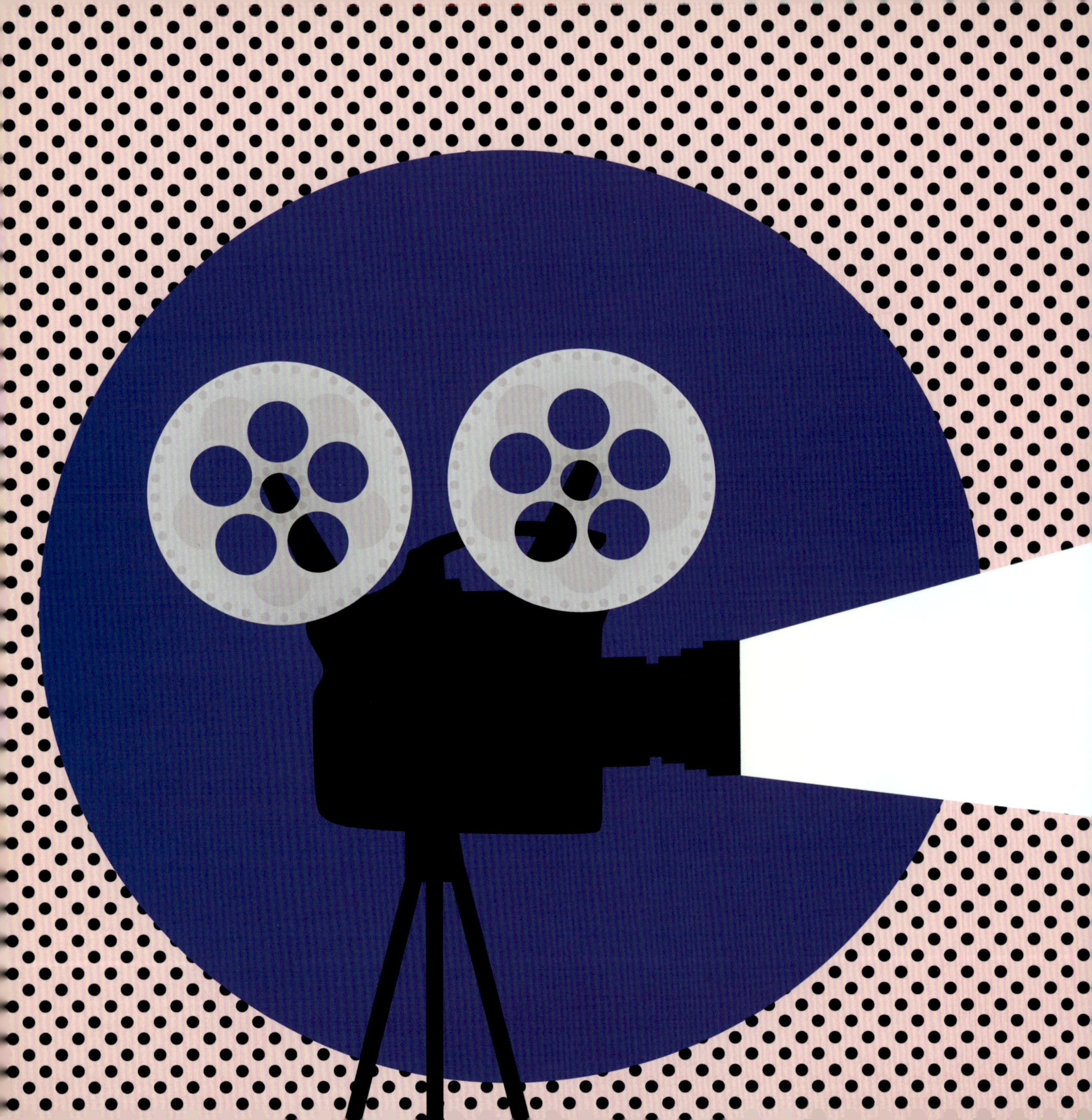

87

Pornography

During the 1960s, Andy Warhol became Pop Art's pornographer-in-chief, his most famous and explicit Pop porno being *Blue Movie*, which premiered in June 1969. Otherwise known by its working title, 'Fuck', it was billed as 'a film about the Vietnam War and what we can do about it' and featured cover girl Viva and actor Louis Waldon advocating, through demonstration, the making of love not war.

Warhol's previous sex-themed movies were genuinely thought-provoking experiments in film-making. *Blow Job* (1964), for example, consisting entirely of facial-reaction shots of actor DeVeren Bookwalter enjoying off-screen fellatio, branded celluloid history with everyday images that had, however, never been seen on film in quite this way before. Similarly, *Flesh* (1968), concerning a male prostitute played by pin-up model Joe Dallesandro, focused on the lead male's body in ways that heterosexual male directors never had. *Blue Movie*, however, was a meditation on sex between men and women with reference made to the Vietnam War. Featuring deliberately everyday dialogue alongside 'real' and explicit sex, it was an ingenious representation of its cultural moment that captured the mood of the changing times. And yet, perhaps predictably, *Blue Movie* was seized by the police for violating obscenity laws only a month after its release. Warhol's 1971 play *Pork* went even further in challenging the boundaries of public taste by discussing other, objectively rather mundane things including defecation and excrement.

Described as 'indigenously American' by *New York Times* critic Vincent Canby, Warhol's films are at once confusing, disturbing, arousing, monotonous and dull. They launched a golden age of porn and prefigured what, in 1973, another *New York Times* critic Ralph Blumenthal called 'porno chic'. For Warhol, however, sex wasn't real and loving, joyful and involved; it was a repetitive, adolescent, voyeuristic fantasy with masturbatory highs and sensational lows. 'Sex is nostalgia for sex,' he claimed. *Flesh* concludes with a threesome in which Dallesandro's disengaged character falls asleep. Reality, according to Warhol, is less attractive than fantasies of perfect bodies and ecstatic sex. In this way, his films weren't really about sex at all, but simply pointed to our collective inability – or unwillingness – to face reality.

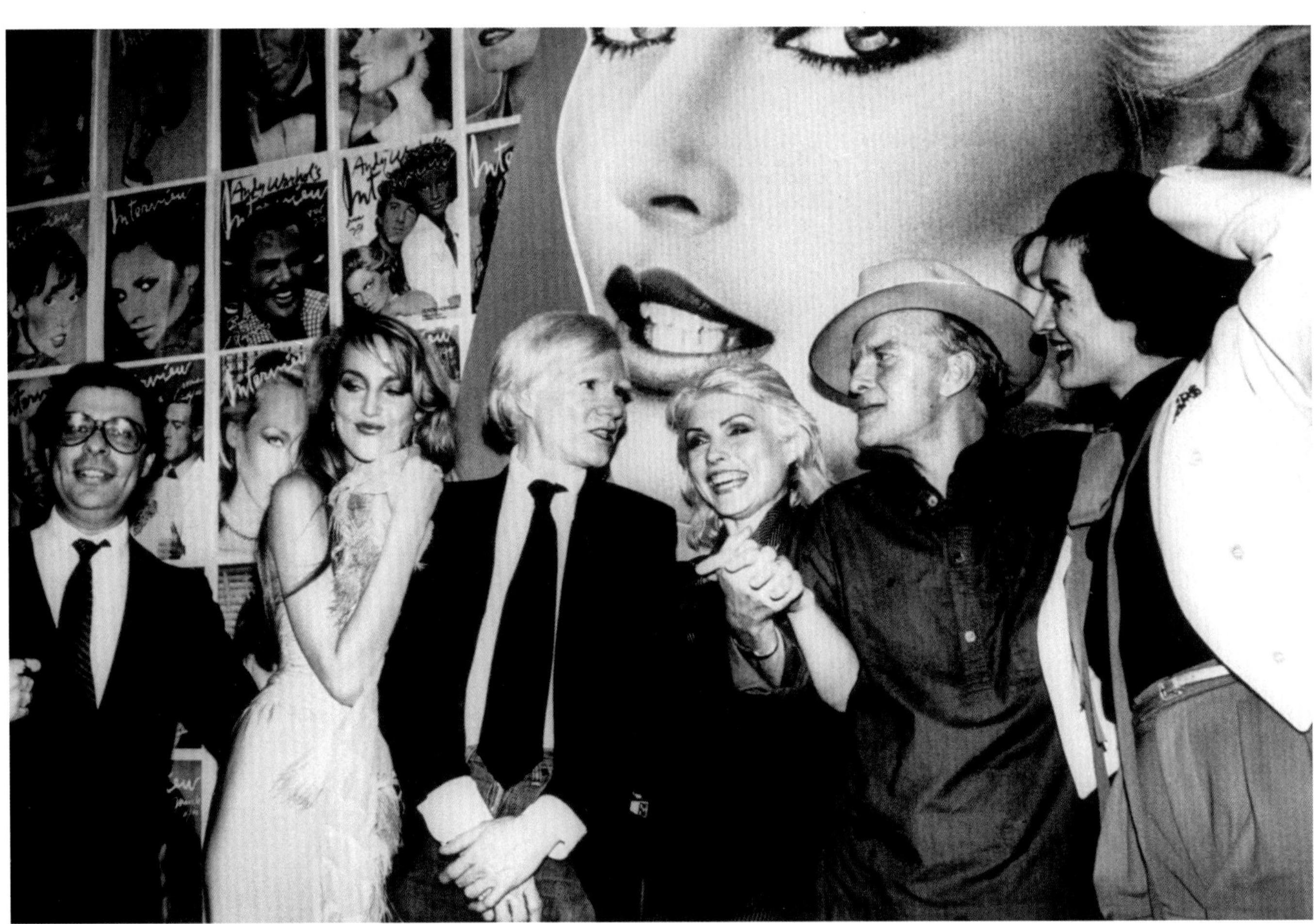

88

Interview magazine

Published in 1969, the inaugural edition of Andy Warhol's *Interview* magazine – billed as a film journal – featured on its front cover a controversial black-and-white production shot from French director Agnès Varda's seminal movie of the same year, *Lions Love (...and Lies)*. Topless Warhol superstar Viva is glimpsed between the two long-haired authors of the 1960s rock musical *Hair*, James Rado and Gerome Ragni, in a self-conscious depiction of bohemian Hollywood life. In *Lions Love (...and Lies)*, the three played out a colourful Warholian Pop dream of scripted reality, sunny sexuality,
25 hard partying, blaring **televisions**
and endless telephone calls. With characteristic irony, both reflecting and commodifying the voice of the hippy generation, Warhol's *Interview*
74 turned this lifestyle into **business** and
eventually succeeded in taking Pop attitudes mainstream.

Starting with a niche following, *Interview* had become a mainstream purveyor of popular celebrity culture within a decade. Although synonymous with Warhol himself, the magazine was in fact co-founded by British journalist John Wilcock, a
regular at the **Factory**, who in 1971 71
published *The Autobiography and Sex Life of Andy Warhol*. For over 15 years, American Pop artist Richard Bernstein created cover designs and celebrity portraits for *Interview*, many of which are now considered works of art in their own right. By the late 1970s, *Interview* had featured on its front cover some of the most fashionable denizens of that period's clubland Valhalla, Studio 54: Diana Ross, Cher, Grace Jones, Jerry Hall and Diane von Furstenberg.

Interview was, in fact, the key vehicle for widening the reach of the Pop Art aesthetic and became an example of
what the author **J. G. Ballard** called 89
'transformational grammar'. If Pop Art began by reordering and transgressing the offerings of the established print media, *Interview* – folded back into, and arguably shaping, the mainstream – marked the end of Pop Art itself.

OPPOSITE
From left, Bob Colacello, Jerry Hall, Andy Warhol, Debbie Harry, Truman Capote and Paloma Picasso at a Studio 54 party for *Interview* magazine, 1978

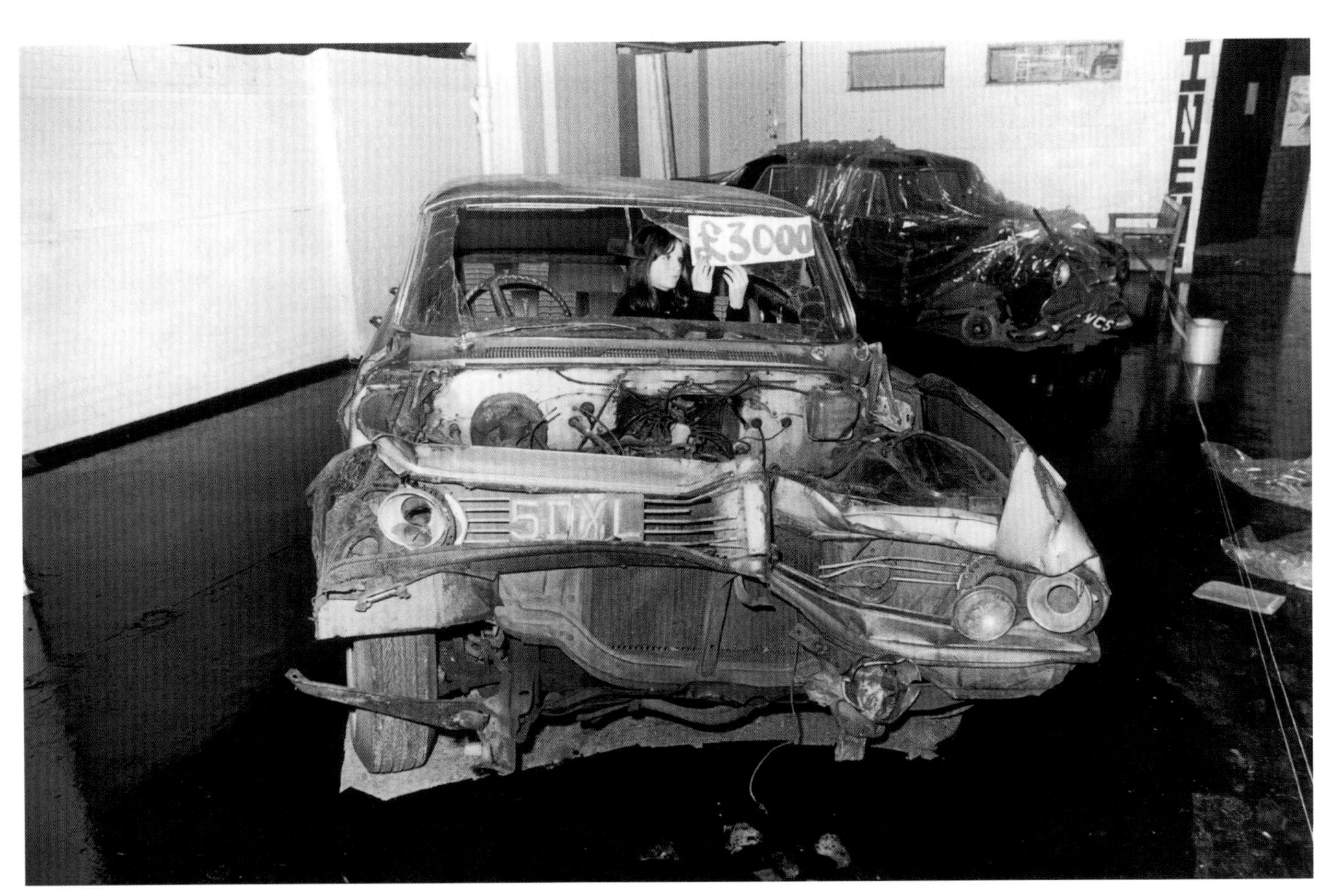
£3000

89

J. G. Ballard and *The Atrocity Exhibition*

1970

Published in 1970 by British writer J. G. Ballard, the bard of postmodernism, *The Atrocity Exhibition* – a zeitgeisty collection of 'condensed novels' – concerned what Ballard called the 'hidden logic' of the 1960s. A fulcrum of Pop Art and contemporary literature, *The Atrocity Exhibition* is a literary collage that intentionally reads like a translation of Pop Art's visual techniques.

A friend of British Pop artists Eduardo Paolozzi and Richard Hamilton, Ballard was a fascinated
6 admirer of the 1950s **Independent Group**. *The Atrocity Exhibition* focuses not just on Pop celebrities
45 (**Marilyn Monroe**, Elizabeth Taylor, the Kennedys and Ronald Reagan) but emphasizes Pop
7 themes and motifs (**cars**,
14 **plastic surgery**, assassination,
51 87 **war** and **pornography**). Describing the *Atrocity* stories as a 'media maze', Ballard highlighted the 'banalisation of
83 **celebrity**'. Reiterating the collective loss of 'reality', Ballard defined the 'unique vocabulary and grammar of late 20th century life'; an addictively confusing (tele)visual simulation or 'waking dream'.

As academic Roger Luckhurst has pointed out, Ballard and his contemporary Andy Warhol were both fascinated by what French philosopher Guy Debord famously called in 1967 the 'society of the spectacle'. Charting our responses to the modern 'technological landscape', the same year Ballard published *The Atrocity Exhibition* he curated a controversial exhibition of crashed cars at the New Arts Laboratory gallery behind London's Euston Station. Three years later he published his controversial novel *Crash*. Thanks to 'the machine dream' of the mass media – that 'unique collision of private and public fantasy' that haunts the 'hyper-
stimulated' **TV** viewer – Ballard saw 25
that even 'sex has become a communal and public activity'. In common with several Pop artists, Ballard felt that even violence and cruelty had become attractively packaged like an 'insidious form of pornography' integral to the commercial world. Since
the **assassination of JFK**, television 59
had become 'an endless background of frightening and challenging images'. For Ballard, modern life was a cacophony of voyeuristic 'emergency scenarios' that induce disorientation, anxiety and neurosis.

OPPOSITE
A wrecked American Pontiac, an exhibit at *The Atrocity Exhibition*, 1970

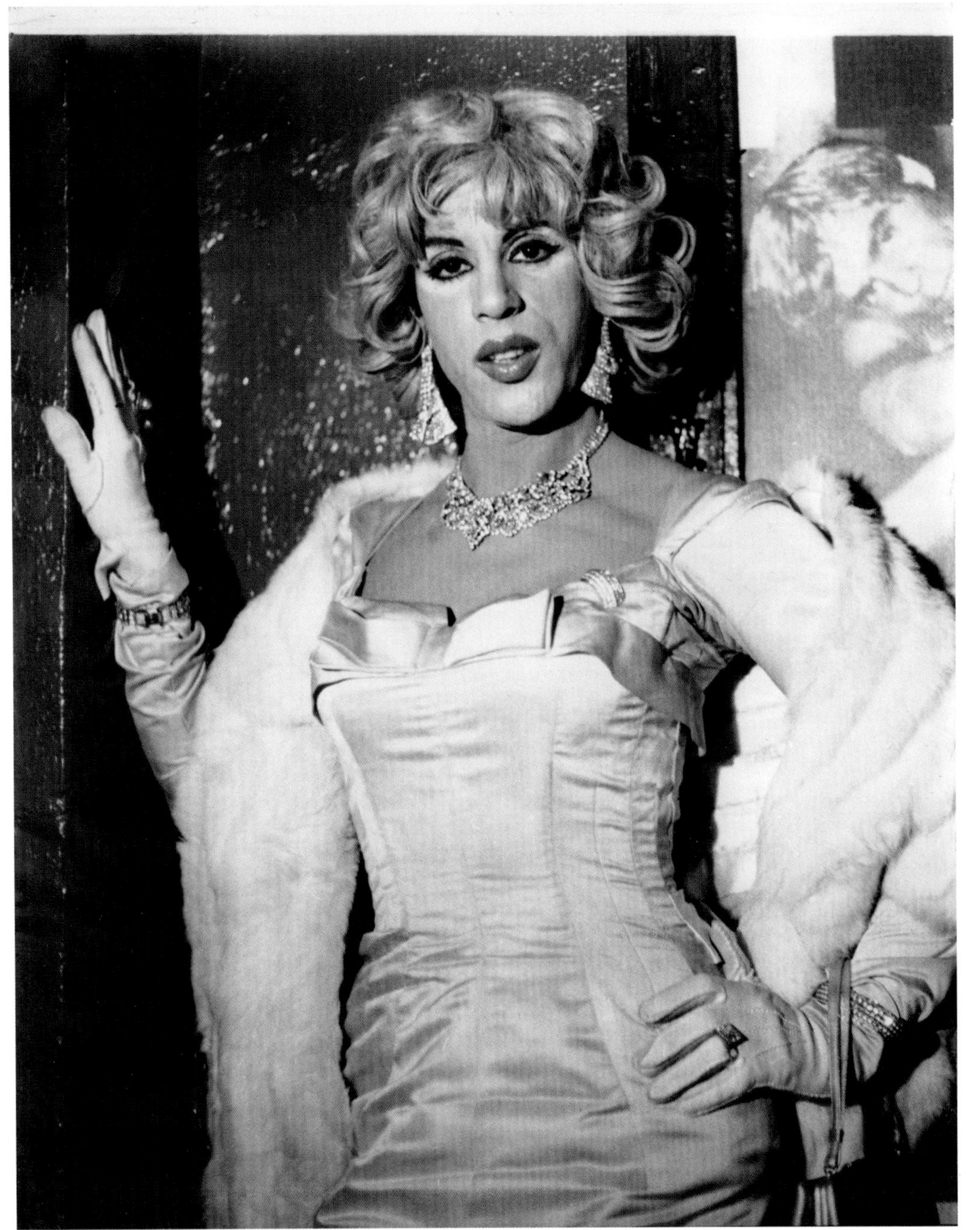

90

Drag

Drag – like Pop Art itself – is a playful imitation of fantasy. Like
65 **Susan Sontag's** notion of life as 'Playing-a-Role', drag challenges the status quo by critiquing the collectively fantasized fictions of gender and
1 convention. **Marcel Duchamp** and Andy Warhol enjoyed using their bodies as radical works of art in order to explore modern ideals of beauty, gender, sex, wealth and celebrity.

Having bestowed a moustache on Leonardo da Vinci's *Mona Lisa* in his 1919 work *L.H.O.O.Q.*, the following year Duchamp bravely began dragging up as his female alter ego Rrose Sélavy (a play on the French phrase 'Eros, c'est la vie'). The elaborately camp Madame Sélavy, an impoverished, aristocratic Russian émigré, soon became Duchamp's artistic alter ego. Immortalized in a deliberately diverse series of black-and-white photographs by Man Ray, she was even depicted as a 'wanted' criminal in Duchamp's 1923 lithograph *Wanted: $2,000 Reward*.

Forty years later, white-blond wigs, sunglasses, everyday make-up and a disengaged voice had become integral to Andrew Warhola's iconic performance as the Pop artist Andy Warhol. Throughout the 1960s and 1970s, he also photographed or filmed himself and his male friends dragging up as women. He described drag queens as fantastical 'ambulatory archives of ideal movie star womanhood', superhuman creations who devoted their lives and endless hours of hard work to looking 'the complete opposite'.
One of his **Polaroid** muses was 19
African-American activist and self-styled 'street queen' Marsha P. Johnson, heroic leader of the 1969 Stonewall Riots. As a film-maker – choosing drag queen Mario Montez to star in *Harlot*, *Camp* and *Chelsea Girls* and transgender performers Candy Darling and Holly Woodlawn to star in *Flesh* and *Trash* respectively –
Warhol turned the **Factory** into his 71
own, countercultural, Pop version of the Hollywood studio system.

OPPOSITE
[illegible]

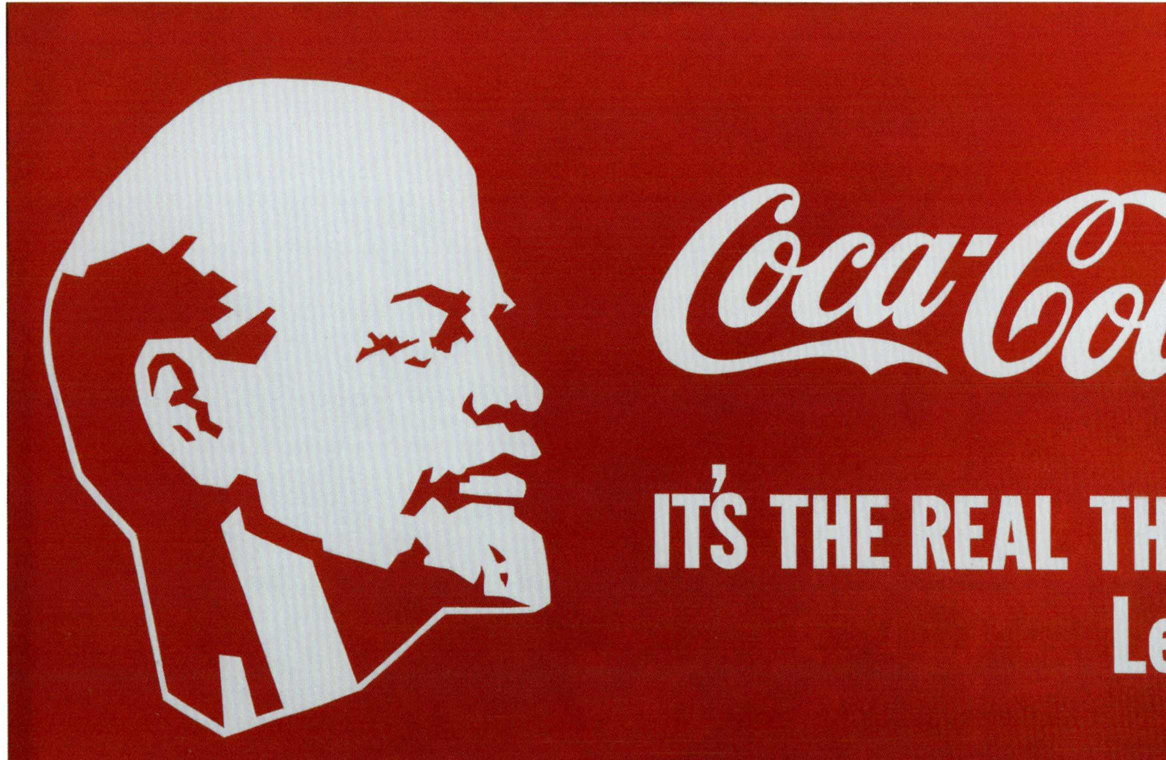
Coca-Cola
IT'S THE REAL THING
Lenin

91

Sots Art

During the winter of 1972, hybridizing the iconographies of Western Pop, or Capitalist Realism, and Soviet Socialist Realism, radical Moscow-born artists Vitaly Komar and Alexander Melamid challenged the prescriptive Soviet style of art to develop the ironic Sots Art – short for Socialist Art and later known as Soviet Pop Art. Just as, in the 1970s, Andy Warhol played with communist emblems and the famous image of Chairman Mao, so Sots artists experimented with the iconographies of capitalist America, which was perceived, in Moscow at least, as an attack on Soviet ideology.

Key figures in Moscow's underground avant-garde, Komar and Melamid hosted illegal 'apartment exhibitions' throughout the 1970s. At one of
19 their **'happenings'** in 1974 they performed the parts of Stalin and Lenin and encouraged their audience to create a canvas that represented the 'heroic labours' of the working class, appropriating and transforming mainstream Soviet Realism in a manner similar to that in which Pop artists had worked with capitalist iconography. When the Soviet police appeared, arrested everyone and interrogated them all night, some assumed – initially at least – that it was just part of the performance.

After his defection to New York in the late 1970s, Komar compared – in an echo of philosopher Herbert Marcuse – the 'consumerist propaganda' of the West with the 'ideological propaganda' of the Soviet Union; Pop Art and Sots Art both erupted out of what Komar described as an 'overproduction' of both kinds of propaganda. Just as Pop artists in the West recognized the mythic status of **Mickey Mouse** and **Marilyn Monroe**, 17 45
Sots artists focussed on fetishized and endlessly reproduced images of Soviet leaders Lenin and Stalin. Whether real or invented, iconic Pop figures – even ideologies themselves – became mythologised, standardized and, as it were, flattened out in parallel visual cultures. Sots Art inaugurated a playful and irreverent cross-cultural Pop equivalencing of both Western and Soviet iconography.

OPPOSITE
Alexander Kosolapov
Lenin and Coca-Cola, 1982
Paint on canvas

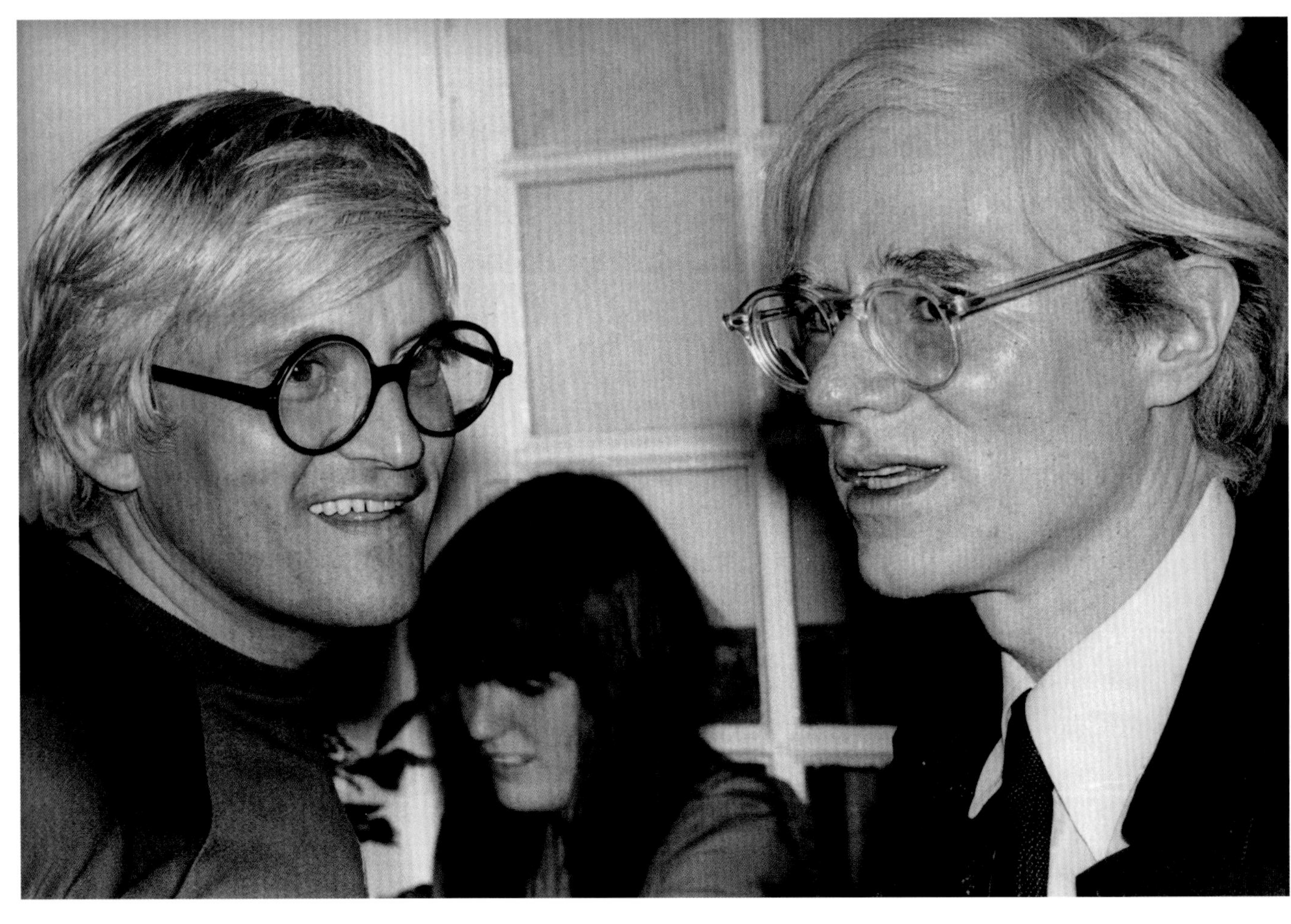

92

David Hockney and Andy Warhol draw each other

1974

Andy Warhol and David Hockney, two of the most famous and recognizable faces in Pop Art, enjoyed a transatlantic friendship and rivalry for over twenty years. The famously guarded New Yorker and the gregarious Brit were separated in age by nearly a decade, but they had much in common – both, for example, as much Pop performers as artists and photographers. The drawings that they made of each other stand out as significant markers of their mutual affection.

While living in Paris in 1974, Hockney received a visit from Warhol and after catching up they decided to draw one another. With a touch of colour, Hockney depicted Warhol as lithe, anxious, forbidding almost – perhaps jetlagged – in a drawing that contrasts with a series of confident photographs of a trench coat-clad Warhol taken on this same trip to Paris by the fashion photographer Helmut Newton. With a simple and assured monochromatic line, Warhol depicted Hockney as thoughtful, with piercing eyes and a coquettish demeanour, in a sitting that inspired a series of Warhol **Polaroids** 19 and a painted diptych. Together, these distinctive pencil sketches provide relatively unguarded glimpses into the lives of two Pop giants.

The pair first met in December 1963, when Hockney – newly arrived in New York from London and en route to **Los Angeles**  for what would prove a four-year sojourn – was taken to the **Factory**  by mutual friend Jeff Goodman. On arrival, Hockney and Goodman found themselves interrupting Warhol and his friend **Henry Geldzahler**,  who was then at the Metropolitan Museum of Art, in conversation with the Hollywood actor Dennis Hopper and his partner Brooke Hayward. The group got along famously, Hopper photographing the four men outside a bar smoking cigars and cigarettes. In later life, and in the period leading up to his death in 1987, Warhol would often spend the day with Hockney in New York, describing his British friend as 'magic'.

OPPOSITE
David Hockney and Andy Warhol, 1970

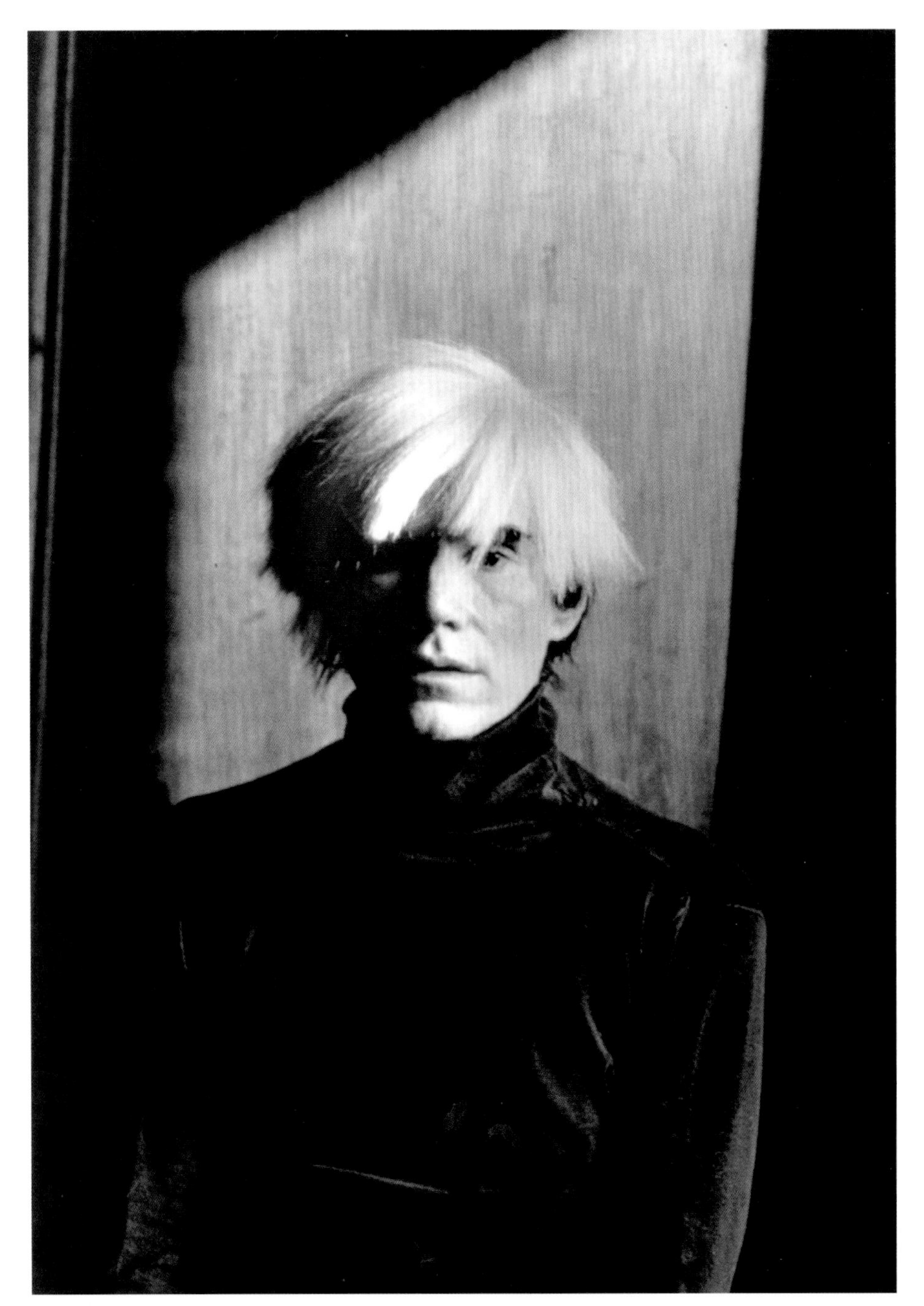

93

The Philosophy of Andy Warhol

1975

Described by *Time* magazine in 1968 as 'the blond guru of a nightmare world', by 1975 Andy Warhol – the self-proclaimed 'deeply superficial person' – had published *The Philosophy of Andy Warhol*. Ever a self-promoter, in September that year Warhol undertook an extensive book tour, much anticipated by the press, around the United States and Europe. It became, like everything he did, a Pop
16 **'happening'**. The Oscar Wilde of the
65 1970s, he embodied what critic **Susan Sontag** called the postmodern 'dandy'.

Enhancing his reputation as the ultimate Pop prophet of postmodernity, the famously aloof Warhol 'wrote' a book of which he wasn't even, strictly speaking, the author. With deliberate and self-conscious irony, Warhol's *Philosophy* was actually a ghostwritten compendium of 'quotable quotes', drawn from taped conversations with his longtime collaborator Pat Hackett
88 and ***Interview* magazine** editor Bob Colacello (or 'Bob Cola', as Warhol preferred to call him). According to Colacello, Warhol's mischievous literary motto was 'Just make it up.'

Despite playing with conventional notions of authorship, Warhol's book has become something of a Pop bible. In a sense, it isn't a book at all – it's another Pop performance. Aside from the desire to make money, after
the **attempt on his life** seven years [illegible]
earlier he also wanted to control his paper legacy, defining his era and the Pop movement he had developed. His 'quotes' are fun, witty, shocking and often very wise. Divided into 15 thematic chapters, with titles such as 'Love', 'Fame', 'Beauty', 'Art' and 'Success', the book's philosophy is sometimes deliberately incoherent, disrupting received notions of intimate confession and rigorous philosophy. Preferring 'low lights and trick mirrors', Warhol mixes up fake information with real misinformation in a way that feels both very Pop and, presciently, very now. It was the 19th-century French poet Charles Baudelaire who famously described the modern artist as an 'observer, philosopher, flâneur'. Warhol cultivated the dandified persona of the (high-minded) observer alongside that of the (seedy) voyeur, all at the same time.

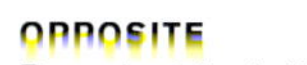

OPPOSITE
Portrait of Andy Warhol

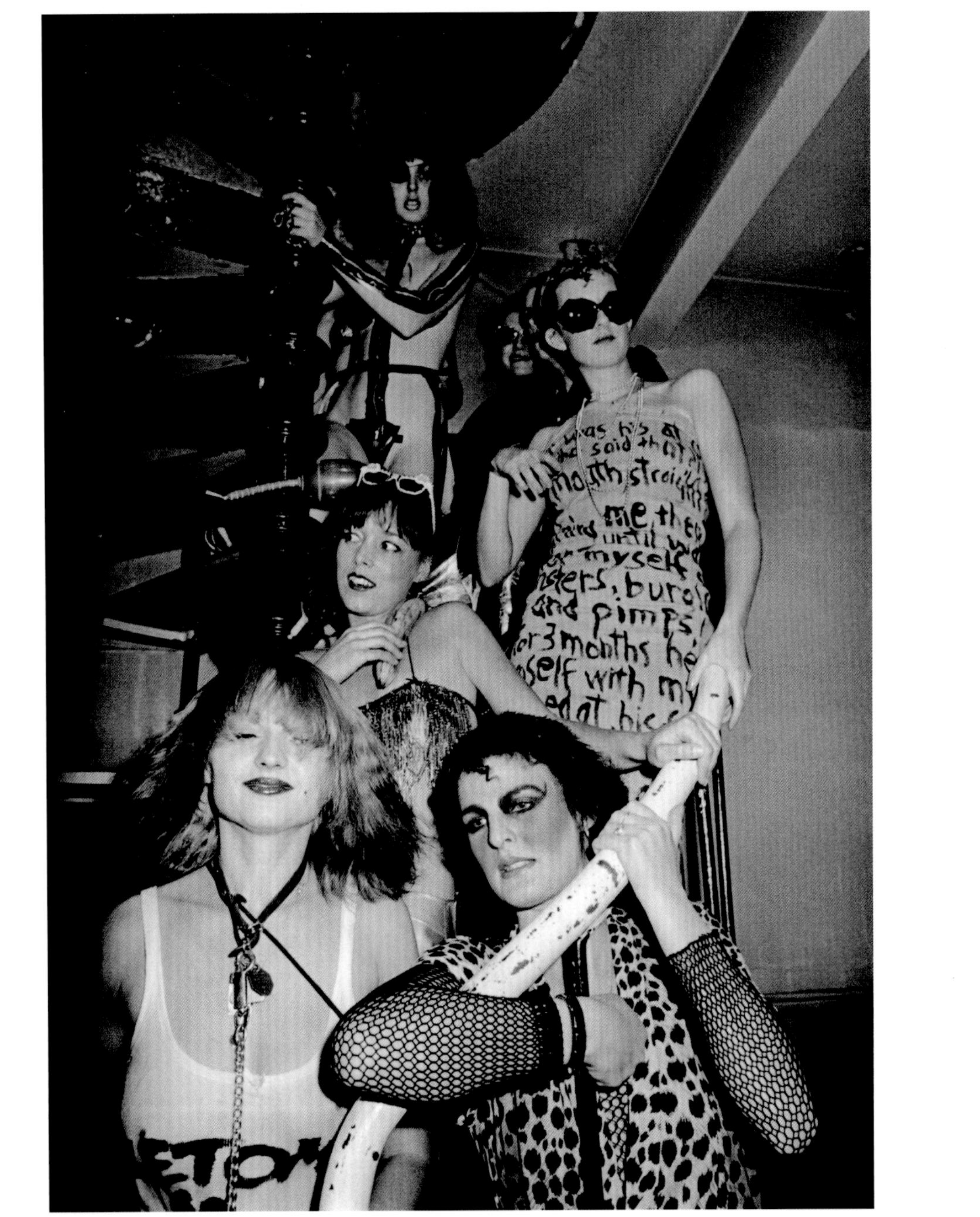

said
me
myself
and pimps!
3 months
with my

94

Punk

Once shorthand for someone young, inexperienced or marginal, by the late 1970s the word 'Punk' described an urgent new form of popular expression in fashion and the arts. Within a decade of the hopeful excesses of the late 1960s, Punk had become the avant-garde attitude of choice for many young people in cities (and suburbs) around the Western world. Youthful and anarchic, Punks responded provocatively to the global social and economic crises of the period, and – primarily in fashion and music – utilized both the motifs and the techniques of Pop Art to develop a form of Punk Pop.

Developing Pop's inherent irony and irreverence into an angry extreme, Punk was a 'fuck you' to an established culture in decline; an anti-art that returned the avant-garde to its Dada roots. But Punk's visceral and confrontational power, perhaps unexpectedly, finds precedents in Andy Warhol's oeuvre: for example, his album designs for the Velvet Underground, which heavily influenced the outrageous visual style of Punk graphics, and his *Piss Painting* series, begun as early as 1976, which features primed canvases stained with urine and foreshadows the provocative content of Punk expression. Some of these canvases were primed with a metallic base that, post-urination, produced seductively beautiful abstract images. The following year Warhol began work on the *Shadow* series of paintings, all featuring erect penises that were both representational and abstract at the same time. Punk Pop attitudes to bodily fluids and the phallus were more fully explored in outrageously provocative British Punk artist Cosey Fanni Tutti's 1976 exhibition *Prostitution* at London's Institute of Contemporary Arts, considered overwhelmingly controversial at the time.

Punk's legacy of anarchic individualism and shock tactics would prove influential in forming the artistic attitudes and public personas of high-profile artists during the 1980s and 1990s.

OPPOSITE
Punks, 1976

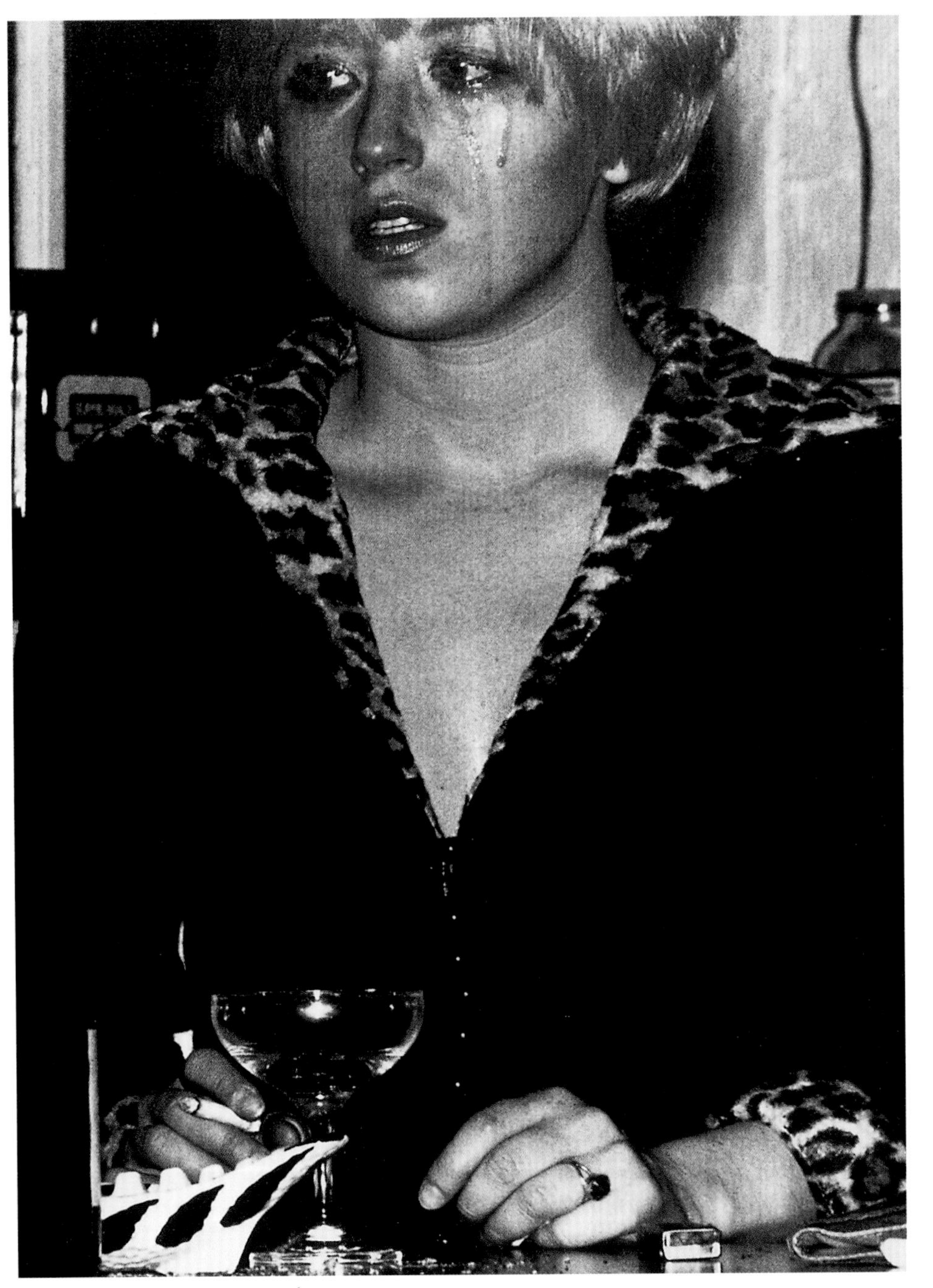

9.5

The Pictures Generation

Postmodern and Neo-Pop, the Pictures Generation was a loosely defined group of nearly thirty American artists and photographers – including Cindy Sherman, Sherrie Levine, Robert Longo and Troy Brauntuch – who used the techniques of advertising to critique popular culture. So called in part because of their return to figurative and representational forms, they were concerned with the slippery and unstable nature of reality as constructed by modern-day media. Such issues would soon be further developed in the work of the French postmodernist philosopher Jean Baudrillard and his seminal 1981 treatise *Simulacra and Simulation*, in which he effectively declared that, thanks to the endless reproduction of modern visual media, truth and reality were dead.

The Pictures Generation can be said to have been defined, at the outset, by the 1977 *Pictures* exhibition at the
94 **Punkish**, non-profit Artists Space gallery in downtown New York, where young American curator and art historian Douglas Crimp chose to showcase the radical, 'post-abstract' early work of Jack Goldstein, Philip Smith, Levine, Brauntuch and Longo. Despite not being featured at *Pictures*, photographer Sherman is now the best-known 'member' of the group, which was arguably less of a movement and more what Crimp called a 'theoretical discussion'. Two years after *Pictures*, in his 1979 essay for the journal *October*, Crimp would in fact expel Smith in favour of Sherman.

Exploring artifice and the ambiguity of gender, Sherman's photographic series *Untitled Film Stills* (1977–80) powerfully challenged the construction of female stereotypes
in advertising, **TV** and Hollywood 25
films. **Dragged up** to 'become' her 90

own subjects, Sherman reflects on oppressive gender expectations and her women often question the roles assigned them. Similarly, Longo's photographic series *Men in the Cities* (1977–83) symbolically explored the painful and disturbing contortions of modern-day masculinity – the images that are glimpsed, with some Pop irony, on the wall of Patrick Bateman's 1980s New York apartment in the 2000 film version of Bret Easton Ellis's novel *American Psycho*.

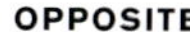

OPPOSITE
Cindy Sherman
Untitled Film Still #27, 1979
GELATIN SILVER PRINT

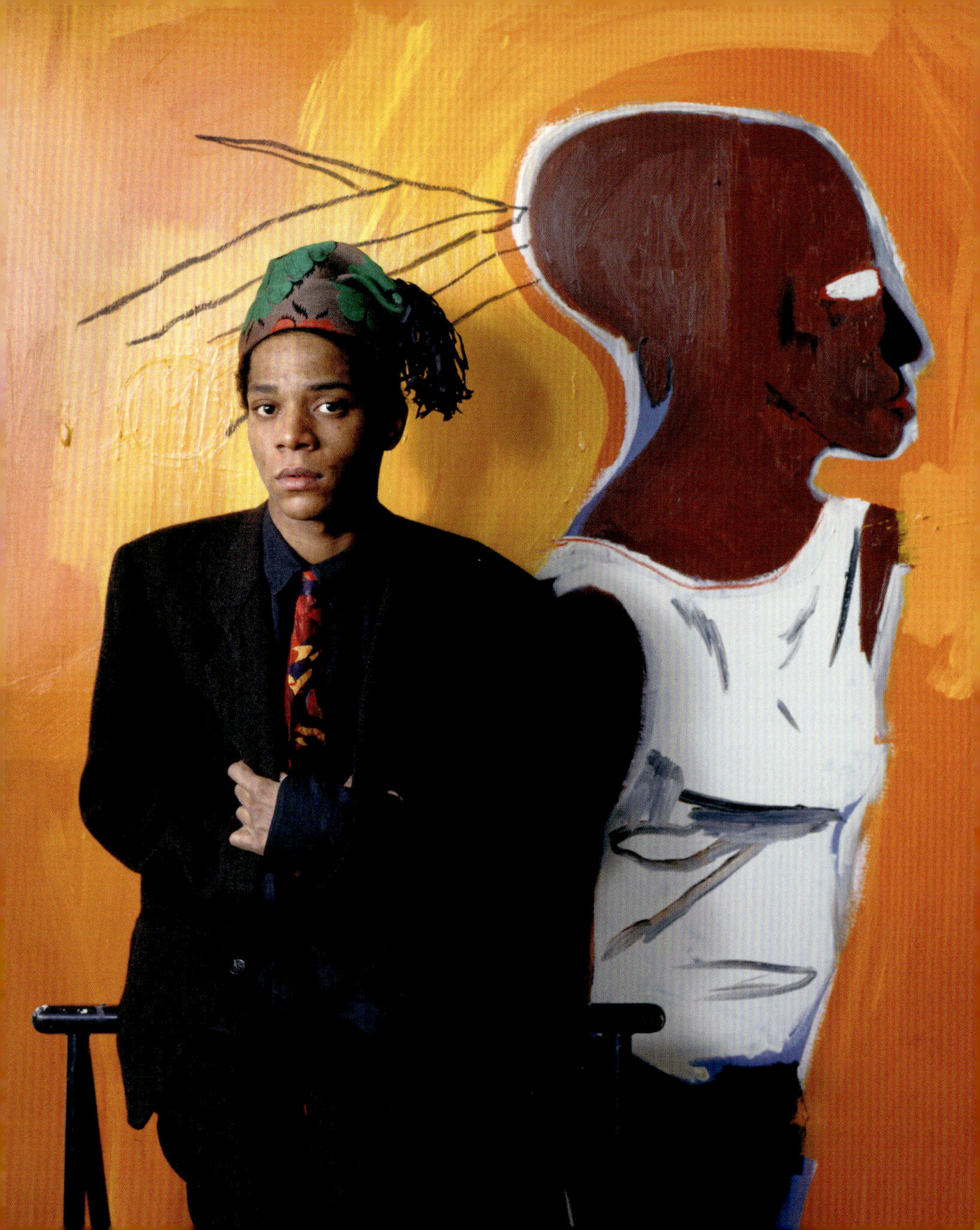

96

Jean-Michel Basquiat

Neo-Pop artist Jean-Michel Basquiat, who died at the age of 27, was the first graffiti artist to gain success as a fine artist. African-American and bisexual, he created powerful Pop-
94 **Punk** figurative abstracts that blended popular iconography and techniques with his own unique expressive style. An art world 'outsider', Basquiat's creative energy and his yearning for fame coalesced into what critic Arthur C. Danto called magnetic 'outlaw aura'.

One of the oldest forms of popular urban expression, graffiti became an urgent and accessible form of cultural protest for young artists like Basquiat in the decaying, crime-ridden New York of the 1970s. As the 1980s dawned, graffiti inched towards the mainstream, soon featuring in the promotional photography and music videos of Punk-inflected bands such as Blondie. After participating in the ground-breaking *Times Square Show*, staged in a vacant building in midtown New York in June 1980, Basquiat held his first European solo exhibition in May 1981 at the Galleria d'Arte Emilio Mazzoli in Modena, Italy. In March 1982, his first solo American exhibition opened at the Annina Nosei Gallery in New York's SoHo.

By most accounts, Basquiat lionized Andy Warhol as an artistic hero. Engineering a meeting with Warhol – just as Warhol himself engineered
a (less successful) **meeting with** 

Marcel Duchamp nearly twenty 

years before – the pair became close friends and rivals. With Warhol worrying to his diary, 'I haven't been creative
since I was **shot**', Basquiat's youth 

and confidence ('I don't listen to what art critics say') was clearly attractive. Recognizing that each could be useful to the other, they collaborated on a joint autumn 1985 exhibition at the Tony Shafrazi Gallery in SoHo. Described by critics as 'inconclusive' and 'infused with banality', Warhol's collaboration with Basquiat – whom the *New York Times* unfairly called an 'art world mascot' – highlighted the problematics of an established white artist working with an 'outsider' black artist. Commodified and appropriated by the art world, Basquiat's position was perhaps – as the *New York Times* suggested at the time – subject to 'manipulation'. Fighting for proper recognition as an autonomous fine artist, Basquiat rejected the 'graffiti' and 'street vernacular' labelling of his work. Crucially, he asserted, 'I am not a black artist, I am an artist.'

OPPOSITE
Jean-Michel Basquiat,
standing in front of [illegible] 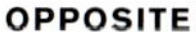
New York, 1985

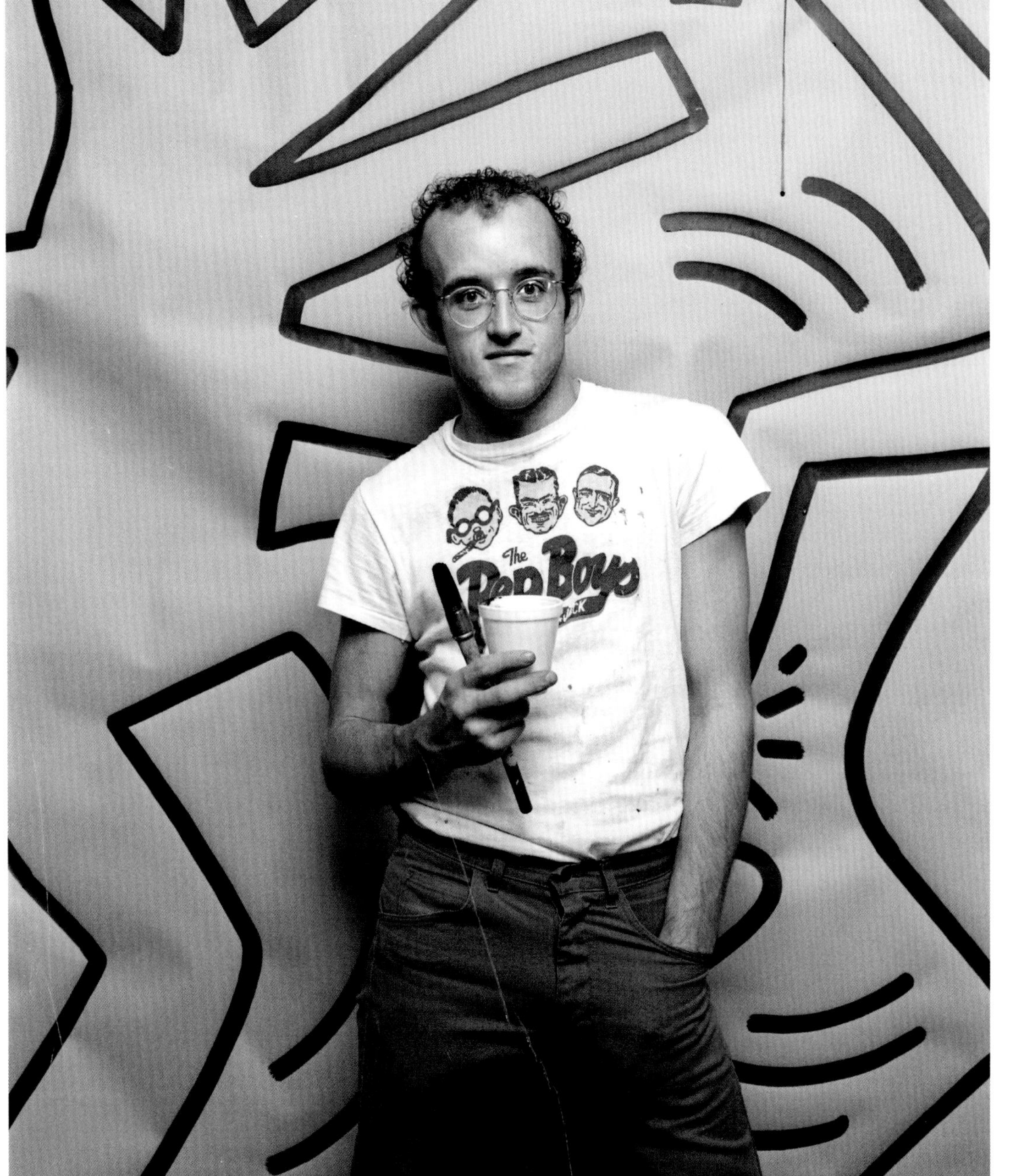
The
Pep Boys

97

Keith Haring

Opening his Pop Shop in New York's SoHo in April 1986, Neo-Pop artist Keith Haring developed Andy Warhol's
74 concept of **art as business** in a socially conscious way. Art, for Haring, wasn't just about making money; it was about progressive communication with as many different people as possible. Concerned that his work was becoming too expensive, sold only from rarefied private galleries, Haring wanted his shop (a second opened in Tokyo the following year) to sell his distinctive, cartoonish work, which was characterized by strong, bold lines and bright, artificial colours, to all comers, most memorably in the form of prints on affordable white T-shirts. The Pop Shop, Haring felt, broke the 'barriers between
30 high and low art'. Inspired by ***The Store***
66 and ***The American Supermarket***, by the immersive environments created by street and subway graffiti, by the branding techniques of advertisers and by the self-promotion of Warhol, it was frequented by celebrities and graffitists alike in a unique coming together of diverse communities.

Having arrived in New York City as an art student in 1978, Haring became friends with graffiti master Fab 5
96 Freddy and artist **Jean-Michel Basquiat**. He began producing white chalk graffiti on unused subway advertising panels and was, on several occasions, arrested for doing so. Metropolitan Museum of Art curator
Henry Geldzahler, however, called 23
Haring's subway pictures 'a tuneful celebration of urban communality'. Working as a busboy, cleaning tables alongside coat-check girl Madonna at 1980s New York hotspot Danceteria, Haring met and became friends with fellow Pennsylvanian Andy Warhol in 1983. Haring took Warhol as his guest to Madonna's wedding to Sean Penn in 1985. As an artist, designer, muralist and graffitist, Haring extended the reach of Pop Art – even into unique fashion collaborations and performance work with, most famously, his old friends Madonna and Grace Jones (whose body he famously graffitied).

Haring appropriated the style and attitude of the street and combined them with a brightly coloured cartoon aesthetic. With his naïve style, he made work that was direct, immediate and easily understood, appealing to a broader audience perhaps than previous Pop Art. In common with
Corita Kent, he incorporated striking [illegible]
political messages into his work and, before his HIV diagnosis in 1988, invented the powerful AIDS campaign slogan *Silence = Death*

OPPOSITE
Keith Haring, 1984

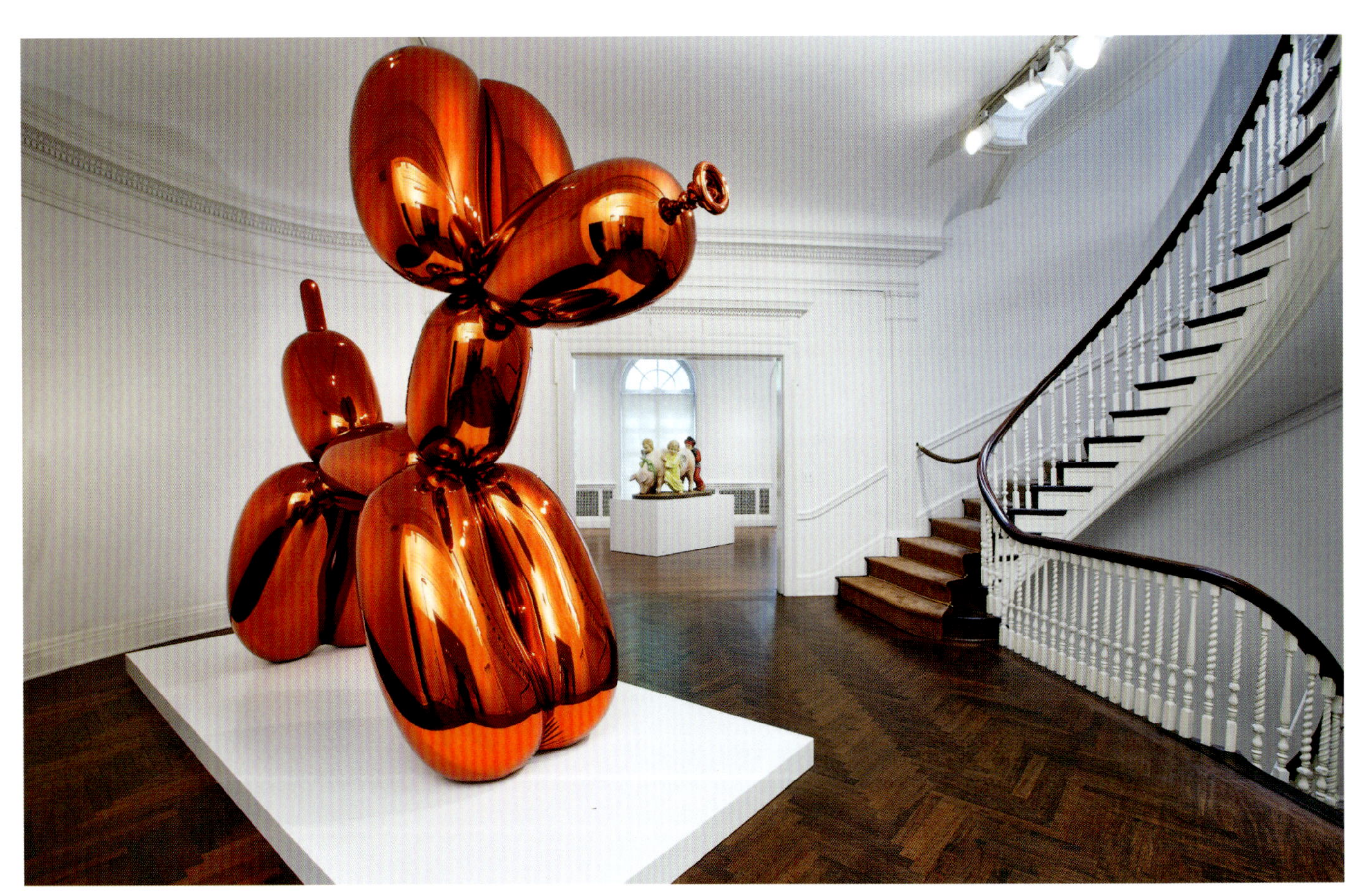

98

Jeff Koons

A year after Andy Warhol's death – at a time of apparently endless credit and the rise of hyper-celebrity – Neo-Pop sculptor and Wall Street broker Jeff Koons encapsulated the outrageous visual excesses of the late 1980s with his radical series *Banality* (1988). Responding to contemporary
65 celebrity culture and developing **Susan Sontag's ironic notion of 'camp'** – of something being 'good *because* it's awful' – Koons's most famous piece from the series was a life-size white-and-gold porcelain sculpture of a reclining Michael Jackson with his then-famous pet chimpanzee Bubbles. Koons wanted Pop icon Jackson, then at the height of his fame, to look god-like as an expensively kitsch ornament.

Pennsylvania-born Koons trained at the Art Institute of Chicago and the Maryland Institute of Art in Baltimore before moving to New York in 1977. After a brief stint working on the front desk at the Museum of Modern Art, he had his first solo exhibition, an installation in the windows of the New Museum of Contemporary Art, in May 1980. To produce the work he really wanted to, however, he needed to be, as he said, 'independent of the art market'. With this resolve, he joined the commodities market, becoming a Wall Street broker, and eventually he created his own
Warhol-inspired **'factory'**, the cut 71
and thrust of 1980s Wall Street clearly influencing his approach to the art world. At the very least, Koons gained a better understanding of what kind of contemporary art bankers actually wanted to buy. Exploring both voyeurism and exhibitionism, in 1989–91 he created a controversial series of explicit works collectively called *Made in Heaven*, featuring the Italian porn star Ilona Staller, who later became his wife. In 2013, his huge *Balloon Dog (Orange)* sold for $58.4 million – the highest price paid at auction for anything made by a living artist.

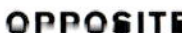

OPPOSITE
Jeff Koons
Balloon Dog (Orange), 1994–2000
MIRROR-POLISHED STAINLESS STEEL WITH TRANSPARENT COLOUR COATING

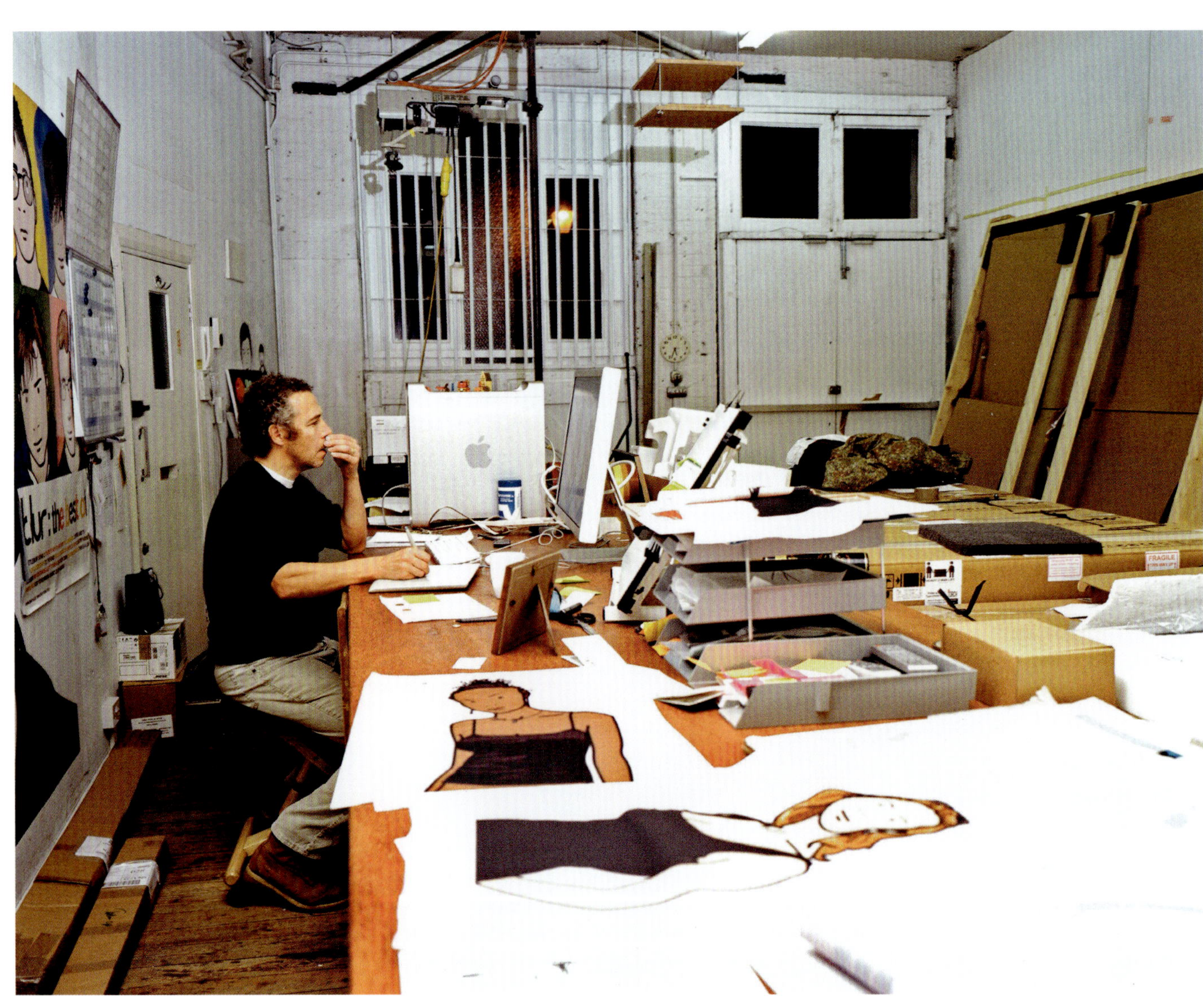
FRAGILE

99

Julian Opie

From their earliest appearance in 1997, British Neo-Pop artist Julian Opie's instantly recognizable bold and striking digital portraits – most famously of celebrities such as the 1990s indie band Blur – both resembled and surpassed Andy
36 Warhol's reductive **silkscreen** portraits of the early 1960s.

A graduate of London's Chelsea and Goldsmiths colleges of art, Opie was initially associated with the 1980s New British Sculpture group and began his career producing cartoonish painted metal sculptures inspired by branded food packaging. Clearly indebted to 1960s Pop Art, he held his first solo exhibition at the age of 25 at the influential Lisson Gallery in London in September 1983. Within a decade, however, perhaps inspired by the nascent internet and Warhol's early experiments in digital portraiture on the 1985 Commodore Amiga 1000, Opie had turned to computer-generated image-making.

Feeding photographs into cutting-edge computer software, Opie created portraits and nudes with block colours and curiously expressive black outlines, some of which would go on to become large public sculptures. For Opie, less is distinctly and dramatically more – the viewer's eye fills in the desired detail. A mark of their direct and accessible popularity, and in common with the work of Warhol and contemporary American street artist Shepard Fairey, Opie's portraits have become iconic, easily copied and parodied. Eliding fame with the mundane by both framing and obscuring contemporary celebrity, Opie's Neo-Pop portraiture heralded a new artistic millennium with a form of anyone-can-do-it,
digital **painting-by-numbers** of 40
which Warhol might have been proud.

OPPOSITE
Julian Opie at his Shoreditch studio in London, 2006

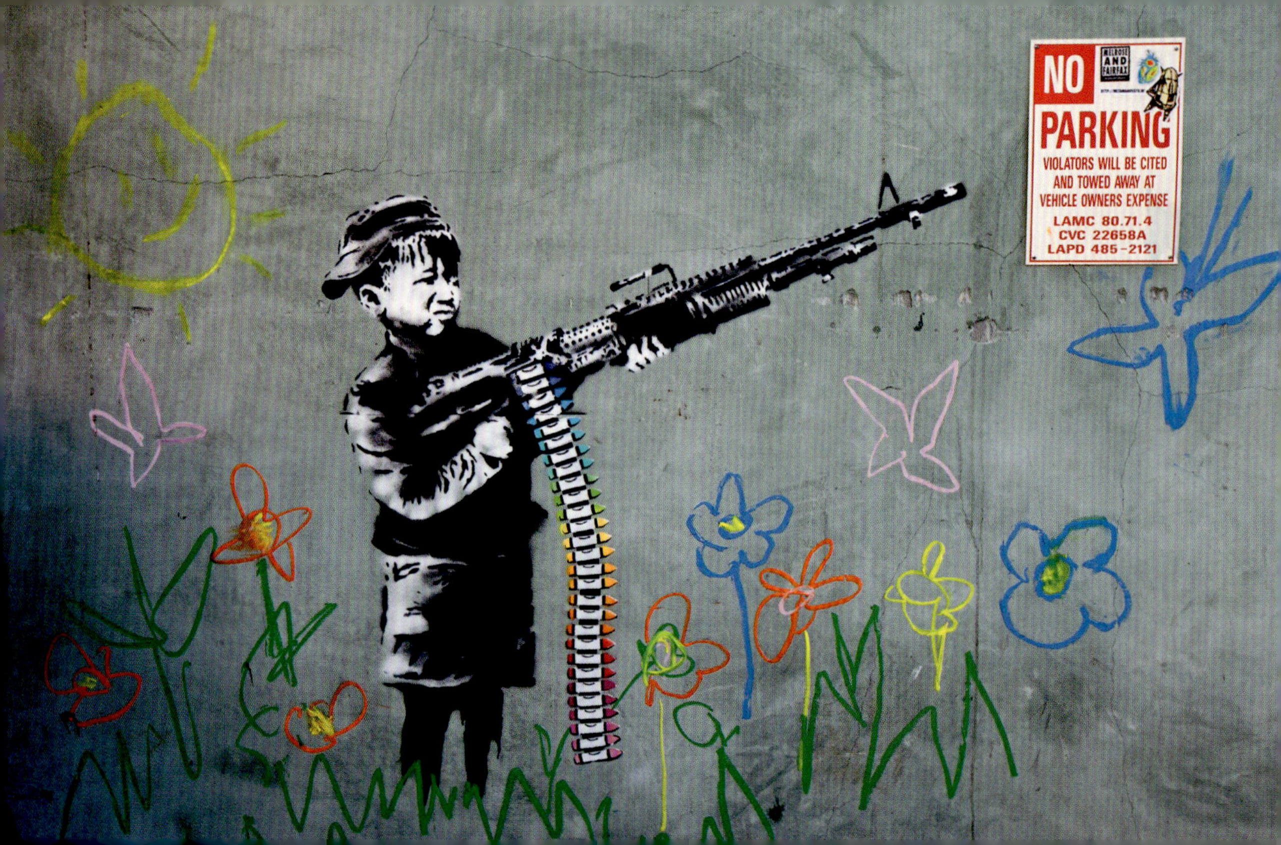
NO
MELROSE AND FAIRFAX
PARKING
VIOLATORS WILL BE CITED
AND TOWED AWAY AT
VEHICLE OWNERS EXPENSE
LAMC 80.71.4
CVC 22658A
LAPD 485-2121

100

Banksy

Anonymously mononymous, British Neo-Pop graffiti artist Banksy's real identity remains the subject of intense speculation, their latest stencil creation eagerly anticipated. The apparently spontaneous, almost-magical appearance of a Banksy has become a public event, a spectacle that can disappear just as quickly and without warning. Produced with spray paint and stencils, Banksy's work echoes the technical efficiency and clean finish of 1960s 'Peak Pop'. Diverse and recurring motifs include anthropomorphized rodents, well-known figures from popular culture and even Old Master paintings. The natural successor to the provocations of Dada protest and Pop satire, Banksy's diverse compositions feature re-appropriated popular imagery and political slogans juxtaposed so as to be funny, whimsical, disturbing and often haunting.

One of the oldest forms of popular expression, since the 1949 invention of aerosol paint by American salesman Edward Seymour, graffiti has taken on a new life – and, for Banksy, 'a wall is a very big weapon'. Inspired by Russian artist Dmitri Vrubel's subversive 1990
 51 image sprayed on the **Berlin Wall**,
Banksy's *Kissing Coppers* from 2004 explores themes of love and peace. Reminiscent of Warhol's series of Elvis
silkscreens from the early 1960s, 36
Banksy's *Elvis with a Gun* from 2008, suggests, however, that conflict has become entertainment. One of Banksy's most arresting images, *Crayon Boy* from 2011, articulates the loss of innocence in a brutalizing world. Developing the tradition of direct graffiti protest, in 2016 Banksy produced a graffiti QR code on a wall of the French Embassy in London that linked users to video evidence of police abuse at Calais's migrant 'jungle'. For Banksy, art should always 'comfort the disturbed and disturb the comfortable'.

Rejecting art history's obsession with authenticity, permanence, ownership and what critic Walter Benjamin called 'aura', Banksy's work is a challenge to the social, political and economic assumptions that underpin and outline modern culture. Despite the art market's attempts to commodify and sanitize Banksy's work, the artist remains resistant to a corporate culture where 'nothing has a right to exist unless it makes a profit'. As such, Banksy's work exemplifies contemporary Guerrilla Pop and gestures hopefully towards a fairer world.

OPPOSITE
Banksy
Crayon Boy, Westwood, Los Angeles, 2011

GRAFFITI

Select bibliography

Demilly, C.
Pop Art
Prestel (2007)

Finlay, J.
Pop! The World of Pop Art
Goodman (2016)

Francis, M. (ed.)
Pop
Phaidon (2010)

Frigeri, F.
Pop Art
Thames & Hudson (2018)

Gualdoni, F.
Pop Art
Skira (2008)

McCarthy, D.
Pop Art
Tate (2000)

Osterwold, T.
Pop Art
Taschen (2011)

Sooke, A.
Pop Art: A Colourful History
Viking (2015)

Wilson, S.
Pop
Thames & Hudson (1974)

Index

Picture credits

10 © Man Ray Trust/ADAGP, Paris and DACS, London 2020; © Association Marcel Duchamp/ADAGP, Paris and DACS, London 2020; 12 Joerg Hejkal/ Bridgeman Images © The Heartfield Community of Heirs/DACS 2019; 14 akg-images; 16 J. R. Eyerman/The LIFE Picture Collection/Getty Images;18 © Estate of Nathan Gluck; courtesy Luis De Jesus Los Angeles; 20 Image © Tate London 2020 © Trustees of the Paolozzi Foundation. Licensed by DACS 2020; 22 Chronicle/Alamy Stock Photo; 26 Bettmann/Getty Images; 28 Martin Shields/Alamy Stock Photo © Jasper Johns/VAGA at ARS, NY and DACS, London 2020; 30 Boltin Picture Library/Bridgeman Images Photo © Robert Rauschenberg Foundation/VAGA at ARS, NY and DACS, London 2020; 32 Architectural Press Archive/RIBA Collections; 34 Kunsthalle, Tubingen/ Bridgeman Images © Richard Hamilton. All Rights Reserved, DACS 2020; 36 The Doris and Donald Fisher Collection at the San Francisco Museum of Modern Art © 2020 The Andy Warhol Foundation for the Visual Arts, Inc. Licensed by DACS, London; 40 Fred W. McDarrah/Getty Images; 42 © Board of Trustees, National Gallery of Art, Washington; 44 Henry Groskinsky/The LIFE Images Collection/ Getty Images; 48, 49 © Yale Center for British Art, Gift of Magda Cordell McHale; 52 Christie's Images/Bridgeman Images; 54 © ARS, NY and DACS, London 2020. Photo courtesy Ray Johnson Estate; 56 Jack Robinson/Hulton Archive/Getty Images; 58 Christie's Images/Bridgeman Images © ADAGP, Paris and DACS, London 2020; 60 Sheri Blaney/Alamy Stock Photo; 62 akg-images © 2020 The Andy Warhol Foundation for the Visual Arts, Inc. Licensed by DACS, London; 64 Museu Coleção Berardo/photo Bruno Lopes © Peter Blake. All rights reserved, DACS 2020; 66 Heritage Image Partnership/Alamy Stock Photo; 70 Christie's Images/Bridgeman Images; © Estate of Tom Wesselmann/VAGA at ARS, NY and DACS, London 2020; 72 The Estate of David Gahr/Getty Images; 74 Mary Sisler Bequest, The Museum of Modern Art, New York/Scala, Florence © 1961 Claes Oldenburg; 75 Courtesy Oldenburg van Bruggen Studio/photo Robert McElroy © 1961 Claes Oldenburg; 76 Christie's Images/Bridgeman Images © Ed Ruscha. Courtesy of the artist and Gagosian; 78 Christie's Images/Bridgeman Images © 2020 The Andy Warhol Foundation for the Visual Arts, Inc. Licensed by DACS, London; 80 Rheinisches Bildarchiv Köln/photo Britta Schlier © Jasper Johns/VAGA at ARS, NY and DACS, London 2020; 84 Keystone-France/Gamma-Keystone via Getty Images © Niki de Saint Phalle Charitable Art Foundation/ADAGP, Paris and DACS, London 2020; 86 Rana/Alamy Stock © 2020 The Andy Warhol Foundation for the Visual Arts, Inc. Licensed by DACS, London; 88 Chronicle/Alamy Stock Photo; 90 akg-images © 2020 The Andy Warhol Foundation for the Visual Arts, Inc. Licensed by DACS, London; 92 Walter Sanders/The LIFE Picture Collection via Getty Images; 94 akg-images © 2020 The Andy Warhol Foundation for the Visual Arts, Inc. Licensed by DACS, London; 96 The Sidney and Harriet Janis Collection, The Museum of Modern Art, New York/Scala, Florence © Jim Dine/ARS, NY and DACS, London 2020; 98 Phillip Harrington/Alamy Stock Photo; 100 Image © Tate, London 2020 © 2020 The Andy Warhol Foundation for the Visual Arts, Inc. Licensed by DACS, London; 101 NY Daily News Archive via Getty Images; 102 Fred W. McDarrah/Getty Images © The George and Helen Segal Foundation/VAGA at ARS, NY and DACS London 2020; 104 Arts Council Collection, Southbank Centre, London/Bridgeman Images; 106 Wolverhampton Art Gallery/Bridgeman Images © Jann Haworth; 108 Fred W. McDarrah/Getty Images; 110 Mel Ramos © Mel Ramos/VAGA at ARS, NY and DACS, London 2020; 112 © 1962 Kiki Kogelnik Foundation. All rights reserved. Photo courtesy Kiki Kogelnik Foundation; 114 Photo Reiner Ruthenbeck © DACS 2020; 116 © Estate of Roy Lichtenstein/DACS/Artimage 2020; 118 Oldenburg van Bruggen Studio © 1963 Claes Oldenburg; 120 Philip Johnson Fund and gift of Mr. and Mrs. Bagley Wright, The Museum of Modern Art, New York/Scala, Florence © Estate of Roy Lichtenstein/DACS 2020; 122 © 2020 Rosalyn Drexler/ Artists Rights Society, New York and Garth Greenan Gallery, New York; 124 Image © Tate, London 2020 © Estate of Roy Lichtenstein/DACS 2020; 126 Christie's Images/Bridgeman Images © Estate of Marisol/ARS, NY and DACS, London 2020; 128 NY Daily News Archive via Getty Images; 130 akg-images © ADAGP, Paris and DACS, London 2020; 132 Collection of Luciano Lanfanchi, Switzerland. Courtesy Hollis Taggart. Photo Joshua Nefsky, New York © Estate of Marjorie Strider; 134 Photo courtesy Allan Stone Collection, New York; 136 Mondadori Portfolio/Mario De Biasi/Bridgeman Images © 2020 The Andy Warhol Foundation for the Visual Arts, Inc. Licensed by DACS, London; 138 Tony Evans/Timelapse Library Ltd/Getty Images; 140 Fred W. McDarrah/ Getty Images; 142 Photographer unknown. Lucy R. Lippard papers, Archives of American Art, Smithsonian Institution © 2020 The Andy Warhol Foundation for the Visual Arts, Inc. Licensed by DACS, London, and © James Rosenquist/VAGA at ARS, NY and DACS, London; 144 Christie's Images/Bridgeman Images © Wayne Thiebaud/VAGA at ARS, NY and DACS, London 2020; 148 Jack Mitchell/Getty Images; 150 Mario Tama/Getty Images © James Rosenquist/VAGA at ARS, NY and DACS, London 2020; 152 Fred W. McDarrah/Getty Images; 154 © Lewis Morley/National Science and Media Museum/Science and Society Picture Library. Photo National Portrait Gallery, London; 156 Photo Nat Finkelstein. Courtesy and © Nat Finkelstein Estate; 160 © Derek Boshier. All Rights Reserved, DACS/Artimage 2020. Image courtesy Flowers Gallery; 162 © Ron Herron Archive. All Rights Reserved, DACS/Artimage 2020; 164 Christie's Images/Bridgeman Images © 2020 The Andy Warhol Foundation for the Visual Arts, Inc. Licensed by DACS, London; 166 Giovanni Coruzzi/Bridgeman Images; 168 Image © Tate, London 2020 © David Hockney; 170 Reprinted with permission of the Corita Art Center, Immaculate Heart Community, Los Angeles; 172 Reproduced by permission of The Velvet Underground Trust; 174 NY Daily News Archive via Getty Images;178 The LIFE Picture Collection/Getty Images; 180 © Martha Rosler. Courtesy of the artist and Mitchell-Innes & Nash, New York; 182 John Hedgecoe/TopFoto/Bridgeman Images © Estate of Tom Wesselmann/VAGA at ARS, NY and DACS, London 2020; 184 Henry Groskinsky/The LIFE Premium Collection via Getty Images; 188 Robin Platzer/Twin Images/The LIFE Images Collection via Getty Images; 190 Wesley/Keystone/Getty Images; 192 The Andy Warhol Museum, Pittsburgh. Founding Collection, Contribution The Andy Warhol Foundation for the Visual Arts, Inc; 194 Courtesy Tsukanov Art Collection; 196 Hulton-Deutsch Collection/Corbis via Getty Images; 198 Moviestore Collection/Alamy Stock Photo; 200 Erica Echenberg/Redferns/Getty Images; 202 Courtesy of the artist and Metro Pictures, New York; 204 Estate of Evelyn Hofer/Getty Images © The Estate of Jean-Michel Basquiat/ADAGP, Paris and DACS, London 2020; 206 Jack Mitchell/Getty Images; 208 © Jeff Koons. Photo Tom Powel Publishing; 210 Tom Stoddart/Getty Images; 212 Ted Soqui/Corbis via Getty Images.

Every effort has been made to establish copyright ownership of works included in this publication and the publishers apologise if any errors or omissions have been made. Please contact us with any corrections for future editions.

Acknowledgement

My partner, Adam,
who generously lived the writing
of this book as much as I.